SAS® Programming I: Essentials

Course Notes

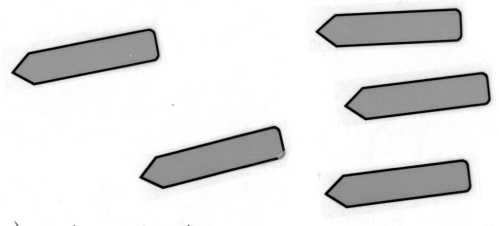

travis.masters@sas.com

Trainer : Travis Masters

SAS® Programming I: Essentials Course Notes was developed by Michelle Buchecker, Sarah Calhoun, and Larry Stewart. Additional contributions were made by Warren Repole. Editing and production support was provided by the Curriculum Development and Support Department.

SAS® Programming I: Essentials Course Notes

Book code 59728, course code PROG1, prepared date 29Apr04.

Table of Contents

Course Description

This three-day course focuses on how to

- read raw data files and SAS data sets

- investigate and summarize data by generating frequency tables and descriptive statistics

- create SAS variables and recode data values

- subset data

- combine multiple SAS files

- create listing, summary, HTML, and graph reports.

After completing this course, you should be able to

- read a SAS data set

- read a raw data file

- combine SAS data sets through concatenation and merging

- create a SAS variable through the assignment statement and conditional logic

- investigate and summarize your data

- calculate simple statistics

- create list, summary, HTML, and graph reports.

To learn more...

SAS Education

A full curriculum of general and statistical instructor-based training is available at any of the Institute's training facilities. Institute instructors can also provide on-site training.

For information on other courses in the curriculum, contact the SAS Education Division at 1-919-531-7321, or send e-mail to training@sas.com. You can also find this information on the Web at **support.sas.com/training/** as well as in the Training Course Catalog.

SAS Publishing

For a list of other SAS books that relate to the topics covered in this Course Notes, USA customers can contact our SAS Publishing Department at 1-800-727-3228 or send e-mail to sasbook@sas.com. Customers outside the USA, please contact your local SAS office.

Also, see the Publications Catalog on the Web at **support.sas.com/pubs** for a complete list of books and a convenient order form.

Prerequisites

Before attending this course, you should have completed the Introduction to Programming Concepts Using SAS® Software course or have at least six months of programming experience.

Specifically, you should be able to

- understand file structures and system commands on your operating systems

- write system commands to create and access system files

- understand programming logic.

General Conventions

This section explains the various conventions used in presenting text, SAS language syntax, and examples in this book.

Typographical Conventions

You will see several type styles in this book. This list explains the meaning of each style:

UPPERCASE ROMAN	is used for SAS statements and other SAS language elements when they appear in the text.
italic	identifies terms or concepts that are defined in text. Italic is also used for book titles when they are referenced in text, as well as for various syntax and mathematical elements.
bold	is used for emphasis within text.
`monospace`	is used for examples of SAS programming statements and for SAS character strings. Monospace is also used to refer to variable and data set names, field names in windows, information in fields, and user-supplied information.
<u>**select**</u>	indicates selectable items in windows and menus. This book also uses icons to represent selectable items.

Syntax Conventions

The general forms of SAS statements and commands shown in this book include only that part of the syntax actually taught in the course. For complete syntax, see the appropriate SAS reference guide.

> **PROC CHART** DATA = *SAS-data-set*;
>   **HBAR | VBAR** *chart-variables </ options>*;
> **RUN**;

This is an example of how SAS syntax is shown in text:

- **PROC** and **CHART** are in uppercase bold because they are SAS keywords.
- DATA= is in uppercase to indicate that it must be spelled as shown.
- *SAS-data-set* is in italic because it represents a value that you supply. In this case, the value must be the name of a SAS data set.
- **HBAR** and **VBAR** are in uppercase bold because they are SAS keywords. They are separated by a vertical bar to indicate they are mutually exclusive; you can choose one or the other.
- *chart-variables* is in italic because it represents a value or values that you supply.
- *</ options>* represents optional syntax specific to the HBAR and VBAR statements. The angle brackets enclose the slash as well as *options* because if no options are specified you do not include the slash.
- **RUN** is in uppercase bold because it is a SAS keyword.

Chapter 1   Introduction

1.1   An Overview of the SAS System

Objectives

- Understand the structure and design of the SAS System.
- Introduce the course scenario.

3

Components of the SAS System

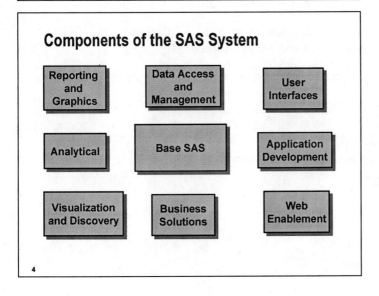

4

Data-Driven Tasks

The functionality of the SAS System is built around the
four data-driven tasks common to virtually any application:

1. data access
2. data management
3. data analysis
4. data presentation.

5

---

data access	addresses the data required by the application.
data management	shapes data into a form required by the application.
data analysis	summarizes, reduces, or otherwise transforms raw data into meaningful and useful information.
data presentation	communicates information in ways that clearly demonstrate its significance.

Turning Data into Information

Process of delivering meaningful information:

- 80% data-related
  - access
  - scrub
  - transform
  - manage
  - store and retrieve
- 20% analysis.

6

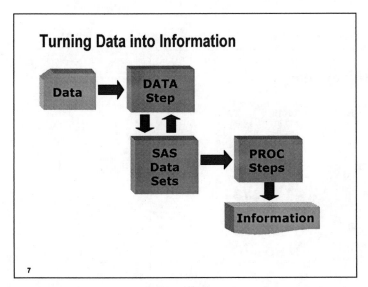

Turning Data into Information

7

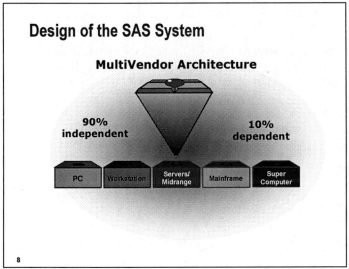

Design of the SAS System

8

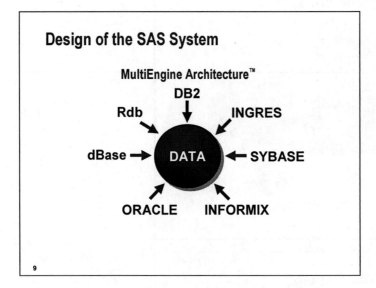

Design of the SAS System

MultiEngine Architecture™

DB2 · Rdb · INGRES · dBase · DATA · SYBASE · ORACLE · INFORMIX

In order to access databases such as ORACLE, the SAS/ACCESS product for your given Database Management System (DBMS) must be licensed, in addition to Base SAS software.

Course Scenario

In this course, you will be working with business data from International Airlines (IA). The various kinds of data IA maintains are

- flight data
- passenger data
- cargo data
- employee data
- revenue data.

Course Scenario

Some tasks you will be performing are

- importing data
- creating a list of employees
- producing a frequency table of job codes
- summarizing data
- creating a report of salary information.

11

Chapter 2   Getting Started with the SAS® System

2.1   Introduction to SAS Programs

Objectives

- State the components of a SAS program.
- State the modes in which you can run a SAS program.

3

SAS Programs

A *SAS program* is a sequence of steps that the user submits for execution.

DATA steps are typically used to create SAS data sets.

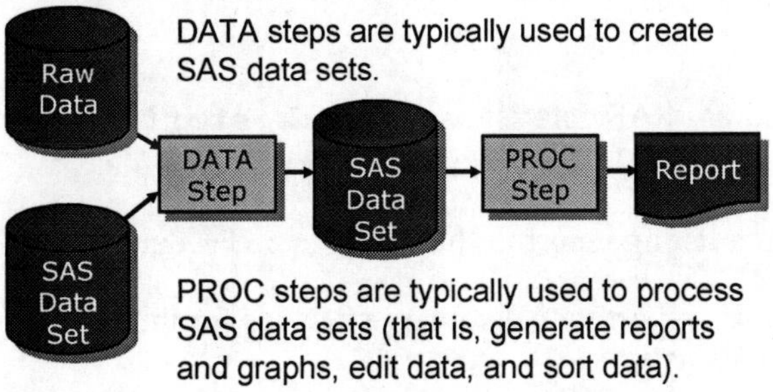

Raw Data → DATA Step → SAS Data Set → PROC Step → Report

SAS Data Set

PROC steps are typically used to process SAS data sets (that is, generate reports and graphs, edit data, and sort data).

4

Proc = Procedure

*each step
processed
independently*

```
SAS Programs

data work.staff;
    infile 'raw-data-file';
    input LastName $ 1-20 FirstName $ 21-30    ⎫ DATA
          JobTitle $ 36-43 Salary 54-59;       ⎬ Step
run;                                            ⎭

proc print data=work.staff;                    ⎫
run;                                            ⎬
                                               ⎬ PROC
proc means data=work.staff;                    ⎬ Steps
    class JobTitle;                            ⎬
    var Salary;                                ⎬
run;                                            ⎭

5
```

Examples of raw data file names:

z/OS[1] (OS/390)	*userid*.prog1.rawdata(emplist)
Windows	c:\workshop\winsas\prog1\emplist.dat
UNIX	/users/*userid*/emplist.dat

The DATA step creates a temporary SAS data set named **work.staff** by reading the four variables described in the INPUT statement from the raw data file.

The PROC PRINT step creates a listing report of the **work.staff** data set.

The PROC MEANS step creates a report with summary statistics for the variable **Salary** for each value of **JobTitle**.

---

[1] Any reference to z/OS applies to OS/390, unless otherwise noted.

Step Boundaries

SAS steps begin with a

- DATA statement
- PROC statement.

SAS detects the end of a step when it encounters

- a RUN statement (for **most** steps)
- a QUIT statement (for **some** procedures)
- the beginning of another step (DATA statement or PROC statement).

6

A SAS program executed in batch or noninteractive mode can contain RUN statements, but does not require any RUN statements to execute successfully because the entire program is executed by default. The presence of the RUN statement depends on the programmer's preference.

Step Boundaries

```
data work.staff;
    infile 'raw-data-file';
    input LastName $ 1-20 FirstName $ 21-30
          JobTitle $ 36-43 Salary 54-59;
run;

proc print data=work.staff;

proc means data=work.staff;
    class JobTitle;
    var Salary;
run;
```

7

try not to
use implied
step boundaries.
b/c
processing may only be
program part
if

Examples of raw data file names:

z/OS (OS/390)	`userid.prog1.rawdata(emplist)`
Windows	`c:\workshop\winsas\prog1\emplist.dat`
UNIX	`/users/userid/emplist.dat`

Running a SAS Program

You can invoke SAS in

- interactive windowing mode (SAS windowing environment)

- interactive menu-driven mode (SAS Enterprise Guide, SAS/ASSIST, SAS/AF, or SAS/EIS software)

- batch mode

- noninteractive mode.

8

enterprise guide is point + click

SAS Windowing Environment

Interactive windows enable you to interface with SAS.

9

z/OS (OS/390, MVS) Batch Execution

Place the JCL appropriate for your location before
your SAS statements.

```
//jobname JOB accounting info,name …
// EXEC SAS
//SYSIN DD *
data work.staff;
   infile 'raw-data-file';
   input LastName $ 1-20 FirstName $ 21-30
         JobTitle $ 36-43 Salary 54-59;
run;

proc print data=work.staff;
run;

proc means data=work.staff;
   class JobTitle;
   var Salary;
run;
```

10

Noninteractive Execution (Optional)

To execute a SAS program in noninteractive mode,

■ use an editor to store the program in a file. (Directory-
based users should use a filetype or extension of SAS.)

■ identify the file when you invoke SAS.

Directory-based:

SAS *filename*

z/OS (OS/390, TSO):

SAS INPUT(*filename*)

11

The command for invoking SAS at your site may be different from the
default shown above. Ask your SAS administrator for the command to
invoke SAS at your site.

2.2   Running SAS Programs

Objectives

- Invoke the SAS System and include a SAS program into your session.
- Submit a program and browse the results.
- Navigate the SAS windowing environment.

13

Submitting a SAS Program

When you execute a SAS program, the output generated by SAS is divided into two major parts:

SAS log   contains information about the processing of the SAS program, including any warning and error messages.

SAS output   contains reports generated by SAS procedures and DATA steps.

14

SAS Log

```
1     data work.staff;
2        infile 'raw-data-file';
3        input LastName $ 1-20 FirstName $ 21-30
4              JobTitle $ 36-43 Salary 54-59;
5     run;
NOTE: The infile 'raw-data-file' is:
      File Name= 'raw-data-file',
      RECFM=V,LRECL=256
NOTE: 18 records were read from the infile 'raw-data-file'.
      The minimum record length was 59.
      The maximum record length was 59.
NOTE: The data set WORK.STAFF has 18 observations and 4 variables.

6     proc print data=work.staff;
7     run;
NOTE: There were 18 observations read from the dataset WORK.STAFF.

8     proc means data=work.staff;
9        class JobTitle;
10       var Salary;
11    run;
NOTE: There were 18 observations read from the dataset WORK.STAFF.
```

15

Examples of raw data file names:

z/OS (OS/390)	userid.prog1.rawdata(emplist)
Windows	c:\workshop\winsas\prog1\emplist.dat
UNIX	/users/userid/emplist.dat

PROC PRINT Output

```
                    The SAS System

                    First
Obs   LastName      Name        JobTitle     Salary

 1    TORRES        JAN         Pilot         50000
 2    LANGKAMM      SARAH       Mechanic      80000
 3    SMITH         MICHAEL     Mechanic      40000
 4    LEISTNER      COLIN       Mechanic      36000
 5    WADE          KIRSTEN     Pilot         85000
 6    TOMAS         HARALD      Pilot        105000
 7    WAUGH         TIM         Pilot         70000
 8    LEHMANN       DAGMAR      Mechanic      64000
 9    TRETTHAHN     MICHAEL     Pilot        100000
10    TIETZ         OTTO        Pilot         45000
11    O'DONOGHUE    ART         Mechanic      52000
12    WALKER        THOMAS      Pilot         95000
13    NOROVIITA     JOACHIM     Mechanic      78000
14    OESTERBERG    ANJA        Mechanic      80000
15    LAUFFER       CRAIG       Mechanic      40000
16    TORR          JUGDISH     Pilot         45000
17    WAGSCHAL      NADJA       Pilot         77500
18    TOERMOEN      JOCHEN      Pilot         65000
```

16

PROC MEANS Output

```
                         The SAS System

                       The MEANS Procedure

                   Analysis Variable : Salary

              N
JobTitle    Obs      N         Mean        Std Dev        Minimum

Mechanic      8      8     58750.00       19151.65       36000.00

Pilot        10     10     73750.00       22523.14       45000.00


                   Analysis Variable : Salary

                            N
             JobTitle      Obs        Maximum

             Mechanic       8        80000.00

             Pilot         10       105000.00
```

17

Running a SAS Program – Windows

File: c02s2d1.sas

- Start a SAS session.
- Include and submit a program.
- Browse the results.

Starting a SAS Session

1. Double-click the SAS icon to start your SAS session.

    🖉   How you invoke SAS varies by your operating environment and any customizations in effect at your site.

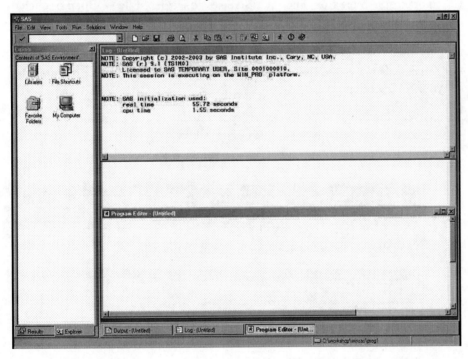

All operating environments support the Program Editor. The Microsoft Windows operating environment supports an additional editor, the Enhanced Editor. Because the Program Editor is available on all operating environments, it will be used throughout class.

   Microsoft Windows users need to close the Enhanced Editor by selecting ☒. To open the Program Editor, select **View** ⇨ **Program Editor**.

Refer to the end of this chapter for a discussion on the Enhanced Editor.

The Results window and Explorer window have slightly different functionality in different operating environments. Refer to the end of this chapter for a discussion on these windows.

Including and Submitting a SAS Program

1. To open a SAS program into your SAS session, select **File** ⇨ **Open** or click on 📂 and then select the file you want to include. To open a program, your Program Editor must be active.

   You can also issue the INCLUDE command to open (include) a program into your SAS session.

   a. With the Program Editor active, type **include** and the name of the file containing the program on the command bar.

   b. Press Enter.

The program is included in the Program Editor window.

```
Program Editor - c02s2d1.sas
data work.staff;
    infile 'emplist.dat';
    input LastName $ 1-20 FirstName $ 21-30
          JobTitle $ 36-43 Salary 54-59;
run;

proc print data=work.staff;
run;

proc means data=work.staff;
    class Jobtitle;
    var Salary;
run;
```

You can use the Program Editor window to

- access and edit existing SAS programs
- write new SAS programs
- submit SAS programs
- save SAS programs to a file.

Within the Program Editor, the syntax in your program is color-coded to show

- step boundaries
- keywords
- variable and data set names.

2. Issue the SUBMIT command or click on or select **Run** ⇨ **Submit** to submit the program for execution. The output from the program is displayed in the Output window.

Examining Your Program Results

The Output window

- is one of the primary windows and is open by default.
- becomes the active window each time it receives output.
- automatically accumulates output in the order in which it is generated. You can issue the CLEAR command or select **Edit** ⇨ **Clear All** to clear the contents of the window, or you can click on the NEW icon 📄 .

To scroll horizontally within the Output window, use the horizontal scrollbar or issue the RIGHT and LEFT commands.

In the Windows environment, the Output window displays the last page of output generated by the program submitted.

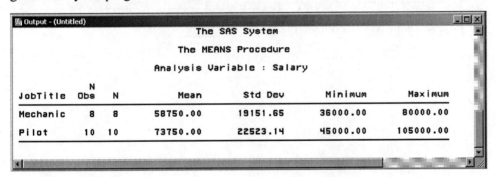

To scroll vertically within the Output window, use the vertical scrollbar or issue the FORWARD and BACKWARD commands or use the PAGE UP or PAGE DOWN keys on the keyboard.

✎   You also can use the TOP and BOTTOM commands to scroll vertically within the Output window.

1. Scroll to the top to view the output from the PRINT procedure.

```
Output - (Untitled)                                                    _ □ ×
                              The SAS System

                         First
         Obs    LastName      Name        JobTitle    Salary

          1    TORRES        JAN         Pilot        50000
          2    LANGKAMM      SARAH       Mechanic     80000
          3    SMITH         MICHAEL     Mechanic     40000
          4    LEISTNER      COLIN       Mechanic     36000
          5    WADE          KIRSTEN     Pilot        85000
          6    TOMAS         HARALD      Pilot       105000
          7    WAUGH         TIM         Pilot        70000
          8    LEHMANN       DAGMAR      Mechanic     64000
          9    TRETTHAHN     MICHAEL     Pilot       100000
         10    TIETZ         OTTO        Pilot        45000
         11    O'DONOGHUE    ART         Mechanic     52000
         12    WALKER        THOMAS      Pilot        95000
         13    NOROVIITA     JOACHIM     Mechanic     78000
         14    OESTERBERG    ANJA        Mechanic     80000
         15    LAUFFER       CRAIG       Mechanic     40000
         16    TORR          JUGDISH     Pilot        45000
         17    WAGSCHAL      NADJA       Pilot        77500
         18    TOERMOEN      JOCHEN      Pilot        65000
```

2. Issue the LOG command or select **Window** ⇨ **Log** or click on the log to display the Log window and browse the messages that the program generated.

    The Log window

    - is one of the primary windows and is open by default.

    - acts as an audit trail of your SAS session; messages are written to the log in the order in which they are generated by the program.

3. To clear the contents of the window, issue the CLEAR command, select

    Edit ⇨ **Clear All**, or click on the NEW icon [ ].

Partial Log

```
Log - (Untitled)                                                    _ |□| X
1    data work.staff;
2       infile 'emplist.dat';
3       input LastName $ 1-20 FirstName $ 21-30
4              JobTitle $ 36-43 Salary 54-59;
5    run;

NOTE: The infile 'emplist.dat' is:
      File Name=C:\workshop\winsas\prog1\emplist.dat,
      RECFM=V,LRECL=256

NOTE: 18 records were read from the infile 'emplist.dat'.
      The minimum record length was 59.
      The maximum record length was 59.
NOTE: The data set WORK.STAFF has 18 observations and 4 variables.
NOTE: DATA statement used:
      real time           0.03 seconds
      cpu time            0.03 seconds


6
7    proc print data=work.staff;
8    run;

NOTE: There were 18 observations read from the data set WORK.STAFF.
NOTE: PROCEDURE PRINT used:
      real time           0.02 seconds
      cpu time            0.02 seconds


9
10   proc means data=work.staff;
11      class Jobtitle;
12      var Salary;
13   run;

NOTE: There were 18 observations read from the data set WORK.STAFF.
NOTE: PROCEDURE MEANS used:
      real time           0.02 seconds
```

The Log window contains the programming statements that are submitted, as well as notes about

- any files that were read
- the records that were read
- the program execution and results.

In this example, the Log window contains no warning or error messages. If the program contains errors, relevant warning and error messages are also written to the SAS log.

4. Issue the END command or select **Window** ⇨ **Program Editor** to return to the Program Editor window.

Running a SAS Program – UNIX (Optional)

File: c02s2d1.sas

- Start a SAS session.
- Include and submit a program.
- Browse the results.

Starting a SAS Session

1. In your UNIX session, type in the appropriate command to start a SAS session.

    How you invoke SAS varies by your operating environment and any
    customizations in effect at your site.

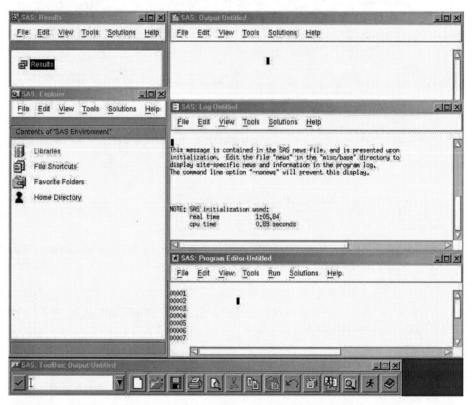

The Results window and Explorer window have slightly different functionality in
different operating environments. Refer to the end of this chapter for a discussion
of these windows.

Including and Submitting a SAS Program

1. To open (include) a SAS program into your SAS session, select **File** ⇨ **Open** or
    click on [icon] and then select the file you want to include.

    You can also issue the INCLUDE command to open (include) a SAS program.

    a. Type **include** and the name of the file containing your program on the
        command bar.
    b. Press Enter.

    You can use the Program Editor window to

    -   access and edit existing SAS programs
    -   write new SAS programs
    -   submit SAS programs
    -   save SAS programs to a file.

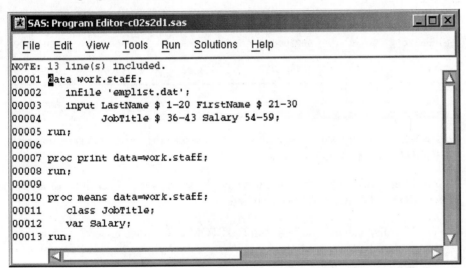

    ✎   The program contains three steps: a DATA step and two PROC steps.

2. Click on [icon] or select **Run** ⇨ **Submit** or issue the SUBMIT command to
    submit your program for execution. The output from your program is displayed
    in the Output window.

Examining Your Program Results

The Output window

- is one of the primary windows and is open by default.
- becomes the active window each time it receives output.
- automatically accumulates output in the order in which it is generated. You can issue the CLEAR command or select **Edit** ⇨ **Clear All** or click 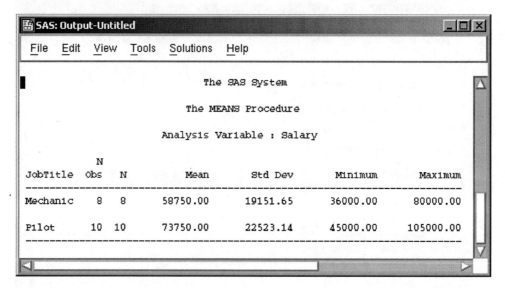 to clear the contents of the window.

To scroll horizontally within the Output window, use the horizontal scrollbar or issue the RIGHT and LEFT commands.

To scroll vertically within the Output window, use the vertical scrollbar or issue the FORWARD and BACKWARD commands.

    You also can use the TOP and BOTTOM commands to scroll vertically within the Output window.

1. Scroll to the top to view the output from the PRINT procedure.

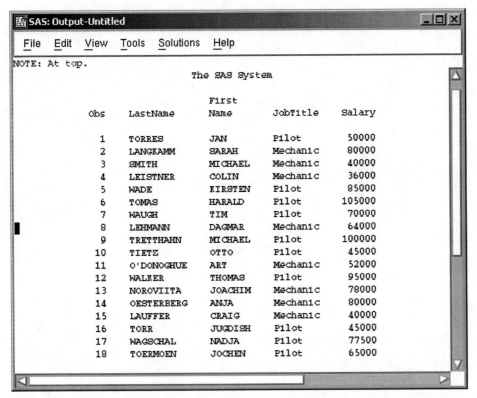

2. Issue the LOG command or select **View** ⇨ **Log** to display the Log window and browse the messages that the program generated.

   The Log window
   - is one of the primary windows and is open by default
   - acts as a record of your SAS session; messages are written to the log in the order in which they are generated by the program.

3. Issue the CLEAR command or select **Edit** ⇨ **Clear All** or click 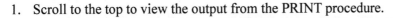 to clear the contents of the window.

Partial Log

```
┌─────────────────────────────────────────────────────────────────────────┐
│ 🖹 SAS: Log-Untitled                                          [_][□][✕]    │
├─────────────────────────────────────────────────────────────────────────┤
│   File    Edit    View    Tools    Solutions    Help                       │
├─────────────────────────────────────────────────────────────────────────┤
│1    data work.staff;                                                       │
│2       infile 'emplist.dat';                                               │
│3       input LastName $ 1-20 FirstName $ 21-30              █              │
│4            JobTitle $ 36-43 Salary 54-59;                                 │
│5    run;                                                                   │
│                                                                           │
│NOTE: The infile 'emplist.dat' is:                                         │
│      File Name=/users/edu99/emplist.dat,                                   │
│      Owner Name=edu99, Group Name=UNKNOWN,                                 │
│      Access Permission=rw-rw-r--,                                          │
│      File Size (bytes)=1080                                                │
│                                                                           │
│NOTE: 18 records were read from the infile 'emplist.dat'.                   │
│      The minimum record length was 59.                                     │
│      The maximum record length was 59.                                     │
│NOTE: The data set WORK.STAFF has 18 observations and 4 variables.          │
│NOTE: DATA statement used:                                                  │
│      real time            0.07 seconds                                     │
│      cpu time             0.05 seconds                                     │
│                                                                           │
│                                                                           │
│6                                                                          │
│7    proc print data=work.staff;                                           │
│8    run;                                                                   │
│                                                                           │
│NOTE: There were 18 observations read from the dataset WORK.STAFF.          │
│NOTE: PROCEDURE PRINT used:                                                 │
│      real time            0.17 seconds                                     │
│      cpu time             0.13 seconds                                     │
│                                                                           │
│                                                                           │
│9                                                                          │
│10   proc means data=work.staff;                                           │
│11      class JobTitle;                                                     │
│12      var Salary;                                                         │
│13   run;                                                                   │
└─────────────────────────────────────────────────────────────────────────┘
```

The Log window contains the programming statements that were most recently submitted, as well as notes about

- any files that were read
- the records that were read
- the program execution and results.

In this example, the Log window contains no warning or error messages. If your program contains errors, relevant warning and error messages are also written to the SAS log.

4. Issue the END command or select **View** ⇨ **Program Editor** to return to the Program Editor window.

Running a SAS Program – z/OS (OS/390) (Optional)

File: *userid*.prog1.sascode(c02s2d1)

- Start a SAS session.
- Include and submit a program.
- Browse the results.

Starting a SAS Session

Type in the appropriate command to start your SAS session.

 How you invoke SAS varies by your operating environment and any customizations in effect at your site.

```
┌Log─────────────────────────────────────────────────────────────┐
 Command ===>

 NOTE: This session is executing on the z/OS    V01R04M00 platform.

 NOTE: Running on IBM Model 2066 Serial Number 023A7A,
                  IBM Model 2066 Serial Number 123A7A.


   Welcome to the SAS Information Delivery System,

         999        000      Release 9.0!  Installed 12Feb2003.
          9  9      0   0
          9  9      0   0    Problems with this version?  Report in DEFECT
           9999     0   0    as Release 9, level TSOM0, platform OS/390
     v  v    99     0   0
     v v    99    0  0   0   Questions or problems?
      v    99     0    000   Contact Carol Angeli x15088 or Ron Burt x16324
└─────────────────────────────────────────────────────────────────┘
┌Program Editor────────────────────────────────────────────────────┐
 Command ===> █

 00001
 00002
 00003
 00004
 00005
 00006
 00007
 00008
 00009
└──────────────────────────────────────────────────────────────────┘
```

Including and Submitting a SAS Program

1. To include (copy) a SAS program into your SAS session, issue the INCLUDE command.

    a. Type **include** and the name of the file containing your program on the command line of the Program Editor.

    b. Press Enter.

```
┌Program Editor─────────────────────────────────────────────────────
 Command ===> include '.prog1.sascode(c02s2d1)'█

 00001
 00002
 00003
 00004
 00005
 00006
 00007
 00008
 00009
```

The program is included in the Program Editor window.

You can use the Program Editor window to

- access and edit existing SAS programs
- write new SAS programs
- submit SAS programs
- save programming statements in a file.

The program contains three steps: a DATA step and two PROC steps.

Issue the SUBMIT command to execute your program.

```
┌Program Editor─────────────────────────────────────────────────────
 Command ===> submit█

 00001 data work.staff;
 00002    infile '.prog1.rawdata(emplist)';
 00003    input LastName $ 1-20 FirstName $ 21-30
 00004          JobTitle $ 36-43 Salary 54-59;
 00005 run;
 00006
 00007 proc print data=work.staff;
 00008 run;
 00009
 00010 proc means data=work.staff;
 00011    class JobTitle;
 00012    var Salary;
 00013 run;
```

2. The first page of the output from your program is displayed in the Output window.

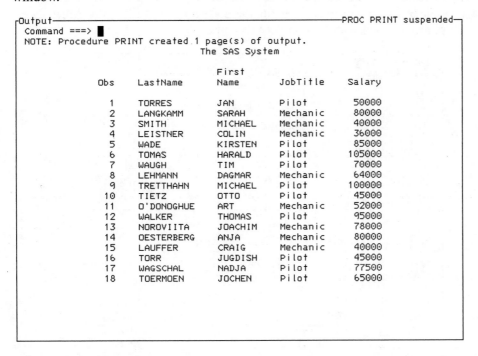

Examining Your Program Results

The Output window

- is one of the primary windows and is open by default.
- becomes the active window each time it receives output.
- automatically accumulates output in the order in which it is generated. You can issue the CLEAR command or select **Edit** ⇨ **Clear All** to clear the contents of the window.

To scroll horizontally within the Output window, issue the RIGHT and LEFT commands.

To scroll vertically within the Output window, issue the FORWARD and BACKWARD commands.

   You also can use the TOP and BOTTOM commands to scroll vertically within the Output window.

1. Issue the END command. If the PRINT procedure produces more than one page
    of output, you are taken to the last page of output. If the PRINT procedure
    produces only one page of output, the END command allows the MEANS
    procedure to execute and produce its output.

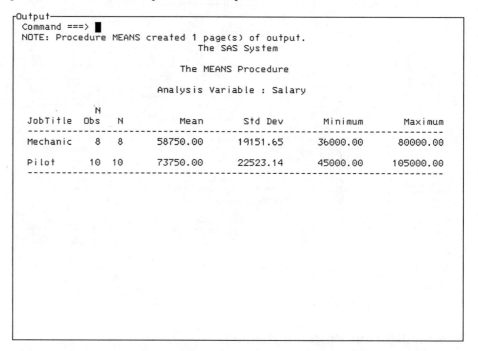

```
┌Output─────────────────────────────────────────────────────────────────────┐
│ Command ===> █                                                             │
│ NOTE: Procedure MEANS created 1 page(s) of output.                        │
│                           The SAS System                                   │
│                                                                            │
│                         The MEANS Procedure                                │
│                                                                            │
│                       Analysis Variable : Salary                           │
│                                                                            │
│              N                                                             │
│ JobTitle   Obs   N        Mean         Std Dev        Minimum      Maximum │
│ ----------------------------------------------------------------------------│
│ Mechanic    8    8     58750.00       19151.65       36000.00     80000.00 │
│                                                                            │
│ Pilot      10   10     73750.00       22523.14       45000.00    105000.00 │
│ ----------------------------------------------------------------------------│
│                                                                            │
│                                                                            │
│                                                                            │
│                                                                            │
│                                                                            │
└────────────────────────────────────────────────────────────────────────────┘
```

You can issue an AUTOSCROLL 0 command on the command line of
the Output window to have all of your SAS output from one submission
placed in the Output window at one time. This eliminates the need to
issue an END command to run each step separately.

The AUTOSCROLL command is in effect for the duration of your SAS
session. If you want this every time you invoke SAS, you can save this
setting by typing **autoscroll 0; wsave** on the command line of
the Output window.

2. Issue the END command to return to the Program Editor window.

After the program executes, you can view messages in the Log window.

Partial Log

```
┌Log─────────────────────────────────────────────────────────────────
 Command ===> █

 1    data work.staff;
 2       infile '.prog1.rawdata(emplist)';
 3       input LastName $ 1-20 FirstName $ 21-30
 4             JobTitle $ 36-43 Salary 54-59;
 5    run;

 NOTE: The infile '.prog1.rawdata(emplist)' is:
       Dsname=EDU403.PROG1.RAWDATA(EMPLIST),
       Unit=3380,Volume=PUB802,Disp=SHR,Blksize=23440,
       Lrecl=80,Recfm=FB

 NOTE: 18 records were read from the infile '.prog1.rawdata(emplist)'.
 NOTE: The data set WORK.STAFF has 18 observations and 4 variables.
 NOTE: The DATA statement used 0.06 CPU seconds and 3158K.

 6
 7    proc print data=work.staff;
 8    run;

 NOTE: There were 18 observations read from the data set WORK.STAFF.
 NOTE: The PROCEDURE PRINT used 0.05 CPU seconds and 3368K.

 9
 10   proc means data=work.staff;
 11      class JobTitle;
 12      var Salary;
 13   run;
```

The Log window

- is one of the primary windows and is open by default.

- acts as a record of your SAS session; messages are written to the log in the order in which they are generated by the program. You can issue the CLEAR command to clear the contents of the window.

The Log window contains the programming statements that were recently submitted, as well as notes about

- any files that were read

- the records that were read

- the program execution and results.

In this example, the Log window contains no warning or error messages. If your program contains errors, relevant warning and error messages are also written to the SAS log.

Issue the END command to return to the Program Editor window.

Running a SAS Program – z/OS (OS/390) Batch (Optional)

File: *userid*.prog1.sascode(batch)

- Submit a program.
- Browse the results.

Submitting a SAS Program

1. To submit a SAS program,
    a. use an editor to create a file containing the necessary JCL and your SAS program
    b. issue a SUBMIT command or perform the steps necessary to submit your program for execution.

```
EDIT       EDU403.PROG1.SASCODE(BATCH) - 01.00          Columns 00001 00072
Command ===> submit                                       Scroll ===> CSR
***** *************************** Top of Data *****************************
000001 //SASCLASS JOB (,STUDENT),'CARY',TIME=(,5),MSGCLASS=H
000002 /*JOBPARM FETCH
000003 // EXEC SAS9
000004 //SYSIN DD *
000005 data work.staff;
000006    infile '.prog1.rawdata(emplist)';
000007    input LastName $ 1-20 FirstName $ 21-30
000008          JobTitle $ 36-43 Salary 54-59;
000009 run;
000010
000011 proc print data=work.staff;
000012 run;
000013
000014 proc means data=work.staff;
000015    class Jobtitle;
000016    var Salary;
000017 run;
****** *************************** Bottom of Data ***************************
```

The program contains three steps: a DATA step and two PROC steps.

Examining Your Program Results

1. Use a utility (for example, IOF) to view the results of your batch job. You can view the output of your program by selecting **SASLIST**.

```
------------------------------- IOF Job Summary -----------------------------
COMMAND ===>                                           SCROLL ===> SCREEN
--JOBNAME--JOBID----STATUS---RAN/RECEIVED------DAY-------DEST----------------
  SASCLASS J028513  OUTPUT   12:28  12/02/2003 TODAY      KHPLJ2
--RC--PGM--------STEP-----PRSTEP---PROC-----COMMENTS------------------------
   0  SAS        SAS                SAS9
--------DDNAME---STEP-----STAT-ACT-C-GRP-D-SIZE-U-DEST--------------UCS------
_    1  LOG      *         HELD     H  1 H    17 L KHPLJ2
_    2  JCL      *         HELD     H  1 H    50 L KHPLJ2
_    3  MESSAGES *         HELD     H  1 H    90 L KHPLJ2
_    4  SASLOG   SAS       HELD     H  1 H    83 L KHPLJ2
_    5  SASCLOG  SAS       DONE     H
s    6  SASLIST  SAS       HELD SEL H  1 H    36 L KHPLJ2
_    7  SYSUDUMP SAS       DONE     H
```

2. The first page of output is displayed.

```
BROWSE - SASLIST          SAS      - Page  1    Line  1        Cols 18-97
COMMAND ===>                                           SCROLL ===> SCREEN
******************************** Top of Data *********************************
                              The SAS System

                              First
            Obs    LastName   Name       JobTitle    Salary

             1     TORRES     JAN        Pilot        50000
             2     LANGKAMM   SARAH      Mechanic     80000
             3     SMITH      MICHAEL    Mechanic     40000
             4     LEISTNER   COLIN      Mechanic     36000
             5     WADE       KIRSTEN    Pilot        85000
             6     TOMAS      HARALD     Pilot       105000
             7     WAUGH      TIM        Pilot        70000
             8     LEHMANN    DAGMAR     Mechanic     64000
             9     TRETTHAHN  MICHAEL    Pilot       100000
            10     TIETZ      OTTO       Pilot        45000
            11     O'DONOGHUE ART        Mechanic     52000
            12     WALKER     THOMAS     Pilot        95000
            13     NOROVIITA  JOACHIM    Mechanic     78000
            14     OESTERBERG ANJA       Mechanic     80000
            15     LAUFFER    CRAIG      Mechanic     40000
            16     TORR       JUGDISH    Pilot        45000
            17     WAGSCHAL   NADJA      Pilot        77500
            18     TOERMOEN   JOCHEN     Pilot        65000
```

3. Because both the PRINT procedure and the MEANS procedure created output,
    SASLIST window contains several reports. Use scrolling commands to see the
    other pages of output.

```
BROWSE - SASLIST            SAS       - Page  2    Line  1       Cols 1-80
COMMAND ===> █                                            SCROLL ===> SCREEN
                         The SAS System

                       The MEANS Procedure

                    Analysis Variable : Salary

               N
JobTitle  Obs   N         Mean       Std Dev      Minimum      Maximum
----------------------------------------------------------------------------
Mechanic    8    8     58750.00     19151.65     36000.00     80000.00

Pilot      10   10     73750.00     22523.14     45000.00    105000.00
----------------------------------------------------------------------------
******************************* Bottom of Data ******************************
```

4. Return to the main job results screen and select **SASLOG** to see a record of your
    SAS session. Messages are written to the log in the order in which they are
    generated by the program.

```
---------------------------- IOF Job Summary ----------------------------
COMMAND ===>                                             SCROLL ===> SCREEN
--JOBNAME---JOBID--STATUS---RAN/RECEIVED------DAY--------DEST-----------------
  SASCLASS J26669  OUTPUT      9:28   7/25/2001 TODAY       SDCMVS
--RC--PGM--------STEP-----PRSTEP---PROC----COMMENTS-------------------------
   0  SASXALV    SAS                SAS8
--------DDNAME---STEP-----STAT-ACT-C-GRP-D-SIZE-U--DEST---------------UCS------
  _   1  LOG        *       HELD    Z  1 H   17 L  SDCMVS
  _   2  JCL        *       HELD    Z  1 H   81 L  SDCMVS
  _   3  MESSAGES   *       HELD    Z  1 H  108 L  SDCMVS
  s█  4  SASLOG    SAS      HELD    Z  1 H   71 L  SDCMVS
  _   5  SASCLOG   SAS      DONE    Z
  _   6  SASLIST   SAS      HELD SEL Z  1 H   36 L  SDCMVS
  _   7  SYSUDUMP  SAS      DONE    D
  _   8  SASSNAP   SAS      DONE    D
      .
```

```
BROWSE - SASLOG             SAS       - Page  1    Line  36      Cols 1-80
COMMAND ===> █                                            SCROLL ===> SCREEN
1            data work.staff;
2                infile 'edu403.prog1.rawdata(emplist)';
3                input LastName $ 1-20 FirstName $ 21-30
4                      JobTitle $ 36-43 Salary 54-59;
5            run;

NOTE: The infile 'edu403.prog1.rawdata(emplist)' is:
      Dsname=EDU403.PROG1.RAWDATA(EMPLIST),
      Unit=3380,Volume=PUB802,Disp=SHR,Blksize=23440,
      Lrecl=80,Recfm=FB

NOTE: 18 records were read from the infile 'edu403.prog1.rawdata(emplist)'.
NOTE: The data set WORK.STAFF has 18 observations and 4 variables.
NOTE: The DATA statement used 0.06 CPU seconds and 2537K.

7            proc print data=work.staff;
8            run;

NOTE: There were 18 observations read from the data set WORK.STAFF.
NOTE: The PROCEDURE PRINT printed page 1.
NOTE: The PROCEDURE PRINT used 0.04 CPU seconds and 2619K.

10           proc means data=work.staff;
11               class JobTitle;
12               var Salary;
```

The SASLOG contains the programming statements that were submitted, as well as notes about

- any files that were read
- the records that were read
- the program execution and results.

In this example, the SASLOG contains no warning or error messages. If your program contains errors, relevant warning and error messages are also written to the SASLOG.

 **Exercises**

1. **Submitting a Program**

   a. With the Program Editor window active, include a SAS program.

      - Windows and UNIX: Select **File** ⇨ **Open** and select the program
        `'c02ex1.sas'` or issue the command: `include 'c02ex1.sas'`

      - z/OS (OS/390): Issue the command
        `include '.prog1.sascode(c02ex1)'`

   b. Submit the program for execution. Based on the report in the Output window,
       how many observations and variables are in the **work.airports** data set?

   c. Examine the Log window. Based on the log notes, how many observations
       and variables are in the **work.airports** data set?

   d. Clear the Log and Output windows.

2. **Issuing the KEYS Command (Optional)**

   The KEYS window is

   - a secondary window

   - used to browse or change function key definitions

   - closed by issuing the END command (Windows, UNIX, z/OS) or by clicking
     on ☒ (Windows, UNIX).

   a. Issue the KEYS command. Browse the contents of the window by scrolling
       vertically.

   b. Close the KEYS window.

2.3 Mastering Fundamental Concepts

Objectives

- Define the components of a SAS data set.
- Define a SAS variable.
- Identify a missing value and a SAS date value.
- State the naming conventions for SAS data sets and variables.
- Explain SAS syntax rules.
- Investigate a SAS data set using the CONTENTS and PRINT procedures.

21

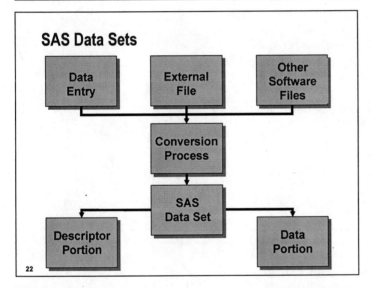

22

descriptor = metadata

Data must be in the form of a SAS data set to be processed by many SAS procedures and some DATA step statements.

A *SAS program* is a file that contains SAS code.

A *SAS data set* is a specially structured file that contains data values.

SAS Data Sets

SAS data sets have a descriptor portion and a data portion.

Descriptor Portion

```
General data set information
* data set name       * data set label
* date/time created * storage information
* number of observations

Information for each variable
* Name   * Type      * Length  * Position
* Format * Informat  * Label
```

Data Portion

23

Browsing the Descriptor Portion

The *descriptor portion* of a SAS data set contains

- general information about the SAS data set (such as data set name and number of observations)
- variable attributes (name, type, length, position, informat, format, label).

The CONTENTS procedure displays the descriptor portion of a SAS data set.

24

Browsing the Descriptor Portion

General form of the CONTENTS procedure:

```
PROC CONTENTS DATA=SAS-data-set;
RUN;
```

Example:

```
proc contents data=work.staff;
run;
```

25   c02s3d1

Partial PROC CONTENTS Output

```
                        The SAS System

                     The CONTENTS Procedure

Data Set Name: WORK.STAFF          Observations:         18
Member Type:   DATA                Variables:            4
Engine         V9                  Indexes               0
Created        Monday, December 01, Observation Length    48
               2003 10:36:59 AM
Last Modified  Monday, December 01, Deleted Observations  0
               2003 10:36:59 AM
Protection:                        Compressed:           NO
Data Set Type:                     Sorted:               NO
Label:

           Alphabetic List of Variables and Attributes

             #     Variable    Type    Len

             2     FirstName   Char     10
             3     JobTitle    Char      8
             1     LastName    Char     20
             4     Salary      Num       8
```

26

This is a partial view of the default PROC CONTENTS output. PROC CONTENTS output also contains information about the physical location of the file and other data set information.

The descriptor portion contains the metadata of the data set.

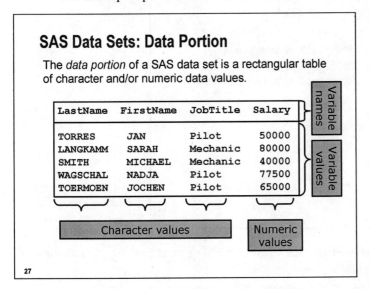

SAS Data Sets: Data Portion

The *data portion* of a SAS data set is a rectangular table of character and/or numeric data values.

LastName	FirstName	JobTitle	Salary
TORRES	JAN	Pilot	50000
LANGKAMM	SARAH	Mechanic	80000
SMITH	MICHAEL	Mechanic	40000
WAGSCHAL	NADJA	Pilot	77500
TOERMOEN	JOCHEN	Pilot	65000

Variable names

Variable values

Character values   Numeric values

27

The **variables** *(columns)* in the table correspond to fields of data, and each data column is named.

The **observations** *(rows)* in the table correspond to records or data lines.

character
limit
32,767

SAS Variable Values

There are two types of variables:

character	contain any value: letters, numbers, special characters, and blanks. Character values are stored with a length of 1 to 32,767 bytes. One byte equals one character.
numeric	stored as floating point numbers in 8 bytes of storage by default. Eight bytes of floating point storage provide space for 16 or 17 significant digits. You are not restricted to 8 digits.

28

In Version 6 and earlier, character values are stored with a length of 1 to 200 bytes.

SAS Data Set and Variable Names

SAS names

- can be 32 characters long.
- can be uppercase, lowercase, or mixed-case.
- must start with a letter or underscore. Subsequent characters can be letters, underscores, or numeric digits.

29

In Version 6 and earlier, data set and variable names can only be a maximum of 8 characters long.

Starting in Version 8, special characters can be used in data set and variable names if you put the name in quotes followed immediately by the letter N.

Example: `class 'Flight#'n;`

In order to use special characters in variable names, the VALIDVARNAME option must be set to ANY (example: `options validvarname=any;`).

Valid SAS Names

Select the valid default SAS names.

- ☑ **data5mon**
- ☐ **5monthsdata**
- ☐ **data#5**
- ☐ **five months data**
- ☑ **fivemonthsdata**

30

SAS Date Values

SAS stores date values as numeric values.

A SAS date value is stored as the number of days between January 1, 1960, and a specific date.

```
←— 01JAN1959 —— 01JAN1960 —— 01JAN1961 —→
              store
←—  -365  ——————  0  ————————  366  ——→
              display
←— 01/01/1959 — 01/01/1960 —— 01/01/1961 —→
```

32

dates stored as numbers

date
time since midnight
datetime - seconds since midnight 1960

Missing Data Values

A value must exist for every variable for each observation. Missing values are valid values.

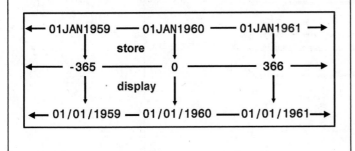

LastName	FirstName	JobTitle	Salary
TORRES	JAN	Pilot	50000
LANGKAMM	SARAH	Mechanic	80000
SMITH	MICHAEL	Mechanic	.
WAGSCHAL	NADJA	Pilot	77500
TOERMOEN	JOCHEN		65000

A character missing value is displayed as a blank. (space)

A numeric missing value is displayed as a period.

no concept of null

33

Browsing the Data Portion

The PRINT procedure displays the data portion of a SAS data set.

By default, PROC PRINT displays
- all observations
- all variables
- an Obs column on the left side.

34

Browsing the Data Portion

General form of the PRINT procedure:

```
PROC PRINT DATA=SAS-data-set;
RUN;
```

Example:

```
proc print data=work.staff;
run;
```

35   c02s3d1

PROC PRINT Output

```
                          The SAS System

                        First
      Obs   LastName     Name        JobTitle    Salary

       1    TORRES       JAN         Pilot        50000
       2    LANGKAMM     SARAH       Mechanic     80000
       3    SMITH        MICHAEL     Mechanic     40000
       4    LEISTNER     COLIN       Mechanic     36000
       5    WADE         KIRSTEN     Pilot        85000
       6    TOMAS        HARALD      Pilot       105000
       7    WAUGH        TIM         Pilot        70000
       8    LEHMANN      DAGMAR      Mechanic     64000
       9    TRETTHAHN    MICHAEL     Pilot       100000
      10    TIETZ        OTTO        Pilot        45000
      11    O'DONOGHUE   ART         Mechanic     52000
      12    WALKER       THOMAS      Pilot        95000
      13    NOROVIITA    JOACHIM     Mechanic     78000
      14    OESTERBERG   ANJA        Mechanic     80000
      15    LAUFFER      CRAIG       Mechanic     40000
      16    TORR         JUGDISH     Pilot        45000
      17    WAGSCHAL     NADJA       Pilot        77500
      18    TOERMOEN     JOCHEN      Pilot        65000
```

36

SAS Data Set Terminology

SAS documentation and text in the SAS windowing environment use the following terms interchangeably:

SAS Data Set	↔	SAS Table
Variable	↔	Column
Observation	↔	Row

37

SAS Syntax Rules

SAS statements

- usually begin with an identifying keyword
- always end with a semicolon.

```
data work.staff;
   infile 'raw-data-file';
   input LastName $ 1-20 FirstName $ 21-30
         JobTitle $ 36-43 Salary 54-59;
run;

proc print data=work.staff;
run;

proc means data=work.staff;
   class JobTitle;
   var Salary;
run;
```
38

Examples of raw data file names:

z/OS (OS/390)	userid.prog1.rawdata(emplist)
Windows	c:\workshop\winsas\prog1\emplist.dat
UNIX	/users/userid/emplist.dat

In most situations, text in quotes is case-sensitive.

SAS Syntax Rules

- SAS statements are free-format.
- One or more blanks or special characters can be used to separate words.
- They can begin and end in any column.
- A single statement can span multiple lines.
- Several statements can be on the same line.

Unconventional Spacing

```
data work.staff;
infile 'raw-data-file';
input LastName $ 1-20 FirstName $ 21-30
JobTitle $ 36-43 Salary 54-59;
run;
    proc means data=work.staff;
class JobTitle;     var Salary;run;
```
40   ...

SAS Syntax Rules

Good spacing makes the program easier to read.

Conventional Spacing

```
data work.staff;
    infile 'raw-data-file';
    input LastName $ 1-20 FirstName $ 21-30
        JobTitle $ 36-43 Salary 54-59;
run;

proc print data=work.staff;
run;

proc means data=work.staff;
    class JobTitle;
    var Salary;
run;
```
45

SAS programming statements are easier to read if you begin DATA, PROC, and RUN statements in column one and indent the other statements

SAS Comments

- Type /* to begin a comment.
- Type your comment text.
- Type */ to end the comment.

```
/* Create work.staff data set */
data work.staff;
   infile 'raw-data-file';
   input LastName $ 1-20 FirstName $ 21-30
         JobTitle $ 36-43 Salary 54-59;
run;

/* Produce listing report of work.staff */
proc print data=work.staff;
run;
```

46   c02s3d2

Avoid placing the /* comment symbols in columns 1 and 2. On some operating environments, SAS may interpret these symbols as a request to end the SAS job or session.

An additional method used for commenting one line of code is to use the asterisk at the beginning of the comment. Everything that is between the asterisk and the semicolon is a comment.

Example: ***infile 'emplist.dat';**

SAS views the entire INFILE statement as a comment.

 **Exercises**

3. **Filling in the Blanks**

   a. SAS statements usually begin with a ___Key word___.

   b. Every SAS statement ends with a ___Semi-colon___.

   c. Character variable values can be up to ___32,767___ characters long and use ___one___ byte(s) of storage per character.

   d. A SAS variable name has ___1___ to ___32___ characters and begins with a ___letter___ or an ___underscore___.

   don't change default

   e. By default, numeric variables are stored in ___8___ bytes of storage.

   f. The internally stored SAS date value for January 1, 1960, is ___0___.

   g. A missing character value is displayed as a ___blank___.

   h. A missing numeric value is displayed as a ___.___

4. **Naming the Pairs**

   a. What are the two kinds of steps? *data + proc*

   b. What are the two portions of every SAS data set? *descriptor data*

   c. What are the two types of variables? *numeric + character*

   d. What are the two major parts of SAS output? *SAS log + output*

5. **Identifying as True or False**

   a. If a SAS program produces output, then the program ran correctly and there is no need to check the SAS log. *FALSE*

   b. Omitting a semicolon never causes errors. *FALSE*

6. **Correcting the Syntax of the SAS Program**

```
data europeflight;
   infile 'testdata.dat';
   input @1 Flt-Num $3. @18 Destination $3. ;
proc print data=europe;
run;
```

underscore not hyphen

2.4 Diagnosing and Correcting Syntax Errors

Objectives

- Identify SAS syntax errors.
- Debug and edit a program with errors.
- Resubmit the corrected program.
- Save the corrected program.

49

Syntax Errors

Syntax errors include

- misspelled keywords
- missing or invalid punctuation
- invalid options.

```
daat work.staff;
    infile 'raw-data-file';
    input LastName $ 1-20 FirstName $ 21-30
          JobTitle $ 36-43 Salary 54-59;
run;

proc print data=work.staff
run;

proc means data=work.staff average max;
    class JobTitle;
    var Salary;
run;
```

50

When SAS encounters a syntax error, SAS underlines the error and the following information is written to the SAS log:

- the word ERROR or WARNING
- the location of the error
- an explanation of the error.

Examples of raw data file names:

z/OS (OS/390)	userid.prog1.rawdata(emplist)
Windows	c:\workshop\winsas\prog1\emplist.dat
UNIX	/users/userid/emplist.dat

Debugging a SAS Program

File: c02s4d1.sas

File: *userid*.prog1.sascode(c02s4d1)

- Submit a SAS program that contains errors.
- Diagnose the errors
- Correct the program.
- Submit the corrected SAS program.
- Save the corrected program.

Submit a SAS Program with Errors

blue = Note
green = Warning
red = Error

```
daat work.staff;
    infile 'raw-data-file';
    input LastName $ 1-20 FirstName $ 21-30
          JobTitle $ 36-43 Salary 54-59;
run;


proc print data=work.staff
run;


proc means data=work.staff average max;
    class JobTitle;
    var Salary;
run;
```

The SAS log contains error messages and warnings.

```
1    daat work.staff;
     ----
     14
WARNING 14-169: Assuming the symbol DATA was misspelled as daat.

2        infile 'raw-data-file';
3        input LastName $ 1-20 FirstName $ 21-30
4              JobTitle $ 36-43 Salary 54-59;
5    run;

NOTE: The infile 'raw-data-file' is:
      File Name='raw-data-file',
      RECFM=V,LRECL=256

NOTE: 18 records were read from the infile 'raw-data-file'.
      The minimum record length was 59.
      The maximum record length was 59.
NOTE: The data set WORK.STAFF has 18 observations and 4
      variables.
```

```
NOTE: DATA statement used (Total process time):
      real time            0.08 seconds
      cpu time             0.07 seconds


6
7    proc print data=work.staff
8    run;
     ---
     22
       -
       200
ERROR 22-322: Syntax error, expecting one of the following: ;,
              (, DATA, DOUBLE, HEADING, LABEL, N, NOOBS, OBS,
              ROUND, ROWS, SPLIT, STYLE, UNIFORM, WIDTH.
ERROR 200-322: The symbol is not recognized and will be ignored.
9

NOTE: The SAS System stopped processing this step because of
      errors.
NOTE: PROCEDURE PRINT used (Total process time):
      real time            0.06 seconds
      cpu time             0.06 seconds



10   proc means data=work.staff average max;
                                 ------- ---
                                 22      202
ERROR 22-322: Syntax error, expecting one of the following: ;,
              (, ALPHA, CHARTYPE, CLASSDATA, CLM,
              COMPLETETYPES, CSS, CV, DATA, DESCEND,
              DESCENDING, DESCENDTYPES, EXCLNPWGT, EXCLNPWGTS,
              EXCLUSIVE, FW, IDMIN, KURTOSIS, LCLM, MAX,
              MAXDEC, MEAN, MEDIAN, MIN, MISSING, N, NDEC,
              NMISS, NONOBS, NOPRINT, NOTHREADS, NOTRAP, NWAY,
              ORDER, P1, P10, P25, P5, P50, P75, P90, P95, P99,
              PCTLDEF, PRINT, PRINTALL, PRINTALLTYPES, PRINTIDS,
              PRINTIDVARS, PROBT, Q1, Q3, QMARKERS, QMETHOD,
              QNTLDEF, QRANGE, RANGE, SKEWNESS, STDDEV,
              STDERR, SUM, SUMSIZE, SUMWGT, T, THREADS, UCLM,
              USS, VAR, VARDEF.
ERROR 202-322: The option or parameter is not recognized and
               will be ignored.
11       class JobTitle;
12       var Salary;
13   run;

NOTE: The SAS System stopped processing this step because of
      errors.
NOTE: PROCEDURE MEANS used (Total process time):
      real time            0.05 seconds
      cpu time             0.05 seconds
```

Debugging Your Program

The log indicates that SAS

- assumed the keyword DATA was misspelled and executed the DATA step
- interpreted the word RUN as an option in the PROC PRINT statement (because there was a missing semicolon), so PROC PRINT was not executed
- did not recognize the word AVERAGE as a valid option in the PROC MEANS statement, so the PROC MEANS step was not executed.

1. If you are using the Enhanced Editor, the program will remain in the editor.

    However, if you are using the Program Editor, the code disappears with each submit. Use the RECALL command or select **Run** ⇨ **Recall Last Submit** to recall the program you submitted back to the Program Editor. The original program is copied into the Program Editor.

2. Edit the program.

    a. Correct the spelling of DATA.

    b. Put a semicolon at the end of the PROC PRINT statement.

    c. Change the word AVERAGE to MEAN in the PROC MEANS statement.

```
data work.staff;
    infile 'raw-data-file';
    input LastName $ 1-20 FirstName $ 21-30
          JobTitle $ 36-43 Salary 54-59;
run;

proc print data=work.staff;
run;

proc means data=work.staff mean max;
    class JobTitle;
    var Salary;
run;
```

3. Submit the program. It runs successfully without errors and generates output.

Saving Your Program

You can use the FILE command to save your program to a file. The program must be in the Enhanced Editor or Program Editor before you issue the FILE command. If the code is not in the Program Editor, recall your program before saving the program.

z/OS (OS/390): `file '.prog1.sascode(myprog)'`

Windows or UNIX: `file 'myprog.sas'`

You can also select **File** ⇨ **Save As**.

A note appears that indicates the statements are saved to the file.

Submitting a SAS Program That Contains Unbalanced Quotes

The closing quote for the INFILE statement is missing.

File: c02s4d2.sas

File: *userid*.prog1.sascode(c02s4d2)

```
data work.staff;
   infile 'raw-data-file;
   input LastName $ 1-20 FirstName $ 21-30
         JobTitle $ 36-43 Salary 54-59;
run;

proc print data=work.staff;
run;

proc means data=work.staff mean max;
   class JobTitle;
   var Salary;
run;
```

Submit the program and browse the SAS log.

```
Log - (Untitled)  DATA STEP running                                    _ □ x

1      data work.staff;
2         infile 'emplist.dat;
3         input LastName $ 1-20 FirstName $ 21-30
4               JobTitle $ 36-43 Salary 54-59;
5      run;
6
7      proc print data=work.staff;
8      run;
9
10     proc means data=work.staff mean max;
11        class JobTitle;
12        var Salary;
13     run;
```

There are no notes in the SAS log because all of the SAS statements after the INFILE statement have become part of the quoted string.

 The banner on the window indicates the DATA step is still running because the RUN statement was not recognized.

Correcting Unbalanced Quotes Programatically

You can correct the unbalanced quotes programmatically by adding the following code before your previous statements:

```
*';*";run;
```

If the quote counter within SAS has an uneven number of quotation marks as seen in the above program, SAS reads the quotation in the comment above as the matching quote in the quote counter. SAS then has an even number of quotes in the quote counter and runs successfully, assuming no other errors occur. Both single quotation marks and double quotation marks are used in case you submitted double quotation marks instead of single quotation marks.

Point-and-Click Approaches to Balancing Quotation Marks

Windows

1. To correct the problem in the Windows environment, click the break icon 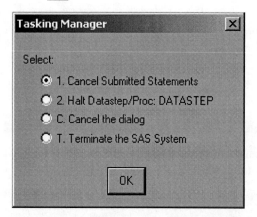 or press the Ctrl and Break keys.

2. Select **1. Cancel Submitted Statements** in the Tasking Manager window and select **OK**.

3. Select **Y to cancel submitted statements,** ⇨ **OK**.

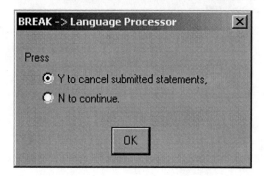

UNIX

1. To correct the problem in the UNIX operating environment, open the
   SAS: Session Management window and select **Interrupt**.

2. Select **1** in the SAS: Tasking Manager window.

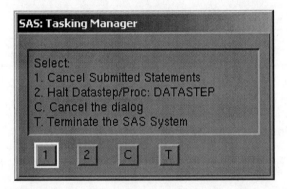

3. Select **Y**.

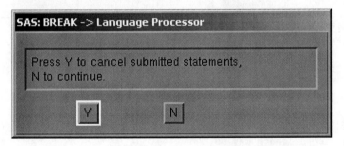

z/OS (OS/390)

1. To correct the problem in the z/OS (OS/390) operating environment, press the Attention key or issue the ATTENTION command.

2. Type **1** to select **1. Cancel Submitted Statements** and press Enter.

```
┌Tasking Manager────────────────────────────────────────────────┐
│ Select:                                                        │
│ 1 █. Cancel Submitted Statements                              │
│    2. Halt Datastep/Proc: DATASTEP                            │
│    C. Cancel the dialog                                       │
│    T. Terminate the SAS System                               │
└────────────────────────────────────────────────────────────────┘
```

3. Type **Y** and press Enter.

```
┌BREAK -> Language Processor─────────────────────────────────────┐
│ Press Y to cancel submitted statements, N to continue.   y █  │
└────────────────────────────────────────────────────────────────┘
```

Resubmitting the Program

1. Recall the program into the Program Editor window.

2. Add a closing quote to the file reference on the INFILE statement.

3. Resubmit the program.

Partial SAS Log

```
27    data work.staff;
28       infile 'raw-data-file';
29       input LastName $ 1-20 FirstName $ 21-30
30              JobTitle $ 36-43 Salary 54-59;
31    run;

NOTE: 18 records were read from the infile 'raw-data-file'.
      The minimum record length was 59.
      The maximum record length was 59.
NOTE: The data set WORK.STAFF has 18 observations and 4 variables.
32
33    proc print data=work.staff;
34    run;

NOTE: There were 18 observations read from the dataset WORK.STAFF.
35
36    proc means data=work.staff mean max;
37       class JobTitle;
38       var Salary;
39    run;

NOTE: There were 18 observations read from the dataset WORK.STAFF.
```

Recall a Submitted Program

Program statements accumulate in a recall buffer each time you issue a SUBMIT command.

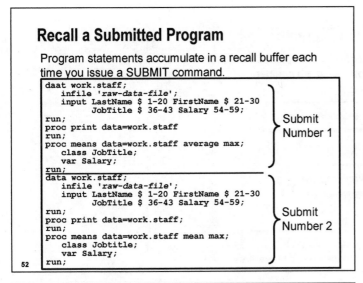

```
daat work.staff;
   infile 'raw-data-file';
   input LastName $ 1-20 FirstName $ 21-30
         JobTitle $ 36-43 Salary 54-59;
run;
proc print data=work.staff
run;
proc means data=work.staff average max;
   class JobTitle;
   var Salary;
run;
```
Submit Number 1

```
data work.staff;
   infile 'raw-data-file';
   input LastName $ 1-20 FirstName $ 21-30
         JobTitle $ 36-43 Salary 54-59;
run;
proc print data=work.staff;
run;
proc means data=work.staff mean max;
   class Jobtitle;
   var Salary;
run;
```
Submit Number 2

52

Recall a Submitted Program

Issue the RECALL command once to recall the most recently submitted program.

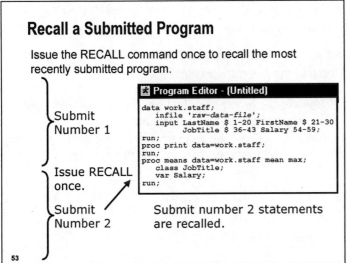

Submit Number 1

Issue RECALL once.

Submit Number 2

Program Editor - (Untitled)
```
data work.staff;
   infile 'raw-data-file';
   input LastName $ 1-20 FirstName $ 21-30
         JobTitle $ 36-43 Salary 54-59;
run;
proc print data=work.staff;
run;
proc means data=work.staff mean max;
   class JobTitle;
   var Salary;
run;
```

Submit number 2 statements are recalled.

53

Recall a Submitted Program

Issue the RECALL command again to recall submit number 1 statements.

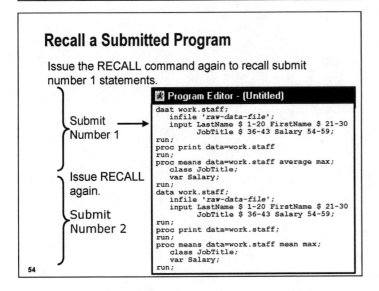

Submit Number 1

Issue RECALL again.

Submit Number 2

Program Editor - (Untitled)
```
daat work.staff;
   infile 'raw-data-file';
   input LastName $ 1-20 FirstName $ 21-30
         JobTitle $ 36-43 Salary 54-59;
run;
proc print data=work.staff
run;
proc means data=work.staff average max;
   class JobTitle;
   var Salary;
run;
data work.staff;
   infile 'raw-data-file';
   input LastName $ 1-20 FirstName $ 21-30
         JobTitle $ 36-43 Salary 54-59;
run;
proc print data=work.staff;
run;
proc means data=work.staff mean max;
   class JobTitle;
   var Salary;
run;
```

54

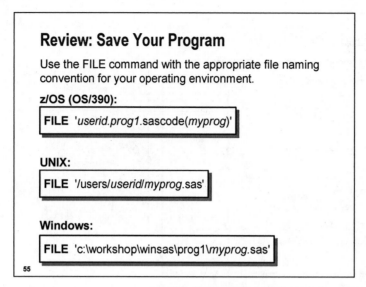

z/OS (OS/390):   A file reference of `'.PROG1.SASCODE(MYPROG)'`
                      assumes *userid* is the first level of the filename.

Windows and UNIX: A file reference of `'myprog.sas'` assumes the file will be
                      stored in the current working folder.

When you make changes to the program in the Enhanced Editor and have not
saved the new version of the program, the window bar and the top border of
the window reflect that you changed the program without saving it by putting
an asterisk (*) beside the window name. When you save the program, the *
disappears.

Exercises

7. Correcting Errors

a. With the Program Editor window active, include the SAS program **c02ex7**.

- Windows and UNIX: Select **File** ⇨ **Open** and select the program `'c02ex7.sas'` or issue the command: `include 'c02ex7.sas'`

- z/OS (OS/390): Issue the command: `include '.prog1.sascode(c02ex7)'`

b. Submit the program.

c. Use the SAS log notes to identify the error, correct the error, and resubmit the program.

2.5   Exploring Your SAS Environment (Self-Study)

Exploring Your SAS Environment under Windows

File: c02s5d1.sas

Enhanced Editor

The Enhanced Editor (the default editor on Windows) provides many helpful features, including color coding and automatically retaining the program after each submit, eliminating the need to recall your program.

In the Enhanced Editor, each program you open will open a new Enhanced Editor. You can have numerous Enhanced Editors open at one time. However, if you are using the Program Editor, you can only have one Program Editor open at a time.

✏   The Enhanced Editor is available only on Windows.

```
c02s5d1.sas                                                    _ □ X
data work.staff;
    infile 'emplist.dat';
    input LastName $ 1-20 FirstName $ 21-30
          JobTitle $ 36-43 Salary 54-59;
run;

proc print data=work.staff;
run;

proc means data=work.staff;
    class Jobtitle;
    var Salary;
run;
```

✏   The program contains three steps: a DATA step and two PROC steps.

As you browse the program, notice the following:
- The syntax is color-coded to show
  - step boundaries
  - keywords
  - variable and data set names.
- A section boundary line separates each step.

With the Enhanced Editor, you have the ability to minimize and maximize each DATA or PROC step. A minus sign ⊟ next to DATA or PROC indicates that the code has been expanded. To minimize the DATA or PROC step, click on the minus sign. Once the step has been minimized, the minus sign turns into a plus sign ⊞. To maximize the step after it has been minimized, click on the plus sign.

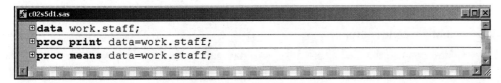

✎ You can customize the appearance and functionality of the Enhanced Editor by selecting **Tools** ⇨ **Options** ⇨ **Enhanced Editor**.

1. Issue the SUBMIT command or click on ⌐⌐ or select **Run** ⇨ **Submit** to submit the program for execution. The output from the program is displayed in the Output window.

✎ You can submit the code when it is collapsed. This is helpful if you want to highlight a portion of the program and submit only that portion. You can highlight the entire line that is visible for a step and submit it. To highlight the entire line, click to the left of the plus sign ⊞.

Navigating in Your SAS Session

1. Open the file **c02s5d1.sas** either by selecting **File** ⇨ **Open**, issuing the INCLUDE command, or by clicking on ⌐⌐ .

2. Submit the program in the Enhanced Editor by issuing the SUBMIT command, selecting **Run** ⇨ **Submit**, or by clicking on ⌐⌐ .

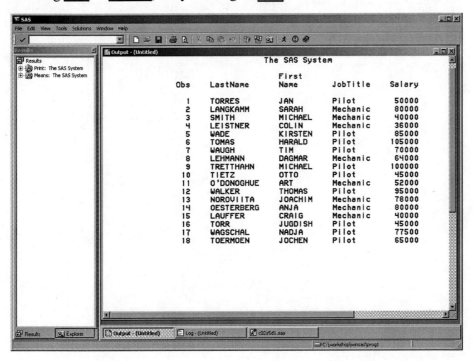

- The Results and Output windows are displayed when you submit a program that generates output.
- You can use the Ctrl and Tab keys to navigate between windows.
- You can use the SAS window bar at the bottom of the workspace to navigate between all of the windows in the SAS windowing environment or to minimize and maximize windows.
- Each window in the workspace has its own menu selections that reflect the actions you can perform when that window is active. This applies to pull-down, pop-up, and tool bar menus.
- The Results window lists all the reports that appear in the Output window. You can double-click and drill down on each procedure in the Results window, which enables you to go to that report in the Output window.
- Starting in Version 8, you can also use the Results window to erase particular reports from the Output window. You can delete each individual report by either right-clicking on the output name and selecting **Delete** or clicking on the ✕ on the tool bar.

3. Return to the Enhanced Editor by selecting [⚄ c02s5d1.sas] from the SAS window bar.

    Unlike the Program Editor, the code is not cleared from the Enhanced Editor after a submit, so you do not need to use a RECALL command.

Exploring SAS Libraries and Files

1. Select the  tab on the SAS window bar to open the Explorer
    window.

    The functionality of the SAS Explorer is similar to explorers for Windows-based
    systems. In addition to the single-pane view of folders and files that opens by
    default, you can specify a tree view.

2. You can also select **View** ⇨ **Explorer**.

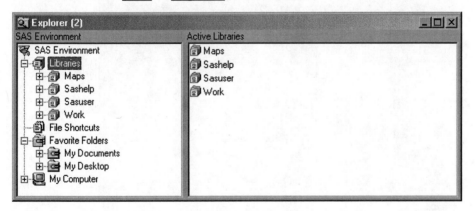

    You can change the size of the windows by positioning the cursor on the window
    divider so that the cursor becomes a double-arrow. Drag the window to the size
    you prefer.

3. Expand and collapse directories on the left. Drill-down and open specific files on
    the right.

4. Toggle this view off by selecting **View** ⇨ **Show Tree**.

    In addition to the tree view, you can view directories and files
    - as large and small icons
    - in a list format
    - by their detail information.

5. Double-click on the **work** library to show all members of that library.

6. Right-click on the **staff** data set and select **Properties**.

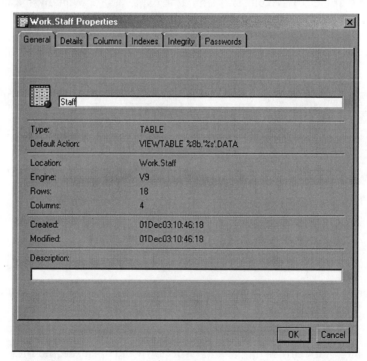

This default view provides general information about the data set, such as the library in which it is stored, the type of information it contains, its creation date, the number of observations and variables, and so on. You can request specific information about the columns in the data table by using the **Columns** tab at the top of the Properties window.

7. Select X to close the Properties window.

8. You can view the data portion of a data set by double-clicking on the file or right-clicking on the file and selecting **Open**. This opens the data set in a VIEWTABLE window. A view of **work.staff** is shown below.

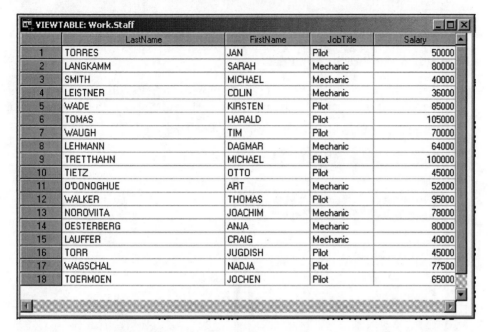

In addition to browsing SAS data sets, you can use the VIEWTABLE window to edit data sets, create data sets, and customize your view of a SAS data set. For example, you can

*   sort your data
*   change the color and fonts of variables
*   display variable labels versus variable names
*   remove and add variables.

9. Select ☒ to close the VIEWTABLE window.

Exploring Your SAS Environment under UNIX

File: c02s5d1.sas

Exploring SAS Libraries and Files

1. When you start your SAS session, the Explorer window is displayed in a single pane view. If the Explorer window is not displayed, you can open it by selecting 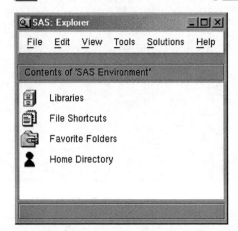 on the SAS Toolbox or selecting **View** ⇨ **Explorer**.

2. Select **View** ⇨ **Show Tree**. This selection toggles the tree view on or off.

The functionality of the SAS Explorer is similar to explorers for GUI-based systems. You can choose to use a tree view or a single-pane view of folders and files. The window above shows the tree view.

3. You can change the size of the windows by positioning the cursor on the window divider so that the cursor becomes a double arrow. Drag the window to the size you prefer.

4. You expand and collapse directories on the left and drill-down and open specific files on the right.

    In addition to the tree view, you can view directories and files

    • as large and small icons

    • in a list format

    • by their detail information.

5. Click on **Libraries** in the left panel to display the active libraries.

6. Right-click on the **work** library and select <u>**Open**</u> to show all members of the library.

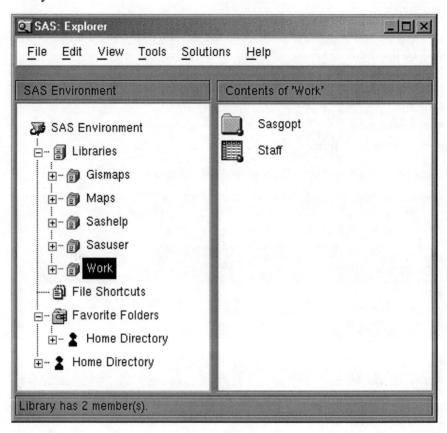

7. Right-click on the **staff** data set and select **Properties**.

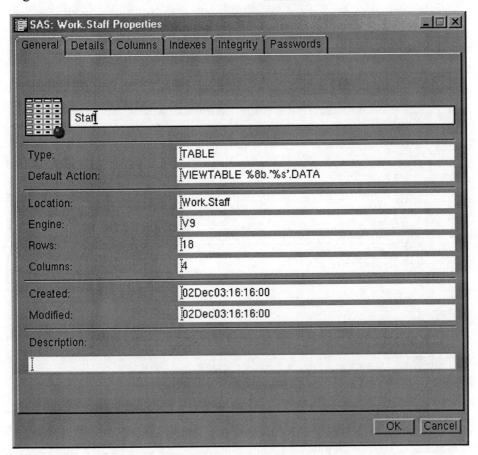

This default view provides general information about the data set, such as the library in which it is stored, the type of information it contains, its creation date, the number of observations and variables, and so on. You can request specific information about the columns in the data table by selecting the **Columns** tab at the top of the Properties window.

8. Select 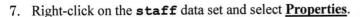 to close the Properties window.

9. View the data portion of a data set by double-clicking on the file or right-clicking on the file and selecting **Open**. This opens the data set in a VIEWTABLE window. A view of **work.staff** is shown below.

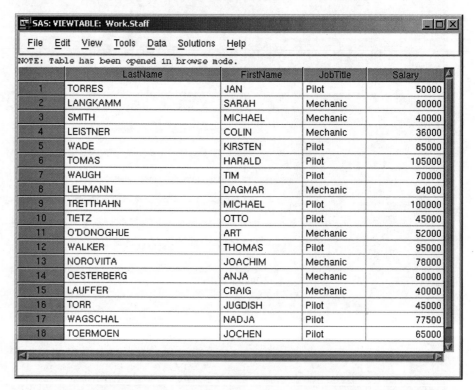

In addition to browsing SAS data sets, you can use the VIEWTABLE window to edit data sets, create data sets, and customize your view of a SAS data set. For example, you can

- sort your data
- change the color and fonts of variables
- display variable labels versus variable names
- remove and add variables.

10. Select **File** ⇨ **Close** to close the VIEWTABLE window.

Exploring Your SAS Environment under z/OS (OS/390)

File: *userid*.prog1.sascode(c02s5d1)

Navigating Your SAS Session

To perform tasks in your interactive SAS session, you can type commands on the command line or you can use

- pull-down menus
- function keys.

1. Type **pmenu** on a command line to turn on pull-down menus.

```
┌Program Editor──────────────────────────────────────
 Command ===> pmenu█

  00001
  00002
```

```
┌Program Editor──────────────────────────────────────
 File Edit View Tools Run Solutions Help

  00001
  00002
```

If you have a mouse to control the cursor, you can click on a word to see the available actions for each pull-down menu item. Click on a word to select an item or click outside the pull-down area to **not** select an action.

You can also use your tab or arrow keys to move through the pull-down menu and action items. Press Enter when the cursor is positioned on the item you want. Move your cursor away from the items and press Enter to **not** select an action.

2. Select **Tools** ⇨ **Options** ⇨ **Turn All Menus Off** to turn off the pull-down menus and return to a command line.

Exploring SAS Libraries and Files

1. Type **explorer** on the command line and press Enter or select
   View ➪ **Explorer** to open the Explorer window.

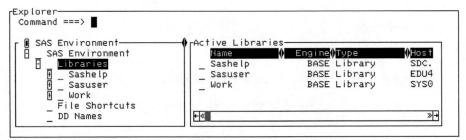

   You can specify a tree view or a single-pane view of folders and files. The
   window above shows the tree view.

2. Issue the TREE command or select **View** ➪ **Show Tree** and press Enter. This
   selection toggles the tree view on or off.

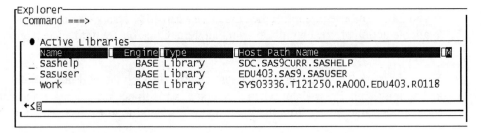

   The window above shows the single pane view.

3. If necessary, toggle the view to show the single pane view.

4. Type **S** next to the **work** library and press Enter to show all members of that
   library.

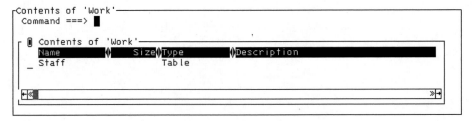

5. Type **?** next to the **staff** data set and press Enter. Select **Properties** and press Enter. You can also type **p** next to **staff** and press Enter.

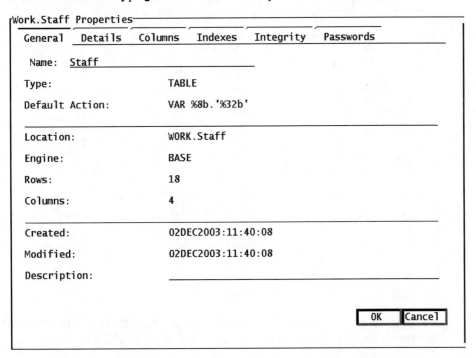

This default view provides general information about the data set, such as the library in which it is stored, the type of information it contains, its creation date, the number of observations and variables, and so on. You can also request specific information about the variables in the data set by selecting the **Columns** tab, or typing **V** next to **staff** and pressing Enter.

6. Select 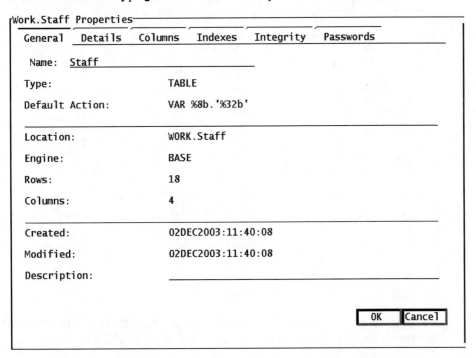 to close the Properties window.

7. To view the data portion of a data set, type **?** next to the filename, press Enter, and select **Open**. This opens the data set in an FSVIEW window. A view of **work.staff** is shown below.

```
┌FSVIEW:    WORK.STAFF  (B)─────────────────────────────────────────────
 Command ===>

   Obs      LastName             FirstName    JobTitle         Salary

    1       TORRES               JAN          Pilot            50000
    2       LANGKAMM             SARAH        Mechanic         80000
    3       SMITH                MICHAEL      Mechanic         40000
    4       LEISTNER             COLIN        Mechanic         36000
    5       WADE                 KIRSTEN      Pilot            85000
    6       TOMAS                HARALD       Pilot           105000
    7       WAUGH                TIM          Pilot            70000
    8       LEHMANN              DAGMAR       Mechanic         64000
    9       TRETTHAHN            MICHAEL      Pilot           100000
   10       TIETZ                OTTO         Pilot            45000
   11       O'DONOGHUE           ART          Mechanic         52000
   12       WALKER               THOMAS       Pilot            95000
   13       NOROVIITA            JOACHIM      Mechanic         78000
   14       OESTERBERG           ANJA         Mechanic         80000
   15       LAUFFER              CRAIG        Mechanic         40000
   16       TORR                 JUGDISH      Pilot            45000
   17       WAGSCHAL             NADJA        Pilot            77500
   18       TOERMOEN             JOCHEN       Pilot            65000


                                         ■
```

In addition to browsing SAS data sets, you can use the FSVIEW window to edit data sets, create data sets, and customize your view of a SAS data set.

8. Issue the END command or select **File** ⇨ **Close** and press Enter to close the FSVIEW window.

2.6 Solutions to Exercises

1. Submitting a Program

    a. Activate the Program Editor window. Issue the appropriate INCLUDE command or select **File** ⇨ **Open** to select the appropriate file.

```
Command ===> include 'operating-system-filename'
```

    b. To submit your program for execution, select [icon] or issue the SUBMIT command or select **Run** ⇨ **Submit**. Based on the report in the Output window, the **work.airports** data set has 15 observations and 3 variables.

    c. To activate the Log window, issue the LOG command or select **Window** ⇨ **Log**. The Log notes report that the **work.airports** data set has 15 observations and 3 variables.

    d. To clear the Log window, issue the CLEAR command or select **Edit** ⇨ **Clear All**. To activate and clear the Output window, issue the OUTPUT command or select **Window** ⇨ **Output**. Then issue the CLEAR command or select **Edit** ⇨ **Clear All**.

2. Issuing the KEYS Command (Optional)

    a. Type **keys** on the command line or command box or select **Tools** ⇨ **Options** ⇨ **Keys**. The KEYS window opens and you can view all function keys.

    b. Close the KEYS window by issuing the END command or selecting [X].

3. Filling in the Blanks

    a. SAS statements usually begin with an **identifying keyword**.

    b. Every SAS statement ends with a **semicolon**.

    c. Character variable values can be up to **32,767** characters long and use **1** byte(s) of storage per character.

    d. A SAS variable name has **1** to **32** characters and begins with a **letter** or an **underscore**.

    e. By default, numeric variables are stored in **8** bytes of storage.

    f. The internally stored SAS date value for January 1, 1960 is **0**.

    g. A missing character value is displayed as a **blank**.

    h. A missing numeric value is displayed as a **period**.

4. **Naming the Pairs**

   a. What are the two kinds of steps? **DATA and PROC**

   b. What are the two portions of every SAS data set? **Descriptor and Data**

   c. What are the two types of variables? **Character and Numeric**

   d. What are the two major parts of SAS output? **SAS Log and Output**

5. **Identifying as True or False**

   a. If a SAS program produces output, then the program ran correctly and there
       is no need to check the SAS log. **False**

   b. Omitting a semicolon never causes errors. **False**

6. **Correcting the Syntax of the SAS Program**

```
data europeflight;
   infile 'testdata.dat';
   input @1 Flt_Num $3. @18 Destination $3.;
run;
proc print data=europeflight;
run;
```

7. **Correcting Errors**

   a. Activate the Program Editor window by issuing the PGM command or
       selecting **Window** ⇨ **Program Editor**. Then issue the appropriate
       INCLUDE command or select **File** ⇨ **Open** to select the appropriate file.

       Command ===> include 'operating-system-filename'

   b. To submit the program for execution, issue the SUBMIT command or select
       Run ⇨ **Submit**.

   c. Activate the Log window by issuing the LOG command or selecting
       Window ⇨ **Log**. Scroll vertically to examine the SAS log notes. These notes
       confirm that the **work.airports** data set was created. However, an error
       occurred in the PROC step. The name of the procedure is misspelled.

       To recall the program into the Program Editor window, activate the Program
       Editor window by issuing the PGM command or selecting
       Window ⇨ **Program Editor**. Then issue the RECALL command or select
       Run ⇨ **Recall Last Submit**.

       Edit the program to correct the spelling of the PRINT procedure.

       Resubmit your program by issuing the SUBMIT command or selecting
       or **Run** ⇨ **Submit**.

If you do not see a report in the Output window, re-examine the SAS log notes, recall
the program, correct the error, and resubmit the program.

Chapter 3   Getting Familiar with SAS® Data Sets

3.1 SAS Data Libraries

Objectives

- Explain the concept of a SAS data library.
- State the difference between a permanent library and a temporary library.
- Use the CONTENTS procedure to investigate a SAS data library.

3

SAS Data Libraries

A *SAS data library* is a collection of SAS files that are recognized as a unit by SAS.

z/OS (OS/390)	A SAS data library is an operating system file.
z/OS (OS/390):	*userid*.mysas.files
Directory-based Systems	A SAS data library is a directory.
Windows:	c:\mysasfiles
UNIX:	/users/dept/mysasfiles

SAS Data Library

SAS File
SAS File
SAS File

A SAS data set is a type of SAS file.

4

SAS Data Libraries

You can think of a SAS data library as a drawer in a filing cabinet and a SAS data set as one of the file folders in the drawer.

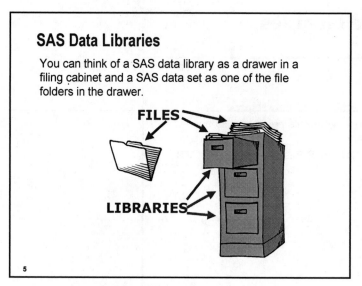

5

Assigning a Libref

Regardless of which host operating system you use, you identify SAS data libraries by assigning each a library reference name (libref).

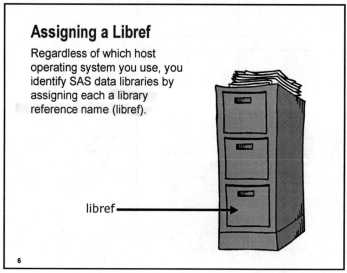

libref

6

SAS Data Libraries

When you invoke SAS, you automatically have access to a temporary and a permanent SAS data library.

work - temporary library ⟶

sasuser - permanent library ⟶

ia - permanent library ⟶

You can create and access your own permanent libraries.

7

The **work** library and its SAS data files are deleted after your SAS session ends.

SAS data sets in permanent libraries, such as the **ia** library, are saved after your SAS session ends.

Assigning a Libref

You can use the LIBNAME statement to assign a libref to a SAS data library.

General form of the LIBNAME statement:

> **LIBNAME** *libref* '*SAS-data-library*' *<options>;*

Rules for naming a libref:
- must be 8 characters or less
- must begin with a letter or underscore
- remaining characters are letters, numbers, or underscores.

8

✎   z/OS (OS/390) users can use a DD statement or TSO ALLOCATE command instead of issuing a LIBNAME statement.

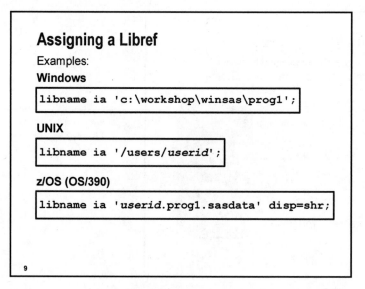

DISP=OLD|SHR specifies the disposition of the file. The default is OLD, which enables both read and write access. SHR enables read-only access.

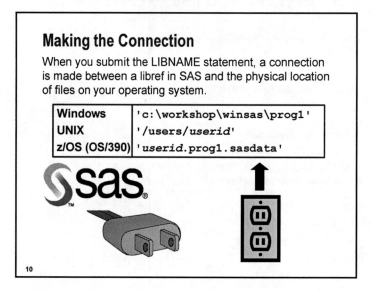

When your session ends, the link between the libref and physical location of your files is broken.

Two-level SAS Filenames

Every SAS file has a two-level name:

libref.filename

The data set **ia.sales** is a SAS file in the **ia** library.

- The first name (libref) refers to the library.

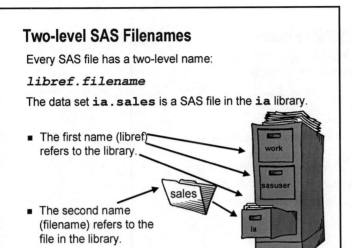

- The second name (filename) refers to the file in the library.

11

Temporary SAS Filename

The libref **work** can be omitted when you refer to a file in the **work** library. The default libref is **work** if the libref is omitted.

| work.employee | ⟷ | employee |

12

Browsing a SAS Data Library

During an interactive SAS session, the LIBNAME window enables you to investigate the contents of a SAS data library.

In the LIBNAME window, you can
- view a list of all the libraries available during your current SAS session
- drill down to see all members of a specific library
- display the descriptor portion of a SAS data set.

13

The LIBNAME command can be abbreviated as LIB.

LIBNAME Window: Windows

LIBNAME				
Active Libraries				
Name	Engine	Type	Host Path Name	Modi
Ila	V9	Library	C:\workshop\winsas\prog1	
Maps	V9	Library	C:\Program Files\SAS\SAS 9.1\maps	
Sashelp	V9	Library	('C:\Program Files\SAS\SAS 9.1\nls\en\SASCFG' 'C:\Program File	
Sasuser	V9	Library	C:\My Documents\V9	
Work	V9	Library	C:\temp\SAS Temporary Files_TD1860	

14

LIBNAME Window: UNIX

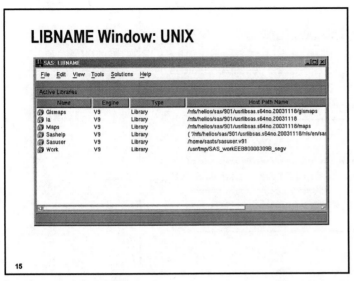

15

LIBNAME Window: z/OS (OS/390)

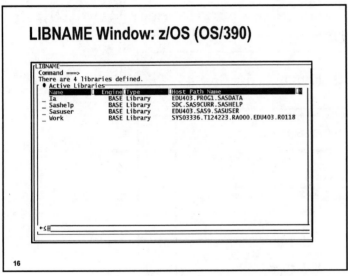

16

Browsing a SAS Data Library

Use the _ALL_ keyword to list all the SAS files in the library and the NODS option to suppress the descriptor portions of the data sets.

General form of the NODS option:

```
PROC CONTENTS DATA=libref._ALL_ NODS;
RUN;
```

NODS must be used in conjunction with the keyword _ALL_.

```
proc contents data=ia._all_ nods;
run;
```

17   c03s1d1

Space after ALL ⟶ nods

🖉 If you are using a noninteractive or batch SAS session, the CONTENTS procedure is an alternative to the LIBNAME command.

PROC CONTENTS Output

Partial Output

```
                         The SAS System

                     The CONTENTS Procedure

                           Directory

            Libref          IA
            Engine          V9
            Physical Name   C:\workshop\winsas\prog1
            File Name       C:\workshop\winsas\prog1

                        Member      File
        #  Name         Type        Size   Last Modified

        1  ALLGOALS     DATA        5120   31Jul01:08:52:34
        2  ALLGOALS2    DATA        5120   31Jul01:08:52:38
        3  ALLSALES     DATA        5120   31Jul01:08:53:28
        4  ALLSALES2    DATA        5120   31Jul01:08:53:46
        5  APRTARGET    DATA       17408   13Aug01:08:41:42
        6  CHICAGO      DATA       17408   31Jul01:08:54:38
        7  CREW         DATA       13312   31Jul01:08:54:44
        8  DELAY        DATA       66560   31Jul01:08:54:46
```

18

Browsing a SAS Data Library

To explore the descriptor portion of a SAS data set, specify the data set name in the DATA= option.

```
PROC CONTENTS DATA=libref.SAS-data-set-name;
RUN;
```

```
proc contents data=ia.crew;
run;
```

19   c03s1d1

PROC CONTENTS Output – Part 1

```
                    The SAS System

                  The CONTENTS Procedure

Data Set Name        IA.CREW          Observations          69
Member Type          DATA             Variables             8
Engine               V9               Indexes               0
Created              Friday, June 29, Observation Length    120
                     2001 03:15:27 PM
Last Modified        Friday, June 29, Deleted Observations  0
                     2001 03:41:07 PM
Protection                            Compressed            NO
Data Set Type                         Sorted                NO
Label
Data Representation  WINDOWS_32
Encoding             Default
```

20

PROC CONTENTS Output – Part 2

```
          Engine/Host Dependent Information

Data Set Page Size          12288
Number of Data Set Pages    1
First Data Page             1
Max Obs per Page           102
Obs in First Data Page     69
Number of Data Set Repairs  0
File Name                   C:\workshop\winsas\
                            prog1\crew.sas7bdat
Release Created             8.0202M0
Host Created                WIN_PRO
```

21

PROC CONTENTS Output – Part 3

#	Variable	Type	Len	Format	Informat
			Alphabetic List of Variables and Attributes		
6	EmpID	Char	6		
3	FirstName	Char	32		
1	HireDate	Num	8	DATE9.	DATE9.
7	JobCode	Char	6		
2	LastName	Char	32		
4	Location	Char	16		
5	Phone	Char	8		
8	Salary	Num	8		

22

Exercises

1. **Assigning a Permanent SAS Data Library**

   a. Submit the LIBNAME statement to provide access to a permanent SAS data library.

   ```
   libname ia 'c:\workshop\winsas\prog1';
   ```

   b. Check the log to confirm that the SAS data library was assigned.

2. **Investigating a SAS Library Interactively**

   a. Issue the LIBNAME command to display the available SAS data libraries.

   b. For Windows and UNIX users, double-click on the **ia** library. For z/OS (OS/390) users, type **s** beside the **ia** library and press Enter. (A partial listing in the Windows environment is shown below.)

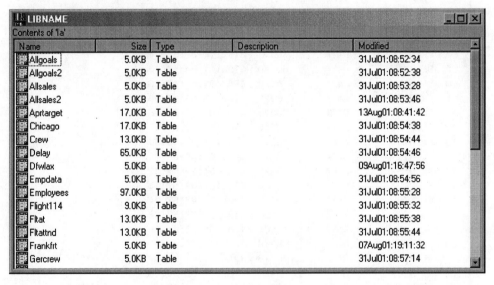

Name	Size	Type	Description	Modified
Allgoals	5.0KB	Table		31Jul01:08:52:34
Allgoals2	5.0KB	Table		31Jul01:08:52:38
Allsales	5.0KB	Table		31Jul01:08:53:28
Allsales2	5.0KB	Table		31Jul01:08:53:46
Aprtarget	17.0KB	Table		13Aug01:08:41:42
Chicago	17.0KB	Table		31Jul01:08:54:38
Crew	13.0KB	Table		31Jul01:08:54:44
Delay	65.0KB	Table		31Jul01:08:54:46
Dfwlax	5.0KB	Table		09Aug01:16:47:56
Empdata	5.0KB	Table		31Jul01:08:54:56
Employees	97.0KB	Table		31Jul01:08:55:28
Flight114	9.0KB	Table		31Jul01:08:55:32
Fltat	13.0KB	Table		31Jul01:08:55:38
Fltattnd	13.0KB	Table		31Jul01:08:55:44
Frankfrt	5.0KB	Table		07Aug01:19:11:32
Gercrew	5.0KB	Table		31Jul01:08:57:14

   c. Close the LIBNAME window.

3. Investigating a SAS Data Set with PROC CONTENTS

a. Submit a PROC CONTENTS step to list all the SAS data sets in the **ia** library. Do not display the descriptor portions of the individual data sets.

```
                            The SAS System

                        The CONTENTS Procedure


                              Directory


              Libref        IA
              Engine        V9
              Physical Name C:\workshop\winsas\prog1
              File Name     C:\workshop\winsas\prog1


                          Member    File
         #   Name          Type     Size   Last Modified

         1   ALLGOALS      DATA      5120  31Jul01:08:52:34
         2   ALLGOALS2     DATA      5120  31Jul01:08:52:38
         3   ALLSALES      DATA      5120  31Jul01:08:53:28
         4   ALLSALES2     DATA      5120  31Jul01:08:53:46
         5   APRTARGET     DATA     17408  13Aug01:08:41:42
         6   CHICAGO       DATA     17408  31Jul01:08:54:38
         7   CREW          DATA     13312  31Jul01:08:54:44
         8   DELAY         DATA     66560  31Jul01:08:54:46
         9   DFWLAX        DATA      5120  09Aug01:16:47:56
        10   EMPDATA       DATA      5120  31Jul01:08:54:56
        11   EMPLOYEES     DATA     99328  31Jul01:08:55:28
        12   FLIGHT114     DATA      9216  31Jul01:08:55:32
        13   FLTAT         DATA     13312  31Jul01:08:55:38
        14   FLTATTND      DATA     13312  31Jul01:08:55:44
        15   FRANKFRT      DATA      5120  07Aug01:19:11:32
        16   GERCREW       DATA      5120  31Jul01:08:57:14
        17   GERSCHED      DATA      5120  31Jul01:08:57:34
        18   GOALS         DATA      5120  31Jul01:08:57:38
        19   JUNTARGET     DATA     17408  13Aug01:08:41:18
        20   MAYTARGET     DATA      9216  13Aug01:08:41:30
        21   MECHANICS     DATA      9216  13Aug01:11:22:32
        22   MIAMIEMP      DATA      5120  31Jul01:08:58:58
        23   NEWMECHS      DATA      9216  31Jul01:08:59:18
        24   PARISEMP      DATA      5120  31Jul01:08:59:22
        25   PASSNGRS      DATA      5120  31Jul01:08:59:24
        26   PERFORMANCE   DATA      5120  31Jul01:08:59:40
        27   PERSONL       DATA     25600  31Jul01:08:59:44
        28   PILOTS        DATA      9216  10Sep01:10:52:56
        29   ROMEEMP       DATA      5120  31Jul01:08:59:56
        30   SALES121999   DATA    115712  31Jul01:09:01:16
        31   SANFRAN       DATA     13312  31Jul01:09:01:24
        32   TARGET121999  DATA    115712  09Aug01:18:38:22
        33   WEEKREV       DATA      5120  31Jul01:09:01:28
```

b. Modify the PROC CONTENTS step submitted above so only the descriptor portion of the data set **ia.pilots** is displayed.

```
                          The SAS System

                      The CONTENTS Procedure

Data Set Name      IA.PILOTS                Observations          20
Member Type        DATA                     Variables             11
Engine             V9                       Indexes               0
Created            Monday, September 10,    Observation Length    96
                   2001 10:52:54 AM
Last Modified      Monday, September 10,    Deleted Observations  0
                   2001 10:52:54 AM
Protection                                  Compressed            NO
Data Set Type                               Sorted                NO
Label
Data Representation WINDOWS_32
Encoding           Default



                  Engine/Host Dependent Information

   Data Set Page Size         8192
   Number of Data Set Pages   1
   First Data Page            1
   Max Obs per Page           84
   Obs in First Data Page     20
   Number of Data Set Repairs 0
   File Name                  C:\workshop\winsas\prog1\pilots.sas7bdat
   Release Created            8.0202M0
   Host Created               WIN_PRO



              Alphabetic List of Variables and Attributes

        #     Variable    Type    Len    Format    Informat

        9     Birth       Num      8     DATE7.    DATE.
        4     City        Char    15
        3     FName       Char    15
        6     Gender      Char     1
       11     HPhone      Char    12
       10     Hired       Num      8     DATE7.    DATE.
        1     IDNum       Char     4
        7     JobCode     Char     3
        2     LName       Char    15
        8     Salary      Num      8
        5     State       Char     2
```

3.2 Solutions to Exercises

1. **Assigning a Permanent SAS Data Library**

   ```
   libname ia 'SAS-data-library';
   ```

2. **Investigating a SAS Library Interactively**

   a. Issue the LIBNAME command to display the available SAS data libraries.

      ```
      Command ===> libname
      ```

   b. For Windows and UNIX users, double-click on the **ia** library. For z/OS (OS/390) users, type **s** beside the **ia** library and press Enter.

   c. Issue the END command or click on ☒ to close the LIBNAME window.

3. **Investigating a SAS Data Set with PROC CONTENTS**

   a.

      ```
      proc contents data=ia._all_ nods;
      run;
      ```

   b.

      ```
      proc contents data=ia.pilots;
      run;
      ```

Chapter 4 Producing List Reports

4.1 Getting Started with the PRINT Procedure

Objectives

- Generate simple list reports using the PRINT procedure.
- Display selected variables (columns) in a list report.
- Display selected observations (rows) in a list report.
- Display a list report with column totals.

3

Overview of PROC PRINT

List reports are typically generated with the PRINT procedure.

```
                       The SAS System

       Emp                             Job
Obs    ID     LastName     FirstName   Code     Salary

 1    0031   GOLDENBERG    DESIREE     PILOT    50221.62
 2    0040   WILLIAMS      ARLENE M.   FLTAT    23666.12
 3    0071   PERRY         ROBERT A.   FLTAT    21957.71
 4    0082   MCGWIER-WATTS CHRISTINA   PILOT    96387.39
 5    0091   SCOTT         HARVEY F.   FLTAT    32278.40
 6    0106   THACKER       DAVID S.    FLTAT    24161.14
 7    0355   BELL          THOMAS B.   PILOT    59803.16
 8    0366   GLENN         MARTHA S.   PILOT   120202.38
```

4

Overview of PROC PRINT

You can display
- titles and footnotes
- descriptive column headings
- formatted data values.

```
                              Salary Report

           Emp                                  Job         Annual
   Obs     ID      LastName        FirstName     Code        Salary

    1     0031     GOLDENBERG      DESIREE       PILOT      $50,221.62
    2     0040     WILLIAMS        ARLENE M.     FLTAT      $23,666.12
    3     0071     PERRY           ROBERT A.     FLTAT      $21,957.71
    4     0082     MCGWIER-WATTS   CHRISTINA     PILOT      $96,387.39
    5     0091     SCOTT           HARVEY F.     FLTAT      $32,278.40
    6     0106     THACKER         DAVID S.      FLTAT      $24,161.14
    7     0355     BELL            THOMAS B.     PILOT      $59,803.16
    8     0366     GLENN           MARTHA S.     PILOT     $120,202.38
```

5

Overview of PROC PRINT

You can display
- column totals
- column subtotals
- page breaks for each subgroup.

```
                            The SAS System

----------------------- JobCode=FLTAT -----------------------

           Emp
   Obs     ID      LastName        FirstName     Salary

    1     0040     WILLIAMS        ARLENE M.     23666.12
    2     0071     PERRY           ROBERT A.     21957.71
    3     0091     SCOTT           HARVEY F.     32278.40
    4     0106     THACKER         DAVID S.      24161.14
  -------                                        --------
  JobCode                                        102063.37
```

6

Overview of PROC PRINT

```
                            The SAS System

----------------------- JobCode=PILOT -----------------------

           Emp
   Obs     ID      LastName        FirstName     Salary

    5     0031     GOLDENBERG      DESIREE       50221.62
    6     0082     MCGWIER-WATTS   CHRISTINA     96387.39
    7     0355     BELL            THOMAS B.     59803.16
    8     0366     GLENN           MARTHA S.    120202.38
  -------                                        --------
  JobCode                                       326614.55
                                                =========
                                                428677.92
```

7

Creating a Default List Report

General form of the PRINT procedure:

```
PROC PRINT DATA=SAS-data-set;
RUN;
```

Example:

```
libname ia 'SAS-data-library';
proc print data=ia.empdata;
run;
```

8   c04s1d1

Creating a Default List Report

`ia.empdata`

EmpID	LastName	FirstName	JobCode	Salary
0031	GOLDENBERG	DESIREE	PILOT	50221.62
0040	WILLIAMS	ARLENE M.	FLTAT	23666.12
0071	PERRY	ROBERT A.	FLTAT	21957.71

PROC Step

Print all variables

```
libname ia 'SAS-data-library';
proc print data=ia.empdata;
run;
```

```
                        The SAS System

         Emp                              Job
Obs       ID    LastName      FirstName   Code     Salary

 1       0031   GOLDENBERG    DESIREE     PILOT    50221.62
 2       0040   WILLIAMS      ARLENE M.   FLTAT    23666.12
 3       0071   PERRY         ROBERT A.   FLTAT    21957.71
```

9

Printing Selected Variables

The VAR statement enables you to
- select variables to include in the report
- define the order of the variables in the report.

General form of the VAR statement:

```
VAR variable(s);
```

10

Printing Selected Variables

`ia.empdata`

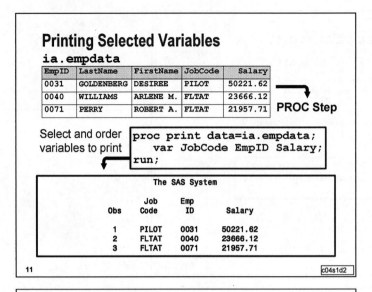

EmpID	LastName	FirstName	JobCode	Salary
0031	GOLDENBERG	DESIREE	PILOT	50221.62
0040	WILLIAMS	ARLENE M.	FLTAT	23666.12
0071	PERRY	ROBERT A.	FLTAT	21957.71

PROC Step

Select and order variables to print

```
proc print data=ia.empdata;
   var JobCode EmpID Salary;
run;
```

```
                  The SAS System

               Job    Emp
        Obs    Code    ID      Salary

         1    PILOT   0031    50221.62
         2    FLTAT   0040    23666.12
         3    FLTAT   0071    21957.71
```

11   c04s1d2

Suppressing the Obs Column

The NOOBS option suppresses the row numbers on the left side of the report.

General form of the NOOBS option:

> **PROC PRINT** DATA=*SAS-data-set* **NOOBS;**
> **RUN;**

12

Suppressing the Obs Column

`ia.empdata`

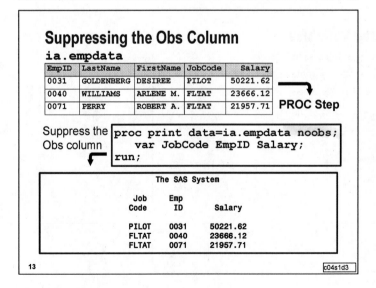

EmpID	LastName	FirstName	JobCode	Salary
0031	GOLDENBERG	DESIREE	PILOT	50221.62
0040	WILLIAMS	ARLENE M.	FLTAT	23666.12
0071	PERRY	ROBERT A.	FLTAT	21957.71

PROC Step

Suppress the Obs column

```
proc print data=ia.empdata noobs;
   var JobCode EmpID Salary;
run;
```

```
                  The SAS System

               Job    Emp
              Code    ID      Salary

             PILOT   0031    50221.62
             FLTAT   0040    23666.12
             FLTAT   0071    21957.71
```

13   c04s1d3

Subsetting Data: WHERE Statement

Produce a listing report that displays information for pilots only.

The WHERE statement

- enables you to select observations that meet a certain condition
- can be used with most SAS procedures.

14

Subsetting Data: WHERE Statement

General form of the WHERE statement:

WHERE *where-expression*;

where-expression is a sequence of operands and operators.

Operands include

- variables
- constants.

15

Subsetting Data: WHERE Statement

Operators include

- comparison operators
- logical operators
- special operators
- functions.

16

Comparison Operators

Mnemonic	Symbol	Definition
EQ	=	equal to
NE	^= ¬= ~=	not equal to
GT	>	greater than
LT	<	less than
GE	>=	greater than or equal to
LE	<=	less than or equal to
IN		equal to one of a list

17

[handwritten note: pulls values from list]

Comparison Operators

Examples:

```
where Salary>25000;

where EmpID='0082';

where Salary=.;

where LastName=' ';

where JobCode in('PILOT','FLTAT');

where JobCode in('PILOT' 'FLTAT');
```

Character comparisons are case-sensitive.

The IN operator allows commas or blanks to separate values.

18

[handwritten note: can't use multiply where clauses but can use where also multiple times .where also .where also .where also also]

Logical Operators

Logical operators include

AND &	if both expressions are true, then the compound expression is true

```
where JobCode='FLTAT' and Salary>50000;
```

OR	if either expression is true, then the compound expression is true

```
where JobCode='PILOT' or JobCode='FLTAT';
```

NOT ^	can be combined with other operators to reverse the logic of a comparison.

```
where JobCode not in('PILOT','FLTAT');
```

19

Special Operators

Special operators include

BETWEEN-AND	selects observations in which the value of the variable falls within a range of values, inclusively.

```
where Salary between 50000 and 70000;
```

CONTAINS ?	selects observations that include the specified substring.

```
where LastName ? 'LAM';
```

(LAMBERT, BELLAMY, and ELAM are selected.)

20

Character constants ? ( )
numeric
no
quotes

Printing Selected Observations

Use the WHERE statement to control which observations are processed.

EmpID	LastName	FirstName	JobCode	Salary
0031	GOLDENBERG	DESIREE	PILOT	50221.62
0040	WILLIAMS	ARLENE M.	FLTAT	23666.12
0071	PERRY	ROBERT A.	FLTAT	21957.71

ia.empdata

→

PROC Step

Select rows to print

```
proc print data=ia.empdata noobs;
    var JobCode EmpID Salary;
    where JobCode='PILOT';
run;
```

```
                    The SAS System

           Job      Emp
           Code      ID       Salary

           PILOT    0031      50221.62
           PILOT    0082      96387.39
           PILOT    0355      59803.16
           PILOT    0366     120202.38
```

21

c04s1d4

Requesting Column Totals

The SUM statement produces column totals.

General form of the SUM statement:

SUM *variable(s);*

The SUM statement also produces subtotals if you print the data in groups.

22

Requesting Column Totals

EmpID	LastName	FirstName	JobCode	Salary
0031	GOLDENBERG	DESIREE	PILOT	50221.62
0040	WILLIAMS	ARLENE M.	FLTAT	23666.12
0071	PERRY	ROBERT A.	FLTAT	21957.71

`ia.empdata`

PROC Step

Produce column totals

```
proc print data=ia.empdata noobs;
     var JobCode EmpID Salary;
     sum Salary;
run;
```

```
                 The SAS System

           Job      Emp
           Code     ID        Salary

           PILOT    0031      50221.62
           FLTAT    0040      23666.12
           FLTAT    0071      21957.71
                      .
                      .
                      =========
                      428677.92
```

23

c04s1d5

 **Exercises**

For these exercises, use SAS data sets stored in a permanent SAS data library.

> Fill in the blank with the location of your SAS data library. Submit the
> LIBNAME statement to assign the libref **ia** to the SAS data library.
>
> ```
> libname ia '_____';
> ```

1. **Printing All Variables and Observations**

    Produce a list report that displays all the variables and observations in the
    ia.passngrs data set. Show column totals for the **FClass**, **BClass**, and
    EClass variables.

    Partial SAS Output

    ```
                                   The SAS System

                 Flight
         Obs       ID      Dest    Depart    FClass    BClass    EClass

           1     IA01802    SEA     15101       10         9       132
           2     IA01804    SEA     15101       11        12       111
           3     IA02901    HNL     15101       13        24       138
           4     IA03100    ANC     15101       13        22       150
           5     IA03101    ANC     15101       14         .       133
           6     IA01802    SEA     15102       12        11       126
           7     IA01804    SEA     15102       12         8       119
           8     IA02901    HNL     15102       14        25       132
           9     IA03100    ANC     15102       16        26       143
          10     IA01802    SEA     15103       12        13       115
          11     IA01804    SEA     15103       12        12       136
          12     IA02901    HNL     15103       12        21       155
          13     IA03100    ANC     15103       14        18       137
           .
           .
           .
          20     IA01804    SEA     15105       11        18       104
          21     IA02901    HNL     15105       13        14       145
          22     IA03100    ANC     15105       15        22        99
          23     IA01802    SEA     15106       12        15       106
          24     IA01804    SEA     15106       10        15       111
          25     IA02901    HNL     15106       13        24       137
          26     IA03100    ANC     15106       15        16       137
          27     IA01802    SEA     15107       12,       17       131
          28     IA01804    SEA     15107       10        13       113
          29     IA02901    HNL     15107       13        19       144
          30     IA03100    ANC     15107       15        23       105
                                              ======    ======    ======
                                                376       485      3859
    ```

2. **Selecting Variables and Observations**

    a. Use the **ia.passngrs** data set to produce a list report that displays only flights to Seattle (**Dest='SEA'**).

    SAS Output

```
                                The SAS System

                Flight
        Obs      ID      Dest    Depart    FClass    BClass    EClass

          1    IA01802    SEA     15101       10         9        132
          2    IA01804    SEA     15101       11        12        111
          6    IA01802    SEA     15102       12        11        126
          7    IA01804    SEA     15102       12         8        119
         10    IA01802    SEA     15103       12        13        115
         11    IA01804    SEA     15103       12        12        136
         14    IA01802    SEA     15104       10        18        128
         15    IA01804    SEA     15104       11        17        105
         19    IA01802    SEA     15105       11        14        131
         20    IA01804    SEA     15105       11        18        104
         23    IA01802    SEA     15106       12        15        106
         24    IA01804    SEA     15106       10        15        111
         27    IA01802    SEA     15107       12        17        131
         28    IA01804    SEA     15107       10        13        113
```

    b. Alter the program so that only the variables **FlightID**, **Depart**, **FClass**, **BClass**, and **EClass** are displayed. Suppress the observation number.

    SAS Output

```
                            The SAS System

        Flight
          ID       Depart    FClass    BClass    EClass

        IA01802    15101       10         9        132
        IA01804    15101       11        12        111
        IA01802    15102       12        11        126
        IA01804    15102       12         8        119
        IA01802    15103       12        13        115
        IA01804    15103       12        12        136
        IA01802    15104       10        18        128
        IA01804    15104       11        17        105
        IA01802    15105       11        14        131
        IA01804    15105       11        18        104
        IA01802    15106       12        15        106
        IA01804    15106       10        15        111
        IA01802    15107       12        17        131
        IA01804    15107       10        13        113
```

c. Alter the program so that only the flights to Seattle with at least 120 **EClass** passengers but fewer than 15 **BClass** passengers are displayed.

SAS Output

```
                        The SAS System

          Flight
            ID      Depart    FClass    BClass    EClass

          IA01802    15101       10         9        132
          IA01802    15102       12        11        126
          IA01804    15103       12        12        136
      IA01802   15105    11    14    131
```

3. **Selecting Variables and Observations (Optional)**

   Write a PROC PRINT step for **ia.employees**.

   - Suppress the observation column.
   - Limit variables to **EmpID**, **Country**, **Division**, **JobCode**, and **Salary**.
   - Add the N option to the PROC PRINT statement. The N option prints the number of output observations at the bottom of the report.
   - Limit output to employees from Canada.
   - Generate a grand total for **Salary**.

   Partial SAS Output

```
                        The SAS System

                                                    Job
    EmpID    Country      Division                  Code        Salary

    E00008   CANADA       CORPORATE OPERATIONS      OFFMGR      $85,000
    E00039   CANADA       HUMAN RESOURCES           FACCLK      $38,000
    E00041   CANADA       SALES & MARKETING         MKTCLK      $45,000
    E00056   CANADA       AIRPORT OPERATIONS        GRCREW      $29,000
    E00079   CANADA       AIRPORT OPERATIONS        GRCREW      $41,000
    E00122   CANADA       HUMAN RESOURCES           RESMGR      $24,000
    E00164   CANADA       AIRPORT OPERATIONS        GRCREW      $36,000
    E00190   CANADA       HUMAN RESOURCES           RECEPT      $22,000
    E00341   CANADA       SALES & MARKETING         MKTMGR      $38,000
    E00359   CANADA       FLIGHT OPERATIONS         MECHO3      $16,000
    E00392   CANADA       AIRPORT OPERATIONS        BAGCLK      $31,000
    E00430   CANADA       FLIGHT OPERATIONS         MECHO3      $20,000
                                                              ==========
                                                              $425,000

                          N = 12
```

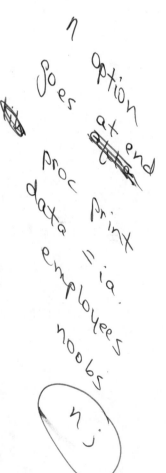

N option
Does at end
Proc Print via
data ia.
employees
noobs

n.

4.2   Sequencing and Grouping Observations

Objectives

- Sequence (sort) observations in a SAS data set.
- Group observations in a list report.
- Print column subtotals in a list report.
- Control page breaks for subgroups.

26

Sorting a SAS Data Set

To request subgroup totals in PROC PRINT, the observations in the data set must be grouped.

The SORT procedure

- rearranges the observations in a SAS data set
- can create a new SAS data set containing the rearranged observations
- can sort on multiple variables
- can sort in ascending (default) or descending order
- does not generate printed output
- treats missing values as the smallest possible value.

27

Sorting a SAS Data Set

General form of the PROC SORT step:

PROC SORT DATA=*input-SAS-data-set*
                    <OUT=*output-SAS-data-set*>;
        BY <DESCENDING> *by-variable(s)*;
RUN;

Examples:

```
proc sort data=ia.empdata;
   by Salary;
run;
```

```
proc sort data=ia.empdata out=work.jobsal;
   by JobCode descending Salary;
run;
```

28

Sorting a SAS Data Set

`ia.empdata`

EmpID	LastName	FirstName	JobCode	Salary
0031	GOLDENBERG	DESIREE	PILOT	50221.62
0040	WILLIAMS	ARLENE M.	FLTAT	23666.12
0071	PERRY	ROBERT A.	FLTAT	21957.71

PROC Step

```
proc sort data=ia.empdata out=work.empdata;
   by JobCode;
run;
```

`work.empdata`

EmpID	LastName	FirstName	JobCode	Salary
0040	WILLIAMS	ARLENE M.	FLTAT	23666.12
0071	PERRY	ROBERT A.	FLTAT	21957.71
0031	GOLDENBERG	DESIREE	PILOT	50221.62

29

Printing Subtotals and Grand Totals

Print the data set grouped by **JobCode** with a subtotal
for the **Salary** column for each **JobCode**.

```
proc sort data=ia.empdata out=work.empdata;
   by JobCode;
run;
proc print data=work.empdata;
   by JobCode;
   sum Salary;
run;
```

Using a BY statement and a SUM statement together in
a PROC PRINT step produces subtotals and grand
totals.

30   c04s2d1 . .

Data must be indexed or in sorted order to use a BY statement in a
PROC PRINT step.

Printing Subtotals and Grand Totals

```
                          The SAS System
---------------------- JobCode=FLTAT ----------------------

          Emp
   Obs    ID     LastName       FirstName      Salary

    1     0040   WILLIAMS       ARLENE M.      23666.12
    2     0071   PERRY          ROBERT A.      21957.71
    3     0091   SCOTT          HARVEY F.      32278.40
    4     0106   THACKER        DAVID S.       24161.14
   -------                                    ---------
   JobCode                                    102063.37

---------------------- JobCode=PILOT ----------------------

          Emp
   Obs    ID     LastName       FirstName      Salary

    5     0031   GOLDENBERG     DESIREE        50221.62
    6     0082   MCGWIER-WATTS  CHRISTINA      96387.39
    7     0355   BELL           THOMAS B.      59803.16
    8     0366   GLENN          MARTHA S.      120202.38
   -------                                    ---------
   JobCode                                    326614.55
                                              =========
                                              428677.92
```

31

Page Breaks

Use the PAGEBY statement to put each subgroup on a separate page.

General form of the PAGEBY statement:

```
PAGEBY by-variable;
```

```
proc print data=work.empdata;
   by JobCode;
   pageby JobCode;
   sum Salary;
run;
```

The PAGEBY statement must be used with a BY statement.

32   c04s2d2

The variable in the PAGEBY statement must appear in the BY statement.

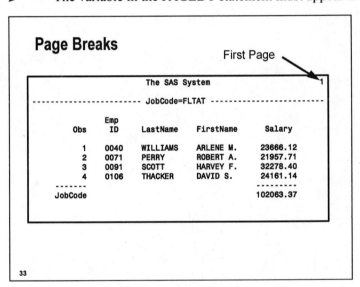

Page Breaks

First Page

```
                    The SAS System                    1

---------------------- JobCode=FLTAT ----------------------

         Emp
   Obs   ID      LastName    FirstName     Salary

    1    0040    WILLIAMS    ARLENE M.    23666.12
    2    0071    PERRY       ROBERT A.    21957.71
    3    0091    SCOTT       HARVEY F.    32278.40
    4    0106    THACKER     DAVID S.     24161.14
   -------                               ---------
   JobCode                               102063.37
```

33

Page Breaks

Second Page

```
                        The SAS System                        2
------------------------ JobCode=PILOT ------------------------

         Emp
  Obs     ID    LastName        FirstName      Salary

    5    0031   GOLDENBERG      DESIREE       50221.62
    6    0082   MCGWIER-WATTS   CHRISTINA     96387.39
    7    0355   BELL            THOMAS B.     59803.16
    8    0366   GLENN           MARTHA S.    120202.38
  -------                                    ---------
  JobCode                                    326614.55
                                             =========
                                             428677.92
```

34

 **Exercises**

For these exercises, use SAS data sets stored in a permanent SAS data library.

> Fill in the blank with the location of your SAS data library. **If you have started a new SAS session since the previous lab,** submit the LIBNAME statement to assign the libref **ia** to the SAS data library.
>
> `libname ia '_____';`

4. **Printing Reports with Page Breaks**

   Create the listing described below using the **ia.passngrs** data set.

   - Sequence the report in ascending order by destination (**Dest**) and place the listing for each destination on a separate page.

   - Print only the variables **Depart**, **FClass**, **BClass**, and **EClass**.

   - Display column totals and subtotals for the variables **FClass**, **BClass**, and **EClass**.

SAS Output

```
                        The SAS System                         1

----------------------------- Dest=ANC -----------------------------

       Obs    Depart    FClass    BClass    EClass

        1     15101       13        22       150
        2     15101       14         .       133
        3     15102       16        26       143
        4     15103       14        18       137
        5     15104       14        17       144
        6     15104       13         .       142
        7     15105       15        22        99
        8     15106       15        16       137
        9     15107       15        23       105
       ----              ------    ------    ------
       Dest               129       144      1190
```

```
                            The SAS System                          2

------------------------------ Dest=HNL -----------------------------

         Obs    Depart    FClass    BClass    EClass

          10    15101       13        24       138
          11    15102       14        25       132
          12    15103       12        21       155
          13    15104       13        22       150
          14    15105       13        14       145
          15    15106       13        24       137
          16    15107       13        19       144
         ----             ------    ------    ------
         Dest              91        149       1001
```

```
                            The SAS System                          3

------------------------------ Dest=SEA -----------------------------

         Obs    Depart    FClass    BClass    EClass

          17    15101       10        9        132
          18    15101       11        12       111
          19    15102       12        11       126
          20    15102       12        8        119
          21    15103       12        13       115
          22    15103       12        12       136
          23    15104       10        18       128
          24    15104       11        17       105
          25    15105       11        14       131
          26    15105       11        18       104
          27    15106       12        15       106
          28    15106       10        15       111
          29    15107       12        17       131
          30    15107       10        13       113
         ----             ------    ------    ------
         Dest             156        192       1668
                         ======    ======    ======
                          376        485       3859
```

5. Producing List Reports (Optional)

Create the listing described below using the **ia.personl** data set.

- Sequence the report in ascending order by **Gender** and last name (**LName**) in ascending order within **Gender**.

- Only print observations (rows) for flight attendants (**JobCode** values **'FA1'**, **'FA2'**, **'FA3'**) who live in New York (**State** value **'NY'**).

- Only print the variables **LName**, **FName**, **Gender**, and **Salary**.

- Suppress the observation number.

SAS Output

```
                        The SAS System

            LName         FName      Gender    Salary

            ARTHUR        BARBARA       F       32886
            DEAN          SHARON        F       33419
            DUNLAP        DONNA         F       28888
            EATON         ALICIA        F       27787
            FIELDS        DIANA         F       23177
            JONES         LESLIE        F       22367
            MCDANIEL      RONDA         F       23738
            MURPHY        ALICE         F       32699
            PATTERSON     RENEE         F       28978
            PEARCE        CAROL         F       22413
            RICHARDS      CASEY         F       22862
            VEGA          ANNA          F       27321
            WALTERS       DIANE         F       27896
            WOOD          DEBORAH       F       23916
            YOUNG         JOANN         F       27956
            CAHILL        MARSHALL      M       28572
            COOPER        ANTHONY       M       32217
            SMART         JONATHAN      M       27761
            VEGA          FRANKLIN      M       28278
```

4.3   Identifying Observations (Self-Study)

Objectives

- Use the ID statement to identify observations.
- Combine the BY and ID statements to produce special formatting.

37

Identifying Observations

The ID statement enables you to
- suppress the Obs column in the report
- specify which variable(s) should replace the Obs column.

General form of the ID statement:

ID *variable(s)*;

38

Creating a Default List Report

`ia.empdata`

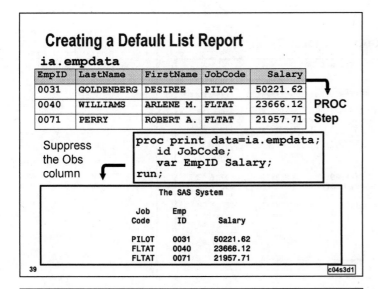

EmpID	LastName	FirstName	JobCode	Salary
0031	GOLDENBERG	DESIREE	PILOT	50221.62
0040	WILLIAMS	ARLENE M.	FLTAT	23666.12
0071	PERRY	ROBERT A.	FLTAT	21957.71

PROC Step

Suppress the Obs column

```
proc print data=ia.empdata;
   id JobCode;
   var EmpID Salary;
run;
```

```
                  The SAS System

         Job      Emp
         Code     ID        Salary

         PILOT    0031      50221.62
         FLTAT    0040      23666.12
         FLTAT    0071      21957.71
```

39   c04s3d1

Special BY-Group Formatting

When the ID and BY statements specify the same variable,

- the Obs column is suppressed
- the BY line is suppressed
- the ID/BY variable prints in the leftmost column
- each ID/BY value only prints at the start of each BY group (and on the subtotal line, if a SUM statement is used).

40

Special BY-Group Formatting

Specify **JobCode** in the BY and ID statements to change the report format.

```
proc sort data=ia.empdata out=work.empdata;
   by JobCode;
run;
proc print data=work.empdata;
   by JobCode;
   id JobCode;
   sum Salary;
run;
```

41   c04s3d2

Special BY-Group Formatting

```
                              The SAS System

        Job     Emp
        Code    ID      LastName        FirstName      Salary

        FLTAT   0040    WILLIAMS        ARLENE M.      23666.12
                0071    PERRY           ROBERT A.      21957.71
                0091    SCOTT           HARVEY F.      32278.40
                0106    THACKER         DAVID S.       24161.14
        -----                                         ---------
        FLTAT                                         102063.37

        PILOT   0031    GOLDENBERG      DESIREE         50221.62
                0082    MCGWIER-WATTS   CHRISTINA       96387.39
                0355    BELL            THOMAS B.       59803.16
                0366    GLENN           MARTHA S.      120202.38
        -----                                         ---------
        PILOT                                         326614.55
                                                      =========
                                                      428677.92
```

42

 **Exercises**

For these exercises, use SAS data sets stored in a permanent SAS data library.

> Fill in the blank with the location of your SAS data library. **If you have started a new SAS session since the previous lab**, submit the LIBNAME statement to assign the libref **ia** to the SAS data library.
>
> `libname ia '`_____`';`

6. **Identifying Observations and Using Page Breaks**

   Create the listing described below using the **ia.passngrs** data set.

   - Sequence the report in ascending order by destination (**Dest**) and place the listing for each destination on a separate page.

   - Only print the variables **Dest**, **Depart**, **FClass**, **BClass**, and **EClass**. Display **Dest** as the leftmost column, suppress the observation number, and suppress redundant values of the **Dest** variable.

   - Display column totals and subtotals for the variables **FClass**, **BClass**, and **EClass**.

   SAS Output

   ```
                         The SAS System                        1

         Dest    Depart    FClass    BClass    EClass

         ANC     15101       13        22        150
                 15101       14         .        133
                 15102       16        26        143
                 15103       14        18        137
                 15104       14        17        144
                 15104       13         .        142
                 15105       15        22         99
                 15106       15        16        137
                 15107       15        23        105

         ----             ------    ------    ------
         ANC               129       144       1190
   ```

```
                        The SAS System                          2

        Dest    Depart    FClass    BClass    EClass

        HNL     15101       13        24        138
                15102       14        25        132
                15103       12        21        155
                15104       13        22        150
                15105       13        14        145
                15106       13        24        137
                15107       13        19        144

        ----              ------    ------    ------
        HNL                 91       149       1001
```

```
                        The SAS System                          3

        Dest    Depart    FClass    BClass    EClass

        SEA     15101       10         9        132
                15101       11        12        111
                15102       12        11        126
                15102       12         8        119
                15103       12        13        115
                15103       12        12        136
                15104       10        18        128
                15104       11        17        105
                15105       11        14        131
                15105       11        18        104
                15106       12        15        106
                15106       10        15        111
                15107       12        17        131
                15107       10        13        113

        ----              ------    ------    ------
        SEA                156       192       1668
                          ======    ======    ======
                           376       485       3859
```

7. Grouping Observations (Optional)

Write a PROC PRINT step for `ia.delay`.

- Observations should appear in ascending order by `Dest` and in descending order by `Mail`. However, the report should be grouped only by `Dest`.

- Print only the variables `Flight`, `Date`, `Dest`, and `Mail`. Display `Dest` in the left column, suppress the observation numbers, and suppress redundant values of `Dest`.

- Create subtotals for `Mail`.

- Add a WHERE statement that prevents rows from printing if the value of `Dest` is missing.

Partial SAS Output – First BY Group

```
                        The SAS System

         Dest     Flight       Date       Mail

         CPH       387       19MAR95       578
                   387       07MAR95       546
                              .
                              .
                              .
                   387       24MAR95       301
                   387       28MAR95       271
                   387       30MAR95         .
         ----                            ------
         CPH                             10436
```

Partial SAS Output – Last BY Group

```
         Dest     Flight       Date       Mail

         YYZ       132       03MAR95       288
                   132       11MAR95       281
                   132       17MAR95       260
                   132       13MAR95       251
                   132       15MAR95       213
         ----                            ------
         YYZ                             24218
                                         ======
                                         241309
```

4.4   Special WHERE Statement Operators (Self-Study)

Objectives

- Use special operators in the WHERE statement to subset data.

45

Special Operators

Additional special operators supported by the WHERE statement are

- LIKE
- sounds like
- IS MISSING (or IS NULL).

46

Special Operators

The following are special operators :

- LIKE selects observations by comparing character values to specified patterns.

  A percent sign (%) replaces any number of characters.

  An underscore (_) replaces one character.

```
where Code like 'E_U%';
```

Selects observations where the value of **Code** begins with an **E**, followed by a single character, followed by a **U**, followed by any number of characters.

47

Special Operators

- The sounds like (=*) operator selects observations that contain spelling variations of the word or words specified.

```
where Name=*'SMITH';
```

Selects names like SMYTHE and SMITT.

- IS NULL or IS MISSING selects observations in which the value of the variable is missing.

```
where Flight is missing;

where Flight is null;
```

48

 **Exercises**

For these exercises, use SAS data sets stored in a permanent SAS data library.

Fill in the blank with the location of your SAS data library. **If you have started a new SAS session since the previous lab**, submit the LIBNAME statement to assign the libref **ia** to the SAS data library.

```
libname ia '_____';
```

8. **Using Special WHERE Statement Operators**

    Create the listing described below using the **ia.personl** data set.

    *   Only print the variables **LName** and **FName**.
    *   Only display observations where the value of **LName** begins with **BR**.

    SAS Output

    ```
                        The SAS System

                   Obs     LName      FName

                    13     BRADLEY    JEREMY
                    14     BRADY      CHRISTINE
                    15     BROWN      JASON
                    16     BRYANT     LEONARD
    ```

4.5 Solutions to Exercises

1. Printing All Variables and Observations

```
libname ia 'SAS-data-library';
proc print data=ia.passngrs;
   sum FClass BClass EClass;
run;
```

2. Selecting Variables and Observations

a.

```
proc print data=ia.passngrs;
   where Dest='SEA';
run;
```

b.

```
proc print data=ia.passngrs noobs;
   where Dest='SEA';
   var FlightID Depart FClass BClass EClass;
run;
```

c.

```
proc print data=ia.passngrs noobs;
   where Dest='SEA' and EClass ge 120 and BClass lt
15;
   var FlightID Depart FClass BClass EClass;
run;
```

3. Selecting Variables and Observations (Optional)

```
proc print data=ia.employees noobs n;
   var EmpId Country Division JobCode Salary;
   sum Salary;
   where Country='CANADA';
run;
```

4. Printing Reports with Page Breaks

```
proc sort data=ia.passngrs out=work.passngrs;
   by Dest;
run;
proc print data=work.passngrs;
   by Dest;
   pageby Dest;
   var Depart FClass BClass EClass;
   sum FClass BClass EClass;
run;
```

5. **Producing List Reports (Optional)**

```
proc sort data=ia.personl out=work.personl;
   by Gender LName;
run;
proc print data=work.personl noobs;
   var LName FName Gender Salary;
   where State='NY' and JobCode in ('FA1' 'FA2'
'FA3');
run;
```

6. **Identifying Observations and Using Page Breaks**

```
proc sort data=ia.passngrs out=work.passngrs;
   by Dest;
run;
proc print data=work.passngrs;
   id Dest;
   by Dest;
   pageby Dest;
   var Depart FClass BClass EClass;
   sum FClass BClass EClass;
run;
```

7. **Grouping Observations (Optional)**

```
proc sort data=ia.delay out=work.delay;
   by Dest descending Mail;
run;

proc print data=work.delay;
   by Dest;
   id Dest;
   sum Mail;
   var Flight Date Mail;
   where dest ne ' ';
run;
```

8. **Using Special WHERE Statement Operators**

```
proc print data=ia.personl;
   where LName like 'BR%';
   var LName Fname;
run;
```

Chapter 5   Enhancing Output

5.1 Customizing Report Appearance

Objectives

- Define titles and footnotes to enhance reports.
- Define descriptive column headings.
- Use SAS system options.

3

Defining Titles and Footnotes

You use titles and footnotes to enhance reports.

General form of the TITLE statement:

TITLE*n* '*text*';

General form of the FOOTNOTE statement:

FOOTNOTE*n* '*text*';

Examples:

```
title1 'Flight Crew Employee Listing';
footnote2 'Employee Review';
```

4

Defining Titles and Footnotes

Features of titles:

- Titles appear at the top of the page.
- The default title is **The SAS System**.
- The value of *n* can be from 1 to 10.
- An unnumbered TITLE is equivalent to TITLE1.
- Titles remain in effect until they are changed, cancelled, or you end your SAS session.
- The null TITLE statement, **title;**, cancels all titles.

5

Defining Titles and Footnotes

Features of footnotes:

- Footnotes appear at the bottom of the page.
- No footnote is printed unless one is specified.
- The value of *n* can be from 1 to 10.
- An unnumbered FOOTNOTE is equivalent to FOOTNOTE1.
- Footnotes remain in effect until they are changed, cancelled, or you end your SAS session.
- The null FOOTNOTE statement, **footnote;**, cancels all footnotes.

6

Changing Titles and Footnotes

TITLE*n* or FOOTNOTE*n*

- replaces a previous title or footnote with the same number
- cancels all titles or footnotes with higher numbers.

7

Defining Titles and Footnotes

PROC PRINT Code	Resultant Title(s)

`proc print data=work.march;`
`    title1 'The First Line';`
`    title2 'The Second Line';`
`run;`	

`proc print data=work.march;`
`    title2 'The Next Line';`
`run;`	

`proc print data=work.march;`
`    title 'The Top Line';`
`run;`	

`proc print data=work.march;`
`    title3 'The Third Line';`
`run;`	

`proc print data=work.march;`
`    title;`
`run;`	

8

Defining Titles and Footnotes

PROC PRINT Code	Resultant Title(s)

`proc print data=work.march;`
`    title1 'The First Line';`
`    title2 'The Second Line';`
`run;`
	The First Line
	The Second Line

`proc print data=work.march;`
`    title2 'The Next Line';`
`run;`
	The First Line
	The Next Line

`proc print data=work.march;`
`    title 'The Top Line';`
`run;`
	The Top Line

`proc print data=work.march;`
`    title3 'The Third Line';`
`run;`
	The Top Line
	
	The Third Line

`proc print data=work.march;`
`    title;`
`run;`	

13   • • •

Assigning Column Labels

General form of the LABEL statement:

> **LABEL** *variable='label'*
> *variable='label'*;

'label' specifies a label up to 256 characters.

Labels are used
- to replace variable names in SAS output
- automatically by many procedures
- by the PRINT procedure when the LABEL or SPLIT= option is specified in the PROC PRINT statement.

14

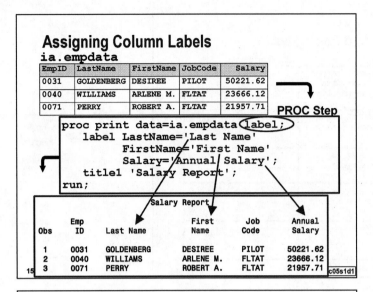

Assigning Column Labels

`ia.empdata`

EmpID	LastName	FirstName	JobCode	Salary
0031	GOLDENBERG	DESIREE	PILOT	50221.62
0040	WILLIAMS	ARLENE M.	FLTAT	23666.12
0071	PERRY	ROBERT A.	FLTAT	21957.71

PROC Step

```
proc print data=ia.empdata label;
   label LastName='Last Name'
         FirstName='First Name'
         Salary='Annual Salary';
   title1 'Salary Report';
run;
```

```
                      Salary Report

           Emp                   First     Job     Annual
Obs        ID      Last Name     Name      Code    Salary

 1        0031    GOLDENBERG    DESIREE    PILOT   50221.62
 2        0040    WILLIAMS      ARLENE M.  FLTAT   23666.12
 3        0071    PERRY         ROBERT A.  FLTAT   21957.71
```

15   c05s1d1

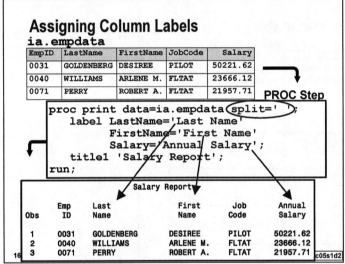

Assigning Column Labels

`ia.empdata`

EmpID	LastName	FirstName	JobCode	Salary
0031	GOLDENBERG	DESIREE	PILOT	50221.62
0040	WILLIAMS	ARLENE M.	FLTAT	23666.12
0071	PERRY	ROBERT A.	FLTAT	21957.71

PROC Step

```
proc print data=ia.empdata split=' ';
   label LastName='Last Name'
         FirstName='First Name'
         Salary='Annual Salary';
   title1 'Salary Report';
run;
```

```
                      Salary Report

           Emp     Last          First     Job     Annual
Obs        ID      Name          Name      Code    Salary

 1        0031    GOLDENBERG    DESIREE    PILOT   50221.62
 2        0040    WILLIAMS      ARLENE M.  FLTAT   23666.12
 3        0071    PERRY         ROBERT A.  FLTAT   21957.71
```

16   c05s1d2

Using SAS System Options

You can use SAS system options to change the appearance of a report.

General form of the OPTIONS statement:

> **OPTIONS** *option . . . ;*

The OPTIONS statement is **not** usually included in a PROC or DATA step.

17

Using SAS System Options

Selected SAS system options:

DATE (default)	specifies to print the date and time the SAS session began at the top of each page of the SAS output.
NODATE	specifies not to print the date and time the SAS session began.
LINESIZE=*width* LS=*width*	specifies the line size for the SAS log and SAS output.
PAGESIZE=*n* PS=*n*	specifies the number of lines (*n*) that can be printed per page of SAS output.

18

Using SAS System Options

Selected SAS system options:

NUMBER (default)	specifies that page numbers be printed on the first line of each page of output.
NONUMBER	specifies that page numbers not be printed.
PAGENO=*n*	specifies a beginning page number (*n*) for the next page of SAS output.

Example:

```
options nodate nonumber ls=72;
```

19

5.2 Formatting Data Values

Objectives

- Display formatted values using SAS formats in a list report.
- Create user-defined formats using the FORMAT procedure.
- Apply user-defined formats to variables in a list report.

21

Using SAS Formats

Enhance the readability of reports by formatting the data values.

```
                        Salary Report

          Emp   Last             First      Job      Annual
   Obs    ID    Name             Name       Code     Salary

    1     0031  GOLDENBERG       DESIREE    PILOT    $50,221.62
    2     0040  WILLIAMS         ARLENE M.  FLTAT    $23,666.12
    3     0071  PERRY            ROBERT A.  FLTAT    $21,957.71
    4     0082  MCGWIER-WATTS    CHRISTINA  PILOT    $96,387.39
    5     0091  SCOTT            HARVEY F.  FLTAT    $32,278.40
    6     0106  THACKER          DAVID S.   FLTAT    $24,161.14
    7     0355  BELL             THOMAS B.  PILOT    $59,803.16
    8     0366  GLENN            MARTHA S.  PILOT    $120,202.38
```

22

Using User-defined Formats

Create custom formats to recode data values in a report.

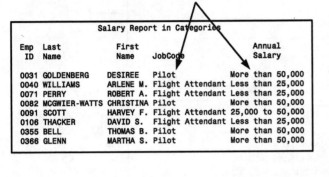

```
                    Salary Report in Categories

Emp  Last            First
 ID  Name            Name      JobCode            Salary

0031 GOLDENBERG      DESIREE   Pilot           More than 50,000
0040 WILLIAMS        ARLENE M. Flight Attendant Less than 25,000
0071 PERRY           ROBERT A. Flight Attendant Less than 25,000
0082 MCGWIER-WATTS   CHRISTINA Pilot           More than 50,000
0091 SCOTT           HARVEY F. Flight Attendant 25,000 to 50,000
0106 THACKER         DAVID S.  Flight Attendant Less than 25,000
0355 BELL            THOMAS B. Pilot           More than 50,000
0366 GLENN           MARTHA S. Pilot           More than 50,000
```

23

Formatting Data Values

You can enhance reports by using SAS formats to format data values.

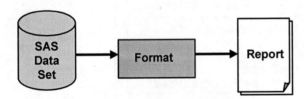

Values in the SAS data set are not changed.

24

Formatting Data Values

To apply a format to a specific SAS variable, use the FORMAT statement.

General form of the FORMAT statement:

FORMAT *variable(s) format*;

Example:

```
proc print data=ia.empdata;
   format Salary dollar11.2;
run;
```

25

 # for character

What Is a SAS Format?

A format is an instruction that SAS uses to write data values.

SAS formats have the following form:

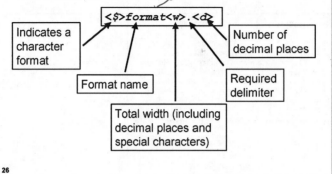

may be dollar & date & etc.

Indicates a character format	Number of decimal places
Format name	Required delimiter
Total width (including decimal places and special characters)	

`<$>format<w>.<d>`

26

SAS Formats

Selected SAS formats:

w.d	standard numeric format
8.2	Width=8, 2 decimal places: 12234.21
$w.	standard character format
$5.	Width=5: KATHY
COMMAw.d	commas in a number
COMMA9.2	Width=9, 2 decimal places: 12,234.21
DOLLARw.d	dollar signs and commas in a number
DOLLAR10.2	Width=10, 2 decimal places: $12,234.21

27

---

includes $ + commas in widths

SAS Formats

If you do not specify a format width large enough to accommodate a numeric value, the displayed value is automatically adjusted to fit into the width.

Stored Value	Format	Displayed Value
27134.2864	COMMA12.2	27,134.29
27134.2864	12.2	27134.29
27134.2864	DOLLAR12.2	$27,134.29
27134.2864	DOLLAR9.2	$27134.29
27134.2864	DOLLAR8.2	27134.29
27134.2864	DOLLAR5.2	27134
27134.2864	DOLLAR4.2	27E3

28

SAS rounds numeric values

Formatting Data Values

EmpID	LastName	FirstName	JobCode	Salary
0031	GOLDENBERG	DESIREE	PILOT	50221.62
0040	WILLIAMS	ARLENE M.	FLTAT	23666.12
0071	PERRY	ROBERT A.	FLTAT	21957.71

ia.empdata

→ PROC Step

```
proc print data=ia.empdata split=' ';
   label LastName='Last Name'
         FirstName='First Name'
         Salary='Annual Salary';
   format Salary dollar11.2;
   title1 'Salary Report';
run;
```

```
                           Salary Report

         Emp   Last                First     Job        Annual
  Obs    ID    Name                Name      Code       Salary

   1    0031   GOLDENBERG          DESIREE   PILOT   $50,221.62
   2    0040   WILLIAMS            ARLENE M. FLTAT   $23,666.12
   3    0071   PERRY               ROBERT A. FLTAT   $21,957.71
```

29   c05s2d1

SAS Formats

Recall that a SAS date is stored as the number of days between 01JAN1960 and the specified date.

SAS date formats display SAS date values in standard date forms.

Selected SAS date formats:

MMDDYY*w*.

Format	Displayed Value
MMDDYY6.	101601
MMDDYY8.	10/16/01
MMDDYY10.	10/16/2001

DATE*w*.

Format	Displayed Value
DATE7.	16OCT01
DATE9.	16OCT2001

30

SAS Formats

Examples:

Stored Value	Format	Displayed Value
0	MMDDYY8.	01/01/60
0	MMDDYY10.	01/01/1960
1	DATE9.	02JAN1960
-1	WORDDATE.	December 31, 1959
365	DDMMYY10.	31/12/1960
366	WEEKDATE.	Sunday, January 1, 1961

31

Exercises

For these exercises, use SAS data sets stored in a permanent SAS data library.

Fill in the blank with the location of your SAS data library. **If you have started a new SAS session since the previous lab**, submit the LIBNAME statement to assign the libref **ia** to the SAS data library.

```
libname ia '_____';
```

1. **Enhanced List Reports**

   Create the listing described below using the **ia.passngrs** data set.

   • Do not display the date and time the SAS session began, set the line size to 64, and start the page number at 1.

   • Sequence the report in ascending order by destination (**Dest**) and place the listing for each destination on a separate page.

   • Print only the variables **Depart**, **FClass**, **BClass**, and **EClass**.

   • Display column totals for the variables **FClass**, **BClass**, and **EClass**.

   • Place the title **San Francisco Passenger Data** on the report.

   • Display the **Depart** values with the DATE9. format and **FClass**, **BClass**, and **EClass** values with commas and zero decimal places.

   • Use the labels below to replace the variable names.

Variable	Label
Dest	Destination
Depart	Departure Date
FClass	First Class
BClass	Business Class
EClass	Economy Class

    Be sure to save your program. You will use your solution to this exercise as the basis of a subsequent workshop.

SAS Output

```
                San Francisco Passenger Data                    1

--------------------- Destination=ANC ----------------------

           Departure    First    Business    Economy
    Obs      Date       Class     Class       Class

     1     06MAY2001     13        22          150
     2     06MAY2001     14         .          133
     3     07MAY2001     16        26          143
     4     08MAY2001     14        18          137
     5     09MAY2001     14        17          144
     6     09MAY2001     13         .          142
     7     10MAY2001     15        22           99
     8     11MAY2001     15        16          137
     9     12MAY2001     15        23          105
    ----               ------    --------     -------
    Dest                129       144         1,190
```

```
                San Francisco Passenger Data                    2

--------------------- Destination=HNL ----------------------

           Departure    First    Business    Economy
    Obs      Date       Class     Class       Class

    10     06MAY2001     13        24          138
    11     07MAY2001     14        25          132
    12     08MAY2001     12        21          155
    13     09MAY2001     13        22          150
    14     10MAY2001     13        14          145
    15     11MAY2001     13        24          137
    16     12MAY2001     13        19          144
    ----               ------    --------     -------
    Dest                 91       149         1,001
```

```
                    San Francisco Passenger Data                    3

--------------------- Destination=SEA -----------------------

              Departure    First     Business    Economy
       Obs      Date       Class      Class       Class

        17    06MAY2001     10          9          132
        18    06MAY2001     11         12          111
        19    07MAY2001     12         11          126
        20    07MAY2001     12          8          119
        21    08MAY2001     12         13          115
        22    08MAY2001     12         12          136
        23    09MAY2001     10         18          128
        24    09MAY2001     11         17          105
        25    10MAY2001     11         14          131
        26    10MAY2001     11         18          104
        27    11MAY2001     12         15          106
        28    11MAY2001     10         15          111
        29    12MAY2001     12         17          131
        30    12MAY2001     10         13          113
       ----                ------    --------    -------
       Dest                 156        192        1,668
                           ======    ========    =======
                            376        485        3,859
```

2. Enhanced List Reports (Optional)

Create the listing described below using the **ia.fltat** data set.

- Do not display the date, time, or page numbers.
- Sequence the report by **HireDate**.
- Suppress the observation column and the title (with a null TITLE statement).
- Print only the variables **EmpID**, **Location**, **JobCode**, and **Salary**.
- Run the report once, and then add the YEAR4. format to the **HireDate** variable.

Partial SAS Output

```
------------------------- HireDate=1980 ---------------------------------

                            Job
       EmpID     Location    Code      Salary

       E03591    LONDON      FLTAT3     47000
       E04064    FRANKFURT   FLTAT2     37000
       E01447    LONDON      FLTAT3     45000
       E00753    LONDON      FLTAT2     34000

------------------------- HireDate=1981 ---------------------------------

                            Job
       EmpID     Location    Code      Salary

       E02679    FRANKFURT   FLTAT1     27000
       E02606    CARY        FLTAT2     36000
       E00364    FRANKFURT   FLTAT1     25000
       E03921    CARY        FLTAT3     47000

                             .
                             .
                             .

------------------------- HireDate=1993 ---------------------------------

                            Job
       EmpID     Location    Code      Salary

       E02766    CARY        FLTAT2     32000
       E03631    FRANKFURT   FLTAT2     35000
       E01968    CARY        FLTAT2     33000
       E02035    FRANKFURT   FLTAT3     48000

------------------------- HireDate=1994 ---------------------------------

                            Job
       EmpID     Location    Code      Salary

       E03022    CARY        FLTAT1     23000
       E02397    FRANKFURT   FLTAT1     22000
```

Creating User-defined Formats

SAS also provides the FORMAT procedure, which enables you to define custom formats.

To create and use your own formats,

1. use the FORMAT procedure to create the format
2. apply the format to specific variable(s) by using a FORMAT statement.

33

Creating User-defined Formats

General form of a PROC FORMAT step:

```
PROC FORMAT;
     VALUE format-name range1='label '
                       range2='label '
                          . . . ;
RUN;
```

34

Creating User-defined Formats

Format-name

- names the format you are creating
- cannot be more than 32 characters in SAS System 9
- for character values, must have a dollar sign ($) as the first character, a letter or underscore as the second character
- for numeric values, must have a letter or underscore as the first character
- cannot end in a number
- cannot be the name of a SAS format
- does not end with a period in the VALUE statement.

35

format to correspond to data type

not user-defined type

Format names in releases prior to SAS 9 are limited to 8 characters.

Creating User-defined Formats

Labels
- can be up to 32,767 characters in length
- are typically enclosed in quotes, although it is not required.

Range(s)
- can be single values
- ranges of values.

36

Creating User-defined Formats

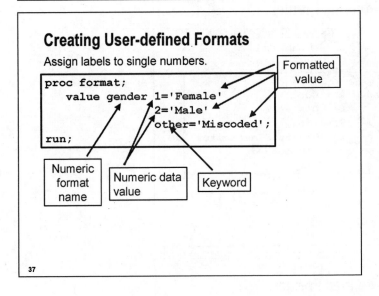

Assign labels to single numbers.

```
proc format;
   value gender 1='Female'
                2='Male'
                other='Miscoded';
run;
```

Formatted value

Numeric format name

Numeric data value

Keyword

37

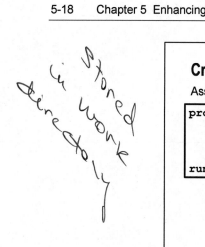

Creating User-defined Formats

Assign labels to ranges of numbers.

```
proc format;
    value boardfmt low-49='Below'
                   50-99='Average'
                   100-high='Above Average';
run;
```

Keyword

Numeric data ranges

38

Creating User-defined Formats

Assign labels to character values and ranges of character values.

Character format name

```
proc format;
    value $grade 'A'='Good'
                 'B'-'D'='Fair'
                 'F'='Poor'
                 'I','U'='See Instructor'
                 other='Miscoded';
run;
```

Character value range

Discrete character values

Keyword

39

Creating User-defined Formats

Step 1: Create the format.

```
proc format;
    value $codefmt 'FLTAT'='Flight Attendant'
                   'PILOT'='Pilot';
run;
```

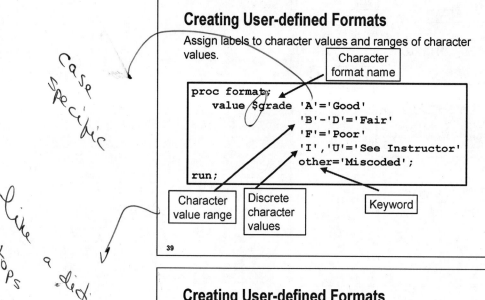

$codefmt

Step 2: Apply the format.

```
proc print data=ia.empdata;
    format JobCode $codefmt.;
run;
```

40

Creating User-defined Formats

Step 1: Create the format.

```
proc format;
   value money low-<25000 ='Less than 25,000'
               25000-50000='25,000 to 50,000'
               50000<-high='More than 50,000';
run;
```

Step 2: Apply the format.

```
proc print data=ia.empdata;
   format Salary money.;
run;
```

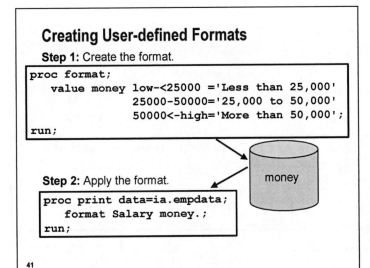

41

Creating User-defined Formats

You can use multiple VALUE statements in a single PROC FORMAT step.

```
proc format;
   value $codefmt 'FLTAT'='Flight Attendant'
                  'PILOT'='Pilot';
   value money low-<25000 ='Less than 25,000'
               25000-50000='25,000 to 50,000'
               50000<-high='More than 50,000';
run;
```

42   c05s2d2

Applying User-defined Formats

```
proc print data=ia.empdata split=' ' noobs;
   label LastName='Last Name'
         FirstName='First Name'
         Salary='Annual Salary';
   format Jobcode $codefmt. Salary money.;
   title1 'Salary Report in Categories';
run;
```

```
                    Salary Report in Categories

    Emp  Last            First                        Annual
    ID   Name            Name       JobCode           Salary

    0031 GOLDENBERG      DESIREE    Pilot             More than 50,000
    0040 WILLIAMS        ARLENE M.  Flight Attendant  Less than 25,000
    0071 PERRY           ROBERT A.  Flight Attendant  Less than 25,000
    0082 MCGWIER-WATTS   CHRISTINA  Pilot             More than 50,000
    0091 SCOTT           HARVEY F.  Flight Attendant  25,000 to 50,000
    0106 THACKER         DAVID S.   Flight Attendant  Less than 25,000
    0355 BELL            THOMAS B.  Pilot             More than 50,000
    0366 GLENN           MARTHA S.  Pilot             More than 50,000
```

43

Exercises

For these exercises, use SAS data sets stored in a permanent SAS data library.

Fill in the blank with the location of your SAS data library. **If you have started a new SAS session since the previous lab**, submit the LIBNAME statement to assign the libref **ia** to the SAS data library.

`libname ia'_____';`

---

3. **Creating User-defined Formats**

   Create a format for the variable **Dest** that assigns

   - **Anchorage** to the value **ANC**
   - **Honolulu** to the value **HNL**
   - **Seattle** to the value **SEA**.

4. **Applying User-defined Formats**

   Alter the program you wrote in the earlier **Enhanced List Reports** exercise to use the format you created in the previous exercise to display city names instead of airport codes. Reset the starting page number for the output to 1.

       Be sure to save your modified program. You will use your solution to this exercise as the basis of a subsequent workshop.

   SAS Output

```
                    San Francisco Passenger Data                    1

------------------- Destination=Anchorage --------------------

            Departure    First    Business    Economy
     Obs      Date       Class     Class       Class


      1     06MAY2001      13        22          150
      2     06MAY2001      14         .          133
      3     07MAY2001      16        26          143
      4     08MAY2001      14        18          137
      5     09MAY2001      14        17          144
      6     09MAY2001      13         .          142
      7     10MAY2001      15        22           99
      8     11MAY2001      15        16          137
      9     12MAY2001      15        23          105
     ----               ------    --------     -------
     Dest                 129       144         1,190
```

```
                    San Francisco Passenger Data              2

-------------------- Destination=Honolulu --------------------

              Departure      First    Business    Economy
     Obs         Date        Class     Class       Class

      10      06MAY2001        13        24          138
      11      07MAY2001        14        25          132
      12      08MAY2001        12        21          155
      13      09MAY2001        13        22          150
      14      10MAY2001        13        14          145
      15      11MAY2001        13        24          137
      16      12MAY2001        13        19          144
     ----                   ------    --------    -------
     Dest                      91       149        1,001
```

```
                    San Francisco Passenger Data              3

-------------------- Destination=Seattle --------------------

              Departure      First    Business    Economy
     Obs         Date        Class     Class       Class

      17      06MAY2001        10         9          132
      18      06MAY2001        11        12          111
      19      07MAY2001        12        11          126
      20      07MAY2001        12         8          119
      21      08MAY2001        12        13          115
      22      08MAY2001        12        12          136
      23      09MAY2001        10        18          128
      24      09MAY2001        11        17          105
      25      10MAY2001        11        14          131
      26      10MAY2001        11        18          104
      27      11MAY2001        12        15          106
      28      11MAY2001        10        15          111
      29      12MAY2001        12        17          131
      30      12MAY2001        10        13          113
     ----                   ------    --------    -------
     Dest                     156       192        1,668
                            ======    ========    =======
                              376       485        3,859
```

5. Creating and Applying User-defined Formats (Optional)

a. Create a user-defined format for **Model** that assigns labels as shown below.

Value(s) of Model	Label
JetCruise LF5100 JetCruise LF5200 JetCruise LF8000 JetCruise LF8100	Large Jet
JetCruise MF2100 JetCruise MF4000	Medium Jet
JetCruise SF1000	Small Jet

b. Apply the user-defined format.

- Write a PROC PRINT step for **ia.sanfran**.
- Use the format you created for **Model**.
- Display only the variables **FlightID**, **DepartDate**, **Destination**, and **Model**.
- Suppress the title (with a null TITLE statement).

Partial SAS Output

```
         Flight    Depart
  Obs      ID       Date     Destination     Model

    1    IA11200   01DEC1999      HND      Large Jet
    2    IA01804   01DEC1999      SEA      Small Jet
    3    IA02901   02DEC1999      HNL      Large Jet
    4    IA03100   02DEC1999      ANC      Large Jet
    5    IA02901   03DEC1999      HNL      Large Jet
    6    IA03100   03DEC1999      ANC      Medium Jet
    7    IA00800   04DEC1999      RDU      Medium Jet
    8    IA01805   04DEC1999      SEA      Small Jet
    9    IA01804   06DEC1999      SEA      Large Jet
   10    IA03101   06DEC1999      ANC      Large Jet
   11    IA01802   07DEC1999      SEA      Small Jet
   12    IA11200   08DEC1999      HND      Large Jet
   13    IA03101   08DEC1999      ANC      Large Jet
   14    IA01804   08DEC1999      SEA      Small Jet
   15    IA11201   09DEC1999      HND      Large Jet
   16    IA03100   09DEC1999      ANC      Medium Jet
   17    IA01805   10DEC1999      SEA      Small Jet
    .
    .
    .
```

5.3   Creating HTML Reports

Objectives

- Create HTML reports using the Output Delivery System (ODS).

46

Business Task

Display a listing report in HTML form.

Salary Report

EmpID	LastName	FirstName	JobCode	Annual Salary
0031	GOLDENBERG	DESIREE	Pilot	More than 50,000
0040	WILLIAMS	ARLENE M.	Flight Attendant	Less than 25,000
0071	PERRY	ROBERT A.	Flight Attendant	Less than 25,000
0082	MCGWIER-WATTS	CHRISTINA	Pilot	More than 50,000
0091	SCOTT	HARVEY F.	Flight Attendant	25,000 to 50,000
0106	THACKER	DAVID S.	Flight Attendant	Less than 25,000
0355	BELL	THOMAS B.	Pilot	More than 50,000
0366	GLENN	MARTHA S.	Pilot	More than 50,000

47

The Output Delivery System

ODS statements enable you to create output in a variety of forms.

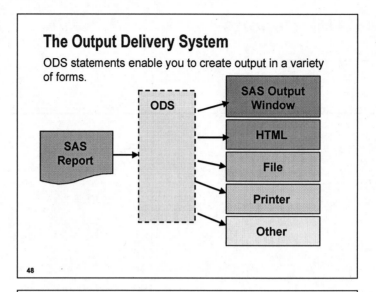

48

Generating HTML Files

The ODS HTML statement opens, closes, and manages the HTML destination.

General form of the ODS HTML statement:

ODS HTML FILE='*HTML-file-specification*' *<options>*;
    SAS code that generates output
ODS HTML CLOSE;

49

Generating HTML Files

Output is directed to the specified HTML file until you
- close the HTML destination
- specify another destination file.

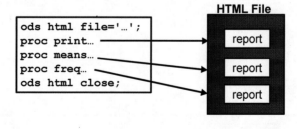

50

can also
use ~~rtf~~
in place of
html
(so can open)
in Word

or

pdf

Creating an HTML Report

1. Open an HTML destination for the listing report.
2. Generate the report.
3. Close the HTML destination.

```
ods html file='c05s3d1.html';
proc print data=ia.empdata label noobs;
    label Salary='Annual Salary';
    format Salary money. Jobcode $codefmt.;
    title1 'Salary Report';
run;
ods html close;
```

51   c05s3d1

style = ____ ;

Creating an HTML Report

Salary Report

EmpID	LastName	FirstName	JobCode	Annual Salary
0031	GOLDENBERG	DESIREE	Pilot	More than 50,000
0040	WILLIAMS	ARLENE M.	Flight Attendant	Less than 25,000
0071	PERRY	ROBERT A.	Flight Attendant	Less than 25,000
0082	MCGWIER-WATTS	CHRISTINA	Pilot	More than 50,000
0091	SCOTT	HARVEY F.	Flight Attendant	25,000 to 50,000
0106	THACKER	DAVID S.	Flight Attendant	Less than 25,000
0355	BELL	THOMAS B.	Pilot	More than 50,000
0366	GLENN	MARTHA S.	Pilot	More than 50,000

52

can also change look of report (colors)

style = water color

proc template;
list styles;
run;

→ to find styles

Exercises

For these exercises, use SAS data sets stored in a permanent SAS data library.

Fill in the blank with the location of your SAS data library. **If you have started a new SAS session since the previous lab**, submit the LIBNAME statement to assign the libref **ia** to the SAS data library.

```
libname ia '_____';
```

6. Creating HTML Reports

Alter the program you wrote in the earlier **Applying User-defined Formats** exercise to create an HTML report using ODS.

San Francisco Passenger Data				
Destination=Anchorage				
Obs	Departure Date	First Class	Business Class	Economy Class
1	06MAY2001	13	22	150
2	06MAY2001	14	.	133
3	07MAY2001	16	26	143
4	08MAY2001	14	18	137
5	09MAY2001	14	17	144
6	09MAY2001	13	.	142
7	10MAY2001	15	22	99
8	11MAY2001	15	16	137
9	12MAY2001	15	23	105
Dest		129	144	1,190

San Francisco Passenger Data

Destination=Honolulu

Obs	Departure Date	First Class	Business Class	Economy Class
10	06MAY2001	13	24	138
11	07MAY2001	14	25	132
12	08MAY2001	12	21	155
13	09MAY2001	13	22	150
14	10MAY2001	13	14	145
15	11MAY2001	13	24	137
16	12MAY2001	13	19	144
Dest		91	149	1,001

San Francisco Passenger Data

Destination=Seattle

Obs	Departure Date	First Class	Business Class	Economy Class
17	06MAY2001	10	9	132
18	06MAY2001	11	12	111
19	07MAY2001	12	11	126
20	07MAY2001	12	8	119
21	08MAY2001	12	13	115
22	08MAY2001	12	12	136
23	09MAY2001	10	18	128
24	09MAY2001	11	17	105
25	10MAY2001	11	14	131
26	10MAY2001	11	18	104
27	11MAY2001	12	15	106
28	11MAY2001	10	15	111
29	12MAY2001	12	17	131
30	12MAY2001	10	13	113
Dest		156	192	1,668
		376	485	3,859

7. Creating a Listing Report (Optional)

Use the `ia.newmechs` data set for this exercise.

a. Create a format for the `Gender` variable that assigns

- `Female` to the value `F`
- `Male` to the value `M`.

b. Create an HTML report of the listing described below.

- Set the line size to 72, do not display the date and time the SAS session began, and do not display page numbers.
- Only print observations that have a value of `MECH01` for the variable `JobCode`.
- Print the variables `EmpID`, `LastName`, `FirstName`, and `Gender` in the order listed here.
- Place the title `Level I Mechanics` on the report.
- Display the values of the variable `Gender` with the format you created in part **a** of this exercise.

Level I Mechanics

Obs	EmpID	LastName	FirstName	Gender
1	E00007	MASSENGILL	ANNETTE M.	Female
6	E00112	WANG	ROBERT B.	Male
8	E00151	BAKER	DONALD A.	Male
16	E00308	RIPPERTON	DAVID D.	Male
19	E00417	BURT	ERICK M.	Male
34	E00449	SIU	MICHELLE	Female

5.4 Solutions to Exercises

1. **Enhanced List Reports**

```
options ls=64 nodate pageno=1;
libname ia 'SAS-data-library';
proc sort data=ia.passngrs out=work.passngrs;
   by Dest;
run;
proc print data=work.passngrs label;
   var Depart FClass BClass EClass;
   by Dest;
   pageby Dest;
   sum FClass BClass EClass;
   format Depart date9. FClass BClass EClass comma6.;
   label Dest='Destination'
         Depart='Departure Date'
         FClass='First Class'
         BClass='Business Class'
         EClass='Economy Class';
   title 'San Francisco Passenger Data';
run;
```

2. **Enhanced List Reports (Optional)**

```
options nodate nonumber;
proc sort data=ia.fltat out=work.fltat;
   by HireDate;
run;

proc print data=work.fltat noobs;
   title;
   by HireDate;
   format HireDate year.;
   var EmpID HireDate Location JobCode Salary;
run;
```

3. **Creating User-defined Formats**

```
proc format;
   value $cities 'ANC'='Anchorage'
                 'HNL'='Honolulu'
                 'SEA'='Seattle';
run;
```

4. Applying User-defined Formats

```
options pageno=1;
proc print data=work.passngrs label;
   var Depart FClass BClass EClass;
   by Dest;
   pageby Dest;
   sum FClass BClass EClass;
   format Depart date9. FClass BClass EClass comma6.
          Dest $cities.;
   label Dest='Destination'
         Depart='Departure Date'
         FClass='First Class'
         BClass='Business Class'
         EClass='Economy Class';
   title 'San Francisco Passenger Data';
run;
```

5. Creating and Applying User-defined Formats (Optional)

a.

```
proc format;
   value $model
      'JetCruise LF5100','JetCruise LF5200',
      'JetCruise LF8000','JetCruise LF8100'
         = 'Large Jet'
      'JetCruise MF2100','JetCruise MF4000'
         = 'Medium Jet'
      'JetCruise SF1000'
         = 'Small Jet'
   ;
run;
```

b.

```
proc print data=ia.sanfran;
   format Model $model.;
   var FlightID DepartDate Destination Model;
run;
```

6. Creating HTML Reports

```
options ls=64 nodate number pageno=1;
ods html file='c05ex04.html';
proc print data=work.passngrs label;
    var Depart FClass BClass EClass;
    by Dest;
    pageby Dest;
    sum FClass BClass EClass;
    format Depart date9. FClass BClass EClass comma6.
           Dest $cities.;
    label Dest='Destination'
          Depart='Departure Date'
          FClass='First Class'
          BClass='Business Class'
          EClass='Economy Class';
    title 'San Francisco Passenger Data';
run;
ods html close;
```

7. Creating a Listing Report (Optional)

a.

```
proc format;
    value $gendfmt 'F'='Female'
                   'M'='Male';
run;
```

b.

```
libname ia 'SAS data library';
options ls=72 nodate nonumber;
ods html file='c05ex05b.html';
proc print data=ia.newmechs;
    where JobCode='MECH01';
    var EmpID LastName FirstName Gender;
    title 'Level I Mechanics';
    format Gender $gendfmt.;
run;
ods html close;
```

Chapter 6 Creating SAS® Data Sets

6.1   Reading Raw Data Files: Column Input

Objectives

- Create a temporary SAS data set from a raw data file.
- Create a permanent SAS data set from a raw data file.
- Explain how the DATA step processes data.
- Read standard data using column input.

3

Accessing Data Sources

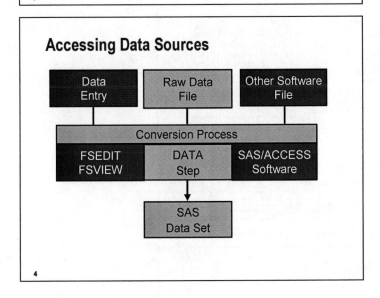

4

Reading Raw Data Files

Data for flights from New York to Dallas (DFW) and Los Angeles (LAX) is stored in a raw data file. Create a SAS data set from the raw data.

```
                 1    1    2
1---5----0----5----0
43912/11/00LAX 20137
92112/11/00DFW 20131
11412/12/00LAX 15170
98212/12/00dfw  5 85
43912/13/00LAX 14196
98212/13/00DFW 15116
43112/14/00LaX 17166
98212/14/00DFW  7 88
11412/15/00LAX    187
98212/15/00DFW 14 31
```

Description	Column
Flight Number	1- 3
Date	4-11
Destination	12-14
First Class Passengers	15-17
Economy Passengers	18-20

5

Creating a SAS Data Set

In order to create a SAS data set from a raw data file, you must

1. start a DATA step and name the SAS data set being created (DATA statement)

2. identify the location of the raw data file to read (INFILE statement)

3. describe how to read the data fields from the raw data file (INPUT statement).

Raw Data File

```
                 1    1    2
1---5----0----5----0
43912/11/00LAX 20137
92112/11/00DFW 20131
11412/12/00LAX 15170
```

⬇

DATA Step

```
data SAS-data-set-name;
   infile 'raw-data-filename';
   input input-specifications;
run;
```

⬇

SAS Data Set

Flight	Date	Dest	First Class	Economy
439	12/11/00	LAX	20	137
921	12/11/00	DFW	20	131
114	12/12/00	LAX	15	170

7

Creating a SAS Data Set

General form of the DATA statement:

```
DATA libref.SAS-data-set(s);
```

Example: This DATA statement creates a temporary SAS data set named **dfwlax**:

```
data work.dfwlax;
```

Example: This DATA statement creates a permanent SAS data set named **dfwlax**:

```
libname ia 'SAS-data-library';
data ia.dfwlax;
```

8

Pointing to a Raw Data File

General form of the INFILE statement:

> **INFILE** *'filename'* *<options>*;

Examples:
```
z/OS (OS/390)
 infile 'userid.prog1.dfwlax';
UNIX
 infile '/users/userid/dfwlax.dat';
Windows
 infile 'c:\workshop\winsas\prog1\dfwlax.dat';
```

The PAD option in the INFILE statement is useful for reading variable-length records typically found in Windows and UNIX environments.

9

Reading Data Fields

General form of the INPUT statement:

> **INPUT** *input-specifications;*

input-specifications
- names the SAS variables
- identifies the variables as character or numeric
- specifies the locations of the fields in the raw data
- can be specified as column, formatted, list or named input.

10

Reading Data Using Column Input

Column input is appropriate for reading
- data in fixed columns
- standard character and numeric data.

General form of a column INPUT statement:

> **INPUT** *variable <$> startcol-endcol . . . ;*

Examples of standard numeric data:
```
15   -15   15.4   +1.23   1.23E3   -1.23E-3
```

11

(handwritten margin notes):
standard numeric data
0 1 2 3 4 5 6 7 8 9 . + - E

3 required attributes
1 name
1 type
1 length

what is standard data?
character anything on keyboard
non-standard leading spaces

The Raw Data

```
                                    1    1    2
                           1---5----0----5----0
                           43912/11/00LAX 20137
                           92112/11/00DFW 20131
                           11412/12/00LAX 15170
                           98212/12/00dfw  5 85
                           43912/13/00LAX 14196
                           98212/13/00DFW 15116
                           43112/14/00LaX 17166
                           98212/14/00DFW  7 88
                           11412/15/00LAX    187
                           98212/15/00DFW 14 31
```

Description	Column
Flight Number	1- 3
Date	4-11
Destination	12-14
First Class Passengers	15-17
Economy Passengers	18-20

12

Reading Data Using Column Input

Raw Data File

```
43912/11/00LAX 20137
92112/11/00DFW 20131
11412/12/00LAX 15170
```

Read the raw data file using column input.

DATA Step

```
data SAS-data-set-name;
   infile 'raw-data-filename';
   input variable <$> startcol-endcol ...;
run;
```

SAS Data Set

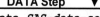

Flight	Date	Dest	FirstClass	Economy
439	12/11/00	LAX	20	137
921	12/11/00	DFW	20	131
114	12/12/00	LAX	15	170

13

(handwritten margin note: b/c slashes in date, reads as characters)

Create Temporary SAS Data Sets

Store the **dfwlax** data set in the **work** library.

```
data work.dfwlax;
   infile 'raw-data-file';
   input Flight $ 1-3 Date $ 4-11
         Dest $ 12-14 FirstClass 15-17
         Economy 18-20;
run;
```

```
NOTE: The data set WORK.DFWLAX has 10 observations and 5
      variables.
```

19   c06s1d1

Examples of raw data file names:

z/OS (OS/390)	`userid.prog1.rawdata(dfwlax)`
Windows	`c:\workshop\winsas\prog1\dfwlax.dat`
UNIX	`/users/userid/dfwlax.dat`

Create Permanent SAS Data Sets

Alter the previous DATA step to permanently store the **dfwlax** data set.

```
libname ia 'SAS-data-library';
data ia.dfwlax;
   infile 'raw-data-file';
   input Flight $ 1-3 Date $ 4-11
         Dest $ 12-14 FirstClass 15-17
         Economy 18-20;
run;
```

```
NOTE: The data set IA.DFWLAX has 10 observations and 5
      variables.
```

20   c06s1d2

Examples of SAS data library names:

z/OS (OS/390)	`userid.prog1.sasdata`
Windows	`c:\workshop\winsas\prog1`
UNIX	`/users/userid`

Looking Behind the Scenes

The DATA step is processed in two phases:
- compilation
- execution.

```
data work.dfwlax;
   infile 'raw-data-file';
   input Flight $ 1-3 Date $ 4-11
         Dest $ 12-14 FirstClass 15-17
         Economy 18-20;
run;
```

21

Looking Behind the Scenes

At compile time, SAS creates

- an input buffer to hold the current raw data file record that is being processed

									1									2
1	2	3	4	5	6	7	8	9	0	1	2	3	4	5	6	7	8	9	0

- a program data vector (PDV) to hold the current SAS observation

Flight	Date	Dest	FirstClass	Economy
$ 3	$ 8	$ 3	N 8	N 8

- the descriptor portion of the output data set.

Flight	Date	Dest	FirstClass	Economy
$ 3	$ 8	$ 3	N 8	N 8

22

Compiling the DATA Step

```
data work.dfwlax;
     infile 'raw-data-file';
     input Flight $ 1-3 Date $ 4-11
           Dest $ 12-14 FirstClass 15-17
           Economy 18-20;
run;
```

23   ...

Compiling the DATA Step

```
data work.dfwlax;
     infile 'raw-data-file';
     input Flight $ 1-3 Date $ 4-11
           Dest $ 12-14 FirstClass 15-17
           Economy 18-20;
run;
```

Input Buffer

									1									2
1	2	3	4	5	6	7	8	9	0	1	2	3	4	5	6	7	8	9	0

24   ...

256 character limit

Compiling the DATA Step

```
data work.dfwlax;
   infile 'raw-data-file';
   input Flight $ 1-3 Date $ 4-11
         Dest $ 12-14 FirstClass 15-17
         Economy 18-20;
run;
```

Input Buffer

| | | | | | | | | | 1 | | | | | | | | | 2 |
|1|2|3|4|5|6|7|8|9|0|1|2|3|4|5|6|7|8|9|0|

PDV

Flight
$ 3

25 ...

Compiling the DATA Step

```
data work.dfwlax;
   infile 'raw-data-file';
   input Flight $ 1-3 Date $ 4-11
         Dest $ 12-14 FirstClass 15-17
         Economy 18-20;
run;
```

Input Buffer

| | | | | | | | | | 1 | | | | | | | | | 2 |
|1|2|3|4|5|6|7|8|9|0|1|2|3|4|5|6|7|8|9|0|

PDV

Flight	Date
$ 3	$ 8

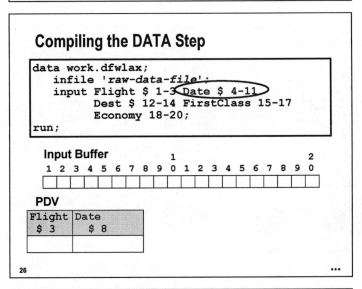

26 ...

Compiling the DATA Step

```
data work.dfwlax;
   infile 'raw-data-file';
   input Flight $ 1-3 Date $ 4-11
         Dest $ 12-14 FirstClass 15-17
         Economy 18-20;
run;
```

Input Buffer

| | | | | | | | | | 1 | | | | | | | | | 2 |
|1|2|3|4|5|6|7|8|9|0|1|2|3|4|5|6|7|8|9|0|

PDV

Flight	Date	Dest
$ 3	$ 8	$ 3

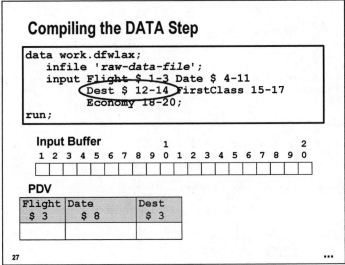

27 ...

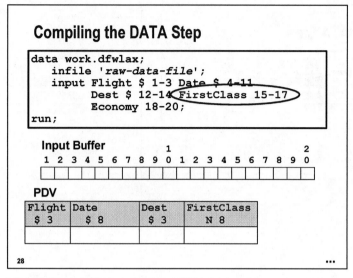

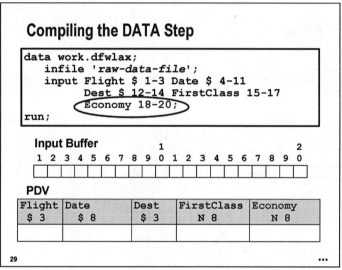

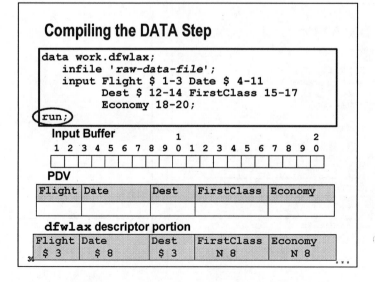

Executing the DATA Step

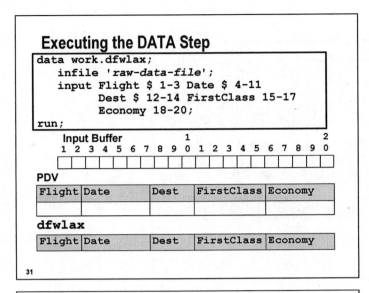

```
data work.dfwlax;
   infile 'raw-data-file';
   input Flight $ 1-3 Date $ 4-11
         Dest $ 12-14 FirstClass 15-17
         Economy 18-20;
run;
```

Input Buffer

1	2	3	4	5	6	7	8	9	0	1	2	3	4	5	6	7	8	9	0

PDV

Flight	Date	Dest	FirstClass	Economy

dfwlax

Flight	Date	Dest	FirstClass	Economy

31

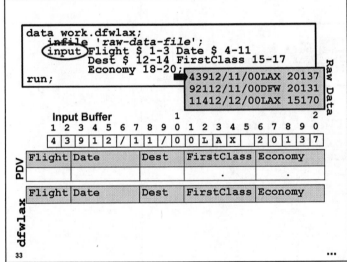

```
data work.dfwlax;
   infile 'raw-data-file';
   input Flight $ 1-3 Date $ 4-11
         Dest $ 12-14 FirstClass 15-17
         Economy 18-20;
run;
```

Raw Data
```
43912/11/00LAX 20137
92112/11/00DFW 20131
11412/12/00LAX 15170
```

Input Buffer

1	2	3	4	5	6	7	8	9	0	1	2	3	4	5	6	7	8	9	0
4	3	9	1	2	/	1	1	/	0	0	L	A	X		2	0	1	3	7

PDV

Flight	Date	Dest	FirstClass	Economy
			.	.

dfwlax

Flight	Date	Dest	FirstClass	Economy

33   ...

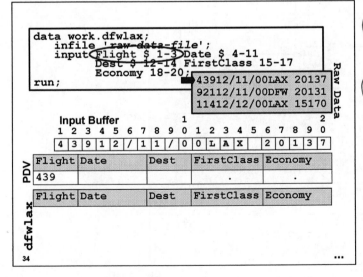

```
data work.dfwlax;
   infile 'raw-data-file';
   input Flight $ 1-3 Date $ 4-11
         Dest $ 12-14 FirstClass 15-17
         Economy 18-20;
run;
```

Raw Data
```
43912/11/00LAX 20137
92112/11/00DFW 20131
11412/12/00LAX 15170
```

Input Buffer

1	2	3	4	5	6	7	8	9	0	1	2	3	4	5	6	7	8	9	0
4	3	9	1	2	/	1	1	/	0	0	L	A	X		2	0	1	3	7

PDV

Flight	Date	Dest	FirstClass	Economy
439			.	.

dfwlax

Flight	Date	Dest	FirstClass	Economy

34   ...

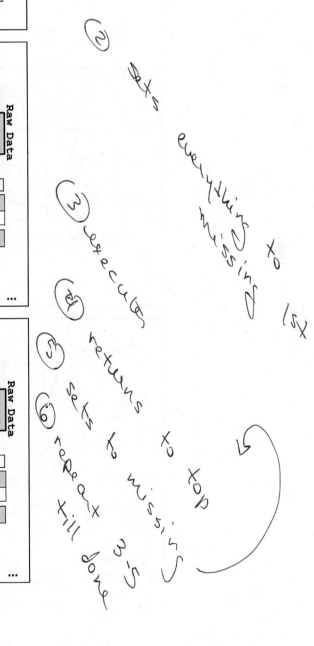

① compile one time

② sets everything to missing 1st

③ execute

④ returns to top

⑤ sets to missing

⑥ repeat 3-5 till done

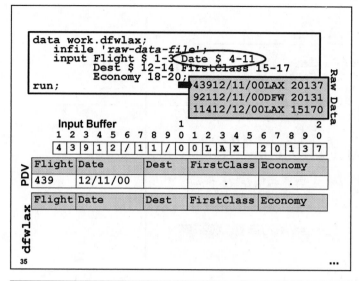

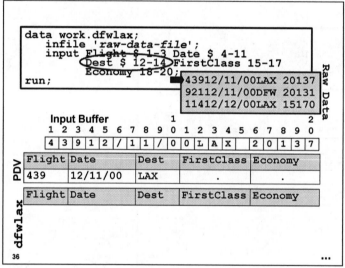

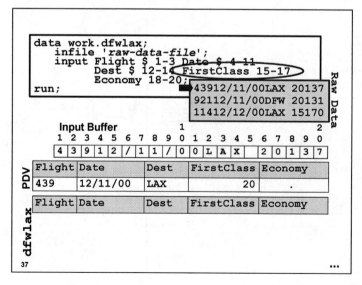

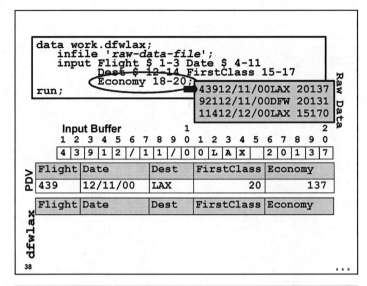

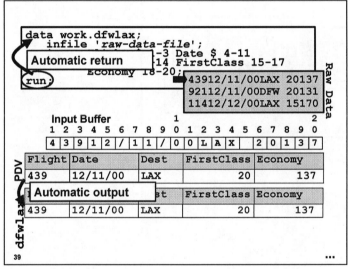

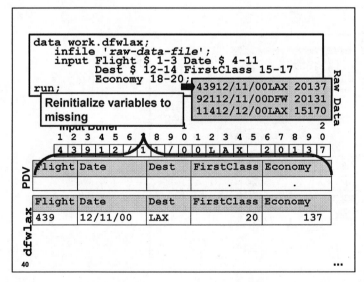

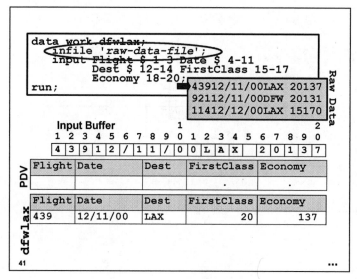

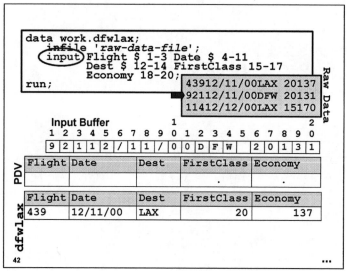

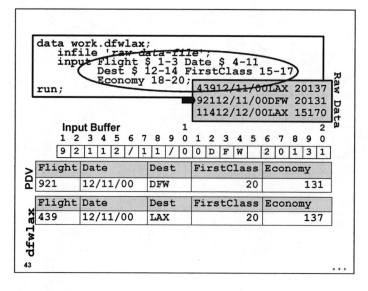

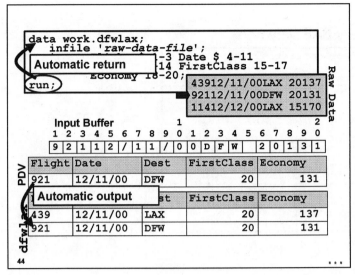

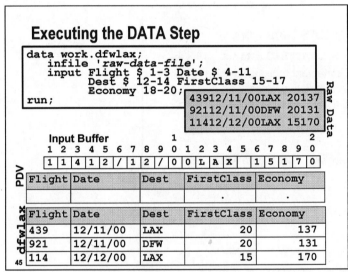

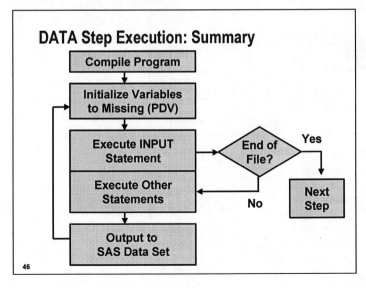

Access Temporary SAS Data Sets

```
proc print data=work.dfwlax;
run;
```

```
                       The SAS System

                                       First
   Obs   Flight   Date      Dest       Class    Economy

    1     439    12/11/00   LAX         20        137
    2     921    12/11/00   DFW         20        131
    3     114    12/12/00   LAX         15        170
    4     982    12/12/00   dfw          5         85
    5     439    12/13/00   LAX         14        196
    6     982    12/13/00   DFW         15        116
    7     431    12/14/00   LaX         17        166
    8     982    12/14/00   DFW          7         88
    9     114    12/15/00   LAX          .        187
   10     982    12/15/00   DFW         14         31
```

47   c06s1d1

Access Permanent SAS Data Sets

To access a permanently stored SAS data set,

- submit a LIBNAME statement to assign a libref to the SAS data library
- use the libref as the first-level name of the SAS data set.

The LIBNAME statement only needs to be submitted once per SAS session.

48

Access Permanent SAS Data Sets

```
libname ia 'SAS-data-library';
proc print data=ia.dfwlax;
run;
```

```
                       The SAS System

                                       First
   Obs   Flight   Date      Dest       Class    Economy

    1     439    12/11/00   LAX         20        137
    2     921    12/11/00   DFW         20        131
    3     114    12/12/00   LAX         15        170
    4     982    12/12/00   dfw          5         85
    5     439    12/13/00   LAX         14        196
    6     982    12/13/00   DFW         15        116
    7     431    12/14/00   LaX         17        166
    8     982    12/14/00   DFW          7         88
    9     114    12/15/00   LAX          .        187
   10     982    12/15/00   DFW         14         31
```

49   c06s1d2

 **Exercises**

For these exercises, write DATA steps that read the raw data file that contains information on flights from San Francisco to various destinations.

Fill in the blank with the location of your raw data file. Use an INFILE statement and an INPUT statement in a DATA step to read the raw file.

```
data ...;
   infile '_____';
   .
   .
   .
```

Each exercise instructs you to read **some** of the fields (identified by **bold** type in the shaded rows below) shown in the following record layout. The complete record layout for the **sfosch** raw data file is shown below.

Variable Name	Field Description	Columns	Data Type
FlightID	Flight ID Number	1-7	Character
RouteID	Route ID Number	8-14	Character
Origin	Flight Origin	15-17	Character
Destination	Flight Destination	18-20	Character
Model	Aircraft Model	21-40	Character
Date	Departure Date	41-49	Character 01JAN2000
DepartDay	Departure Day of Week	51	Numeric 1=Sunday
FClassPass	First Class Passengers	53-55	Numeric
BClassPass	Business Class Passengers	57-59	Numeric
EClassPass	Economy Class Passengers	61-63	Numeric
TotPassCap	Aircraft Capacity – Total Passengers	65-67	Numeric
CargoWt	Weight of Cargo in Pounds	69-73	Numeric
CargoRev	Revenue from Cargo in Dollars	75-79	Numeric

1. **Reading Raw Data Using Column Input**

   a. Create a SAS data set named **work.sanfran** by writing a DATA step that
      uses column input to create only the variables **FlightID**, **RouteID**,
      Destination, **Model**, **DepartDay**, and **TotPassCap**.

   b. Read the log to answer the following questions:

      1) How many records were read from the raw data file?

      2) How many observations does the resulting SAS data set contain?

      3) How many variables does the resulting SAS data set contain?

   c. Use PROC PRINT to display the data portion of the data set. Do not display
      the date and time the SAS session started. Do not display page numbers. Set
      the line size to 72.

   Partial SAS Output (First 10 of 52 Observations)

   ```
                              The SAS System


                                                                Tot
              Flight                                   Depart  Pass
     Obs        ID     RouteID   Destination    Model     Day   Cap

       1     IA11200   0000112      HND     JetCruise LF8100    6    255
       2     IA01804   0000018      SEA     JetCruise SF1000    6    150
       3     IA02901   0000029      HNL     JetCruise LF5200    7    207
       4     IA03100   0000031      ANC     JetCruise LF8100    7    255
       5     IA02901   0000029      HNL     JetCruise LF5200    1    207
       6     IA03100   0000031      ANC     JetCruise MF4000    1    267
       7     IA00800   0000008      RDU     JetCruise MF4000    2    267
       8     IA01805   0000018      SEA     JetCruise SF1000    2    150
       9     IA01804   0000018      SEA     JetCruise LF5100    4    165
      10     IA03101   0000031      ANC     JetCruise LF8100    4    255
   ```

   d. Use PROC CONTENTS to display the descriptor portion of the data set.

   Partial SAS Output

   ```
          Alphabetic List of Variables and Attributes

          #     Variable      Type    Len

          5     DepartDay     Num       8
          3     Destination   Char      3
          1     FlightID      Char      7
          4     Model         Char     20
          2     RouteID       Char      7
          6     TotPassCap    Num       8
   ```

   Your solution to this exercise may be useful in subsequent workshops so you
   should save the program for future reference.

2. Reading Raw Data Using Column Input (Optional)

Write a DATA step to read the **emplist** raw data file.

- Call the new SAS data set **work.emps**.
- Use column input.
- Write the DATA step so that the **EmpID** variable is read first and **HireDate** is not read.

The complete record layout for the **emplist** raw data file is below.

You should read all of the fields except **HireDate**.

Variable Name	Columns	Data Type
LastName	1-20	Character
FirstName	21-30	Character
EmpId	31-35	Character
JobCode	36-43	Character
HireDate	44-51	Numeric
Salary	54-59	Numeric

Write a PROC PRINT step to view the data.

- Suppress the observation column and add a suitable title.

Complete SAS Output

```
          Salary Information for Pilots and Mechanics

                              First
          EmpID    LastName   Name       JobCode    Salary

          E0029    TORRES     JAN        Pilot       50000
          E0045    LANGKAMM   SARAH      Mechanic    80000
          E0106    SMITH      MICHAEL    Mechanic    40000
          E0116    LEISTNER   COLIN      Mechanic    36000
          E0126    WADE       KIRSTEN    Pilot       85000
          E0143    TOMAS      HARALD     Pilot      105000
          E0204    WAUGH      TIM        Pilot       70000
          E0206    LEHMANN    DAGMAR     Mechanic    64000
          E0248    TRETTHAHN  MICHAEL    Pilot      100000
          E0282    TIETZ      OTTO       Pilot       45000
          E0288    O'DONOGHUE ART        Mechanic    52000
          E0304    WALKER     THOMAS     Pilot       95000
          E0310    NOROVIITA  JOACHIM    Mechanic    78000
          E0339    OESTERBERG ANJA       Mechanic    80000
          E0346    LAUFFER    CRAIG      Mechanic    40000
          E0428    TORR       JUGDISH    Pilot       45000
          E0449    WAGSCHAL   NADJA      Pilot       77500
          E0451    TOERMOEN   JOCHEN     Pilot       65000
```

6.2   Reading Raw Data Files: Formatted Input

Objectives

- Read standard and nonstandard character and numeric data using formatted input.
- Read date values and convert them to SAS date values.

52

Reading Data Using Formatted Input

Formatted input is appropriate for reading

- data in fixed columns
- standard and nonstandard character and numeric data
- calendar values to be converted to SAS date values.

53

Reading Data Using Formatted Input

General form of the INPUT statement with formatted input:

INPUT *pointer-control variable informat . . . ;*

Formatted input is used to read data values by

- moving the input pointer to the starting position of the field
- specifying a variable name
- specifying an informat.

54

Reading Data Using Formatted Input

Pointer controls:

@n   moves the pointer to column *n*.

+n   moves the pointer *n* positions.

An *informat* specifies

- the width of the input field
- how to read the data values that are stored in the field.

55

What Is a SAS Informat?

An informat is an instruction that SAS uses to read data values.

SAS informats have the following form:

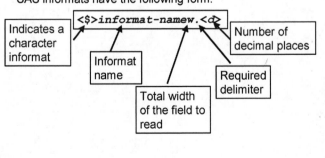

`<$>informat-namew.<d>`

- Indicates a character informat
- Informat name
- Total width of the field to read
- Required delimiter
- Number of decimal places

56

informat like a translator

format → out (display / reading)
informat → in

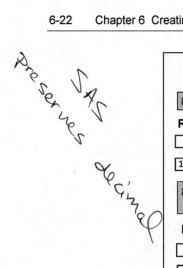

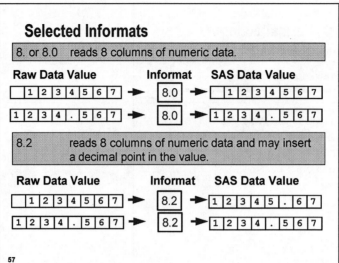

The decimal value specification in the informat is ignored if the data value being read already contains a decimal point.

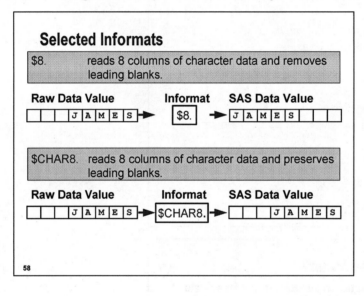

Selected Informats

COMMA7.	reads 7 columns of numeric data and removes selected nonnumeric characters such as dollar signs and commas.

Raw Data Value	Informat	SAS Data Value
$ 1 2 , 5 6 7 →	COMMA7.0 →	1 2 5 6 7

MMDDYY8.	reads dates of the form 10/29/01.

Raw Data Value	Informat	SAS Data Value
1 0 / 2 9 / 0 1 →	MMDDYY8. →	1 5 2 7 7

59

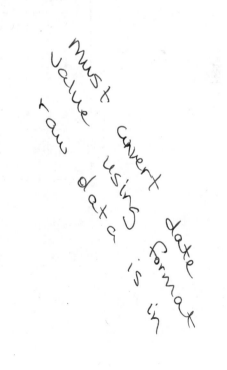
removes both dollar signs commas X

Working with Date Values

Date values that are stored as SAS dates are special numeric values.

A *SAS date value* is interpreted as the number of days between January 1, 1960, and a specific date.

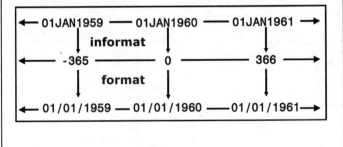

```
←— 01JAN1959 —— 01JAN1960 —— 01JAN1961 —→
              ↓  informat  ↓            ↓
←——  -365  ——————  0  ——————  366  ——→
              ↓   format   ↓            ↓
←— 01/01/1959 — 01/01/1960 —— 01/01/1961 —→
```

60   . . .

must convert date value using raw data format is in

Convert Dates to SAS Date Values

SAS uses date **informats** to **read** and **convert** dates to SAS date values.

Examples:

Raw Data Value	Informat	Converted Value
10/29/2001	MMDDYY10.	15277
10/29/01	MMDDYY8.	15277
29OCT2001	DATE9.	15277
29/10/2001	DDMMYY10.	15277

Number of days between
01JAN1960 and 29OCT2001

61

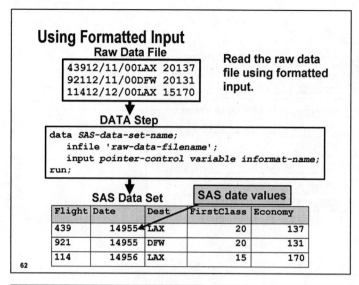

Reading Data: Formatted Input

```
                              1    1    2
                       1---5----0----5----0
       Raw Data File   43912/11/00LAX 20137
                       92112/11/00DFW 20131
                       11412/12/00LAX 15170
```

```
data work.dfwlax;
   infile 'raw-data-file';
   input @1 Flight $3. @4 Date mmddyy8.
         @12 Dest $3. @15 FirstClass 3.
         @18 Economy 3.;
run;
```

68   c06s2d1

Examples of raw data file names:

z/OS (OS/390)	*userid*.prog1.rawdata(dfwlax)
Windows	c:\workshop\winsas\prog1\dfwlax.dat
UNIX	/users/*userid*/dfwlax.dat

Reading Data: Formatted Input

```
proc print data=work.dfwlax;
run;
```

SAS date values

The SAS System

Obs	Flight	Date	Dest	First Class	Economy
1	439	14955	LAX	20	137
2	921	14955	DFW	20	131
3	114	14956	LAX	15	170
4	982	14956	dfw	5	85
5	439	14957	LAX	14	196
6	982	14957	DFW	15	116
7	431	14958	LaX	17	166
8	982	14958	DFW	7	88
9	114	14959	LAX	.	187
10	982	14959	DFW	14	31

69   c06s2d1

Reading Data: Formatted Input

```
proc print data=work.dfwlax;
   format Date date9.;
run;
```

Formatted SAS date values

The SAS System

Obs	Flight	Date	Dest	First Class	Economy
1	439	11DEC2000	LAX	20	137
2	921	11DEC2000	DFW	20	131
3	114	12DEC2000	LAX	15	170
4	982	12DEC2000	dfw	5	85
5	439	13DEC2000	LAX	14	196
6	982	13DEC2000	DFW	15	116
7	431	14DEC2000	LaX	17	166
8	982	14DEC2000	DFW	7	88
9	114	15DEC2000	LAX	.	187
10	982	15DEC2000	DFW	14	31

70   c06s2d2

Can also look @ delimited data (← csv, etc.)

① data work.sanfran;
  infile 'sfosch.dat
     dlm = tab
        ( )

② input   Flight ID $
         Route ID $
         Destination $
         Model $
list   Date   date9,
all   Tot Pass Cap;
variables

③ run;

Exercises

For these exercises, write DATA steps that read the raw data file that contains information on flights from San Francisco to various destinations.

Fill in the blank with the location of your raw data file. Use an INFILE statement and an INPUT statement in a DATA step to read the raw file.

```
data ...;
   infile '_____';
   .
   .
   .
```

Each exercise instructs you to read **some** of the fields (identified by **bold** type in shaded rows below) shown in the following record layout. The complete record layout for the **sfosch** raw data file is shown below.

Variable Name	Field Description	Columns	Data Type
FlightID	Flight ID Number	1-7	Character
RouteID	Route ID Number	8-14	Character
Origin	Flight Origin	15-17	Character
Destination	Flight Destination	18-20	Character
Model	Aircraft Model	21-40	Character
Date	Departure Date	41-49	Character 01JAN2000
DepartDay	Departure Day of Week	51	Numeric 1=Sunday
FClassPass	First Class Passengers	53-55	Numeric
BClassPass	Business Class Passengers	57-59	Numeric
EClassPass	Economy Class Passengers	61-63	Numeric
TotPassCap	Aircraft Capacity – Total Passengers	65-67	Numeric
CargoWt	Weight of Cargo in Pounds	69-73	Numeric
CargoRev	Revenue from Cargo in Dollars	75-79	Numeric

3. Reading Raw Data Using Formatted Input

a. Create a SAS data set named **work.sanfran** by writing a DATA step that uses formatted input to create only the variables **FlightID**, **RouteID**, **Destination**, **Model**, **Date**, and **TotPassCap**. Store the values of **Date** as SAS date values.

> ✎   If you saved your program from the first column input exercise, you can retrieve and modify the code for this workshop.

b. Use PROC PRINT to display the data portion of the data set. Display the values of **Date** in the form **12/15/2000**. Display the following labels for the column headings in place of the variable names:

Variable Name	Label
FlightID	Flight ID
RouteID	Route ID
Model	Aircraft Model
Date	Departure Date
TotPassCap	Total Passenger Capacity

Partial SAS Output (First 10 of 52 Observations)

```
                            The SAS System

                                                           Total
           Flight   Route                         Departure Passenger
   Obs       ID      ID    Destination  Aircraft Model   Date    Capacity

     1   IA11200  0000112      HND      JetCruise LF8100 12/01/2000    255
     2   IA01804  0000018      SEA      JetCruise SF1000 12/01/2000    150
     3   IA02901  0000029      HNL      JetCruise LF5200 12/02/2000    207
     4   IA03100  0000031      ANC      JetCruise LF8100 12/02/2000    255
     5   IA02901  0000029      HNL      JetCruise LF5200 12/03/2000    207
     6   IA03100  0000031      ANC      JetCruise MF4000 12/03/2000    267
     7   IA00800  0000008      RDU      JetCruise MF4000 12/04/2000    267
     8   IA01805  0000018      SEA      JetCruise SF1000 12/04/2000    150
     9   IA01804  0000018      SEA      JetCruise LF5100 12/06/2000    165
    10   IA03101  0000031      ANC      JetCruise LF8100 12/06/2000    255
```

c. Use PROC CONTENTS to display the descriptor portion of the data set.

Partial SAS Output

```
         Alphabetic List of Variables and Attributes

         #    Variable       Type    Len

         5    Date           Num      8
         3    Destination    Char     3
         1    FlightID       Char     7
         4    Model          Char    20
         2    RouteID        Char     7
         6    TotPassCap     Num      8
```

d. Save your program (DATA step, PROC PRINT step, and PROC
CONTENTS step) in a file. You will use this program in a later exercise.

4. Reading Raw Data Using Formatted Input (optional)

Write a DATA step to read the **dfwlax** raw data file.

- Name the new SAS data set **work.dfwlax**.

- Use formatted input.

The complete record layout for the **dfwlax** raw data file is below.

Variable Name	Columns	Data Type
FlightNum	1-3	Character
FlightDate	4-11	Numeric Date style: 01/01/03
Dest	12-14	Character
FirstClass	15-17	Numeric
Economy	18-20	Numeric

Write a PROC PRINT step to view the data.

- Suppress the observation column.

- Format **Economy** and **FirstClass** with commas, and add a suitable date
  format for **FlightDate** (for example, **date9.**, **mmddyy10.**,
  ddmmyy10., or **worddate.**).

- Add a suitable title.

- Suppress the date, time, and page numbers.

- Add grand totals for **FirstClass** and **Economy**.

Complete SAS Output (using the DATE9. format)

```
              Passenger Counts for Flights to LAX and DFW

      Flight       Flight                   First
      Num          Date      Dest           Class       Economy

        439       11DEC2000   LAX             20           137
        921       11DEC2000   DFW             20           131
        114       12DEC2000   LAX             15           170
        982       12DEC2000   dfw              5            85
        439       13DEC2000   LAX             14           196
        982       13DEC2000   DFW             15           116
        431       14DEC2000   LaX             17           166
        982       14DEC2000   DFW              7            88
        114       15DEC2000   LAX              .           187
        982       15DEC2000   DFW             14            31
                                          =========     =========
                                            127           1,307
```

6.3   Examining Data Errors

Objectives

- Define types of data errors.
- Identify data errors.

73

What Are Data Errors?

SAS detects data errors when

- the INPUT statement encounters invalid data in a field
- illegal arguments are used in functions
- impossible mathematical operations are requested.

74

Examining Data Errors

When SAS encounters a data error,

1. a note that describes the error is printed in the SAS log

2. the input record being read is displayed in the SAS log (contents of the input buffer)

3. the values in the SAS observation being created are displayed in the SAS log (contents of the PDV)

4. a missing value is assigned to the appropriate SAS variable

5. execution continues.

75

In log in blue text and won't stop processing

Examining Data Errors

File: c06s3d1.sas

File: *userid*.prog1.sascode(c06s3d1)

- Use column input to read the raw data file.
- Examine the data error in the log.
- Use PROC PRINT to examine the data portion of the data set.

Partial Raw Data File

```
            1    1    2    2    3    3    4    4    5
1---5----0----5----0----5----0----5----0----5----0----
0031GOLDENBERG    DESIREE      PILOT1 50221.62
0040WILLIAMS      ARLENE M.    FLTAT1 23666.12
0071PERRY         ROBERT A.    FLTAT1 21957.71
0082MCGWIER-WATTSCHRISTINA     PILOT3 96387.39
0091SCOTT         HARVEY F.    FLTAT2 32278.40
0106THACKER       DAVID S.     FLTAT1 24161.14
0275GRAHAM        DEBORAH S.   FLTAT2 32024.93
0286DREWRY        SUSAN        PILOT1 55377.00
0309HORTON        THOMAS L.    FLTAT1 23705.12
0334DOWN          EDWARD       PILOT1 56%84.87
0347CHERVENY      BRENDA B.    FLTAT2 38563.45
0355BELL          THOMAS B.    PILOT1 59803.16
0366GLENN         MARTHA S.    PILOT3120202.38
0730BELL          CARLA        PILOT1 37397.93
0739SAYRE         MARCO        PILOT1 59268.61
```

1. Use a DATA step with column input to read the fields from the raw data file and create a SAS data set:

```
data work.empdata2;
   infile 'raw-data-file';
   input EmpID $ 1-4 LastName $ 5-17 FirstName $ 18-30
         JobCode $ 31-36 Salary 37-45;
run;
```

2. Examine the log.

    SAS Log

    ```
    1     options ls=72 nodate nonumber;
    2     data work.empdata2;
    3       infile 'raw-data-file';
    4       input EmpID $ 1-4 LastName $ 5-17 FirstName $ 18-30
    5             JobCode $ 31-36 Salary 37-45;
    6     run;

    NOTE: The infile 'raw-data-file' is:
          File Name=raw-data-file,
          RECFM=V,LRECL=256

    ❶NOTE: Invalid data for Salary in line 10 37-45.
    ❷RULE:       ----+----1----+----2----+----3----+----4----+----5----+----6--
    ❸10        0334DOWN          EDWARD        PILOT1 56%84.87 45
    ❹EmpID=0334 LastName=DOWN FirstName=EDWARD JobCode=PILOT1 Salary=.
    ❺_ERROR_=1 _N_=10
     NOTE: 15 records were read from the infile 'raw-data-file'.
           The minimum record length was 45.
           The maximum record length was 45.
     NOTE: The data set WORK.EMPDATA2 has 15 observations and 5 variables.
    ```

❶ This note indicates that invalid data was found for the variable **Salary** in line 10 of the raw data file, in columns 37-45.

❷ A ruler is drawn above the raw data record that contains the invalid data. The ruler can help you locate the invalid data in the record.

❸ SAS displays the raw data record being read (contents of input buffer).

❹ SAS displays the observation currently being created from the raw data record (contents of PDV). Notice the value of **Salary** is set to missing.

❺ During the processing of every DATA step, SAS automatically creates two variables, _N_ and _ERROR_. They are **not** written to the SAS data set but are available for processing during the execution of the DATA step.

3. Use PROC PRINT to examine the data portion of the SAS data set.

```
proc print data=work.empdata2;
run;
```

SAS Output

```
                          The SAS System

          Emp                                  Job
  Obs     ID     LastName        FirstName      Code       Salary

   1     0031    GOLDENBERG      DESIREE       PILOT1     50221.62
   2     0040    WILLIAMS        ARLENE M.     FLTAT1     23666.12
   3     0071    PERRY           ROBERT A.     FLTAT1     21957.71
   4     0082    MCGWIER-WATTS   CHRISTINA     PILOT3     96387.39
   5     0091    SCOTT           HARVEY F.     FLTAT2     32278.40
   6     0106    THACKER         DAVID S.      FLTAT1     24161.14
   7     0275    GRAHAM          DEBORAH S.    FLTAT2     32024.93
   8     0286    DREWRY          SUSAN         PILOT1     55377.00
   9     0309    HORTON          THOMAS L.     FLTAT1     23705.12
  10     0334    DOWN            EDWARD        PILOT1          .
  11     0347    CHERVENY        BRENDA B.     FLTAT2     38563.45
  12     0355    BELL            THOMAS B.     PILOT1     59803.16
  13     0366    GLENN           MARTHA S.     PILOT3    120202.38
  14     0730    BELL            CARLA         PILOT1     37397.93
  15     0739    SAYRE           MARCO         PILOT1     59268.61
```

A missing numeric value is displayed as a period and a missing character value is displayed as a blank.

File: c06s3d2.sas

File: *userid*.prog1.sascode(c06s3d2)

- Use column input to read the raw data file again, but omit the $ after the variable **JobCode** in the INPUT statement.

- Examine the data error in the log.

1. Use a DATA step with column input to read the fields from the raw data file and create a SAS data set:

```
data work.empdata2;
   infile 'raw-data-file';
   input EmpID $ 1-4 LastName $ 5-17 FirstName $ 18-30
         JobCode 31-36 Salary 37-45;
run;
```

2. Examine the log.

SAS Log

```
1     options ls=72 nodate nonumber;
2     data work.empdata2;
3        infile 'raw-data-file';
4        input EmpID $ 1-4 LastName $ 5-17 FirstName $ 18-30
5             JobCode 31-36 Salary 37-45;
6     run;

NOTE: The infile 'raw-data-file' is:
      File Name=raw-data-file,
      RECFM=V,LRECL=256

NOTE: Invalid data for JobCode in line 1 31-36.
RULE:      ----+----1----+----2----+----3----+----4----+----5----+----6--
1          0031GOLDENBERG   DESIREE      PILOT1 50221.62 45
EmpID=0031 LastName=GOLDENBERG FirstName=DESIREE JobCode=.
Salary=50221.62 _ERROR_=1 _N_=1
NOTE: Invalid data for JobCode in line 2 31-36.
2          0040WILLIAMS     ARLENE M.    FLTAT1 23666.12 45
EmpID=0040 LastName=WILLIAMS FirstName=ARLENE M. JobCode=.
Salary=23666.12 _ERROR_=1 _N_=2
NOTE: Invalid data for JobCode in line 3 31-36.
3          0071PERRY        ROBERT A.    FLTAT1 21957.71 45
EmpID=0071 LastName=PERRY FirstName=ROBERT A. JobCode=. Salary=21957.71
_ERROR_=1 _N_=3
NOTE: Invalid data for JobCode in line 4 31-36.
4          0082MCGWIER-WATTSCHRISTINA     PILOT3 96387.39 45
EmpID=0082 LastName=MCGWIER-WATTS FirstName=CHRISTINA JobCode=.
Salary=96387.39 _ERROR_=1 _N_=4
NOTE: Invalid data for JobCode in line 5 31-36.
5          0091SCOTT        HARVEY F.    FLTAT2 32278.40 45
EmpID=0091 LastName=SCOTT FirstName=HARVEY F. JobCode=. Salary=32278.4
_ERROR_=1 _N_=5
NOTE: Invalid data for JobCode in line 6 31-36.

6          0106THACKER      DAVID S.     FLTAT1 24161.14 45
EmpID=0106 LastName=THACKER FirstName=DAVID S. JobCode=. Salary=24161.14
```

```
_ERROR_=1 _N_=6
NOTE: Invalid data for JobCode in line 7 31-36.
7          0275GRAHAM        DEBORAH S.   FLTAT2 32024.93 45
EmpID=0275 LastName=GRAHAM FirstName=DEBORAH S. JobCode=.
Salary=32024.93 _ERROR_=1 _N_=7
NOTE: Invalid data for JobCode in line 8 31-36.
8          0286DREWRY        SUSAN        PILOT1 55377.00 45
EmpID=0286 LastName=DREWRY FirstName=SUSAN JobCode=. Salary=55377
_ERROR_=1 _N_=8
NOTE: Invalid data for JobCode in line 9 31-36.
9          0309HORTON        THOMAS L.    FLTAT1 23705.12 45
EmpID=0309 LastName=HORTON FirstName=THOMAS L. JobCode=. Salary=23705.12
_ERROR_=1 _N_=9
NOTE: Invalid data for JobCode in line 10 31-36.
NOTE: Invalid data for Salary in line 10 37-45.
10         0334DOWN          EDWARD       PILOT1 56%84.87 45
EmpID=0334 LastName=DOWN FirstName=EDWARD JobCode=. Salary=. _ERROR_=1
_N_=10
NOTE: Invalid data for JobCode in line 11 31-36.
11         0347CHERVENY      BRENDA B.    FLTAT2 38563.45 45
EmpID=0347 LastName=CHERVENY FirstName=BRENDA B. JobCode=.
Salary=38563.45 _ERROR_=1 _N_=11
NOTE: Invalid data for JobCode in line 12 31-36.
12         0355BELL          THOMAS B.    PILOT1 59803.16 45
EmpID=0355 LastName=BELL FirstName=THOMAS B. JobCode=. Salary=59803.16
_ERROR_=1 _N_=12
NOTE: Invalid data for JobCode in line 13 31-36.
13         0366GLENN         MARTHA S.    PILOT3120202.38 45
EmpID=0366 LastName=GLENN FirstName=MARTHA S. JobCode=. Salary=120202.38
_ERROR_=1 _N_=13
NOTE: Invalid data for JobCode in line 14 31-36.
14         0730BELL          CARLA        PILOT1 37397.93 45
EmpID=0730 LastName=BELL FirstName=CARLA JobCode=. Salary=37397.93
_ERROR_=1 _N_=14
NOTE: Invalid data for JobCode in line 15 31-36.
15         0739SAYRE         MARCO        PILOT1 59268.61 45
EmpID=0739 LastName=SAYRE FirstName=MARCO JobCode=. Salary=59268.61
_ERROR_=1 _N_=15
NOTE: 15 records were read from the infile 'raw-data-file'.
      The minimum record length was 45.
      The maximum record length was 45.
NOTE: The data set WORK.EMPDATA2 has 15 observations and 5 variables.
```

 By default, the error message for invalid data for **JobCode** will be printed a maximum of 20 times.

3. Use PROC PRINT to examine the data portion of the SAS data set.

```
proc print data=work.empdata2;
run;
```

SAS Output

```
                          The SAS System

          Emp                                  Job
  Obs      ID    LastName        FirstName     Code      Salary

    1     0031   GOLDENBERG      DESIREE         .       50221.62
    2     0040   WILLIAMS        ARLENE M.       .       23666.12
    3     0071   PERRY           ROBERT A.       .       21957.71
    4     0082   MCGWIER-WATTS   CHRISTINA       .       96387.39
    5     0091   SCOTT           HARVEY F.       .       32278.40
    6     0106   THACKER         DAVID S.        .       24161.14
    7     0275   GRAHAM          DEBORAH S.      .       32024.93
    8     0286   DREWRY          SUSAN           .       55377.00
    9     0309   HORTON          THOMAS L.       .       23705.12
   10     0334   DOWN            EDWARD          .          .
   11     0347   CHERVENY        BRENDA B.       .       38563.45
   12     0355   BELL            THOMAS B.       .       59803.16
   13     0366   GLENN           MARTHA S.       .      120202.38
   14     0730   BELL            CARLA           .       37397.93
   15     0739   SAYRE           MARCO           .       59268.61
```

 **Exercises**

For these exercises, write DATA steps that read the raw data file that contains information on flights from San Francisco to various destinations.

> Fill in the blank with the location of your raw data file. Use an INFILE statement in a DATA step to read the raw file.
>
> ```
> data ...;
>    infile '_____';
>    .
>    .
>    .
> ```

Each exercise instructs you to read **some** of the fields shown (identified by **bold** type in shaded rows below) in the following record layout. The complete record layout for the **sfosch** raw data file is shown below.

Variable Name	Field Description	Columns	Data Type
FlightID	Flight ID Number	1-7	Character
RouteID	Route ID Number	8-14	Character
Origin	Flight Origin	15-17	Character
Destination	Flight Destination	18-20	Character
Model	Aircraft Model	21-40	Character
Date	Departure Date	41-49	Character 01JAN2000
DepartDay	Departure Day of Week	51	Numeric 1=Sunday
FClassPass	First Class Passengers	53-55	Numeric
BClassPass	Business Class Passengers	57-59	Numeric
EClassPass	Economy Class Passengers	61-63	Numeric
TotPassCap	Aircraft Capacity – Total Passengers	65-67	Numeric
CargoWt	Weight of Cargo in Pounds	69-73	Numeric
CargoRev	Revenue from Cargo in Dollars	75-79	Numeric

5. Examining Data Errors

a. Create a SAS data set named **work.passngrs** by writing a DATA step that uses formatted input to create only the variables **FlightID**, **Destination, Date, FClassPass, BClassPass**, and **EClassPass**. Store the values of **Date** as SAS date values.

b. Read the log and answer the following questions:

1) How many records were read from the raw data file?

2) How many observations are in the resulting SAS data set?

3) How many variables are in the resulting SAS data set?

4) What data errors are indicated in the SAS log?

c. Use PROC PRINT to display the data portion of the data set. Do not display the date and time the SAS session started. Do not display page numbers. Set the line size to 72. Use an appropriate format to display the values of **Date**.

Partial SAS Output (First 26 of 52 Observations)

```
                          The SAS System

            Flight                            FClass    BClass
    EClass
    Obs      ID      Destination      Date     Pass      Pass      Pass

      1    IA11200       HND       01DEC2000     19        31        171
      2    IA01804       SEA       01DEC2000     10         .        123
      3    IA02901       HNL       02DEC2000     13        24        138
      4    IA03100       ANC       02DEC2000     13        22        250
      5    IA02901       HNL       03DEC2000     14        25        132
      6    IA03100       ANC       03DEC2000     16         .        243
      7    IA00800       RDU       04DEC2000     16         .        243
      8    IA01805       SEA       04DEC2000     11         .        123
      9    IA01804       SEA       06DEC2000     11        12        111
     10    IA03101       ANC       06DEC2000     14        26        233
     11    IA01802       SEA       07DEC2000     10         .        132
     12    IA11200       HND       08DEC2000     17        33        194
     13    IA03101       ANC       08DEC2000     13        17        242
     14    IA01804       SEA       08DEC2000     12         .        119
     15    IA11201       HND       09DEC2000     15        32        175
     16    IA03100       ANC       09DEC2000     14         .        237
     17    IA01805       SEA       10DEC2000     12         .        126
     18    IA01803       SEA       11DEC2000     12         .        136
     19    IA11201       HND       12DEC2000     18        31        178
     20    IA11200       HND       13DEC2000     17        29        179
     21    IA03100       ANC       13DEC2000     14         .        244
     22    IA01802       SEA       13DEC2000     12         .        115
     23    IA01804       SEA       13DEC2000     11         .        115
     24    IA01805       SEA       13DEC2000     10         .        123
     25    IA11201       HND       14DEC2000     16        35        163
     26    IA00801       RDU       14DEC2000     14         .        222
```

6.4   Assigning Variable Attributes

Objectives

- Assign permanent attributes to SAS variables.
- Override permanent variable attributes.

79

Default Variable Attributes

When a variable is created in a DATA step, the

- name, type, and length of the variable are automatically assigned
- remaining attributes such as label and format are not automatically assigned.

When the variable is used in a later step,

- the name is displayed for identification purposes
- its value is displayed using a system-determined format.

80

Default Variable Attributes

Create the **ia.dfwlax** data set.

```
libname ia 'SAS-data-library';
data ia.dfwlax;
   infile 'raw-data-file';
   input @1 Flight $3. @4 Date mmddyy8.
         @12 Dest $3. @15 FirstClass 3.
         @18 Economy 3.;
run;
```

81   c06s4d1

Examples of raw data file names:

z/OS (OS/390)	userid.prog1.rawdata(dfwlax)
Windows	c:\workshop\winsas\prog1\dfwlax.dat
UNIX	/users/userid/dfwlax.dat

Examples of SAS data library names:

z/OS (OS/390)	userid.prog1.sasdata
Windows	c:\workshop\winsas\prog1
UNIX	/users/userid

Default Variable Attributes

Examine the descriptor portion of the **ia.dfwlax** data set.

```
proc contents data=ia.dfwlax;
run;
```

Partial Output

```
       Alphabetic List of Variables and Attributes

         #     Variable      Type    Len

         2     Date          Num      8
         3     Dest          Char     3
         5     Economy       Num      8
         4     FirstClass    Num      8
         1     Flight        Char     3
```

82   c06s4d1

Specifying Variable Attributes

Use LABEL and FORMAT statements in the

- PROC step to temporarily assign the attributes (for the duration of the step only)
- DATA step to permanently assign the attributes (stored in the data set descriptor portion).

83

Temporary Variable Attributes

Use LABEL and FORMAT statements in a PROC step to temporarily assign attributes.

```
proc print data=ia.dfwlax label;
   format Date mmddyy10.;
   label Dest='Destination'
         FirstClass='First Class Passengers'
         Economy='Economy Passengers';
run;
```

84   c06s4d1

Temporary Variable Attributes

				First Class	Economy
Obs	Flight	Date	Destination	Passengers	Passengers
1	439	12/11/2000	LAX	20	137
2	921	12/11/2000	DFW	20	131
3	114	12/12/2000	LAX	15	170
4	982	12/12/2000	dfw	5	85
5	439	12/13/2000	LAX	14	196
6	982	12/13/2000	DFW	15	116
7	431	12/14/2000	LaX	17	166
8	982	12/14/2000	DFW	7	88
9	114	12/15/2000	LAX	.	187
10	982	12/15/2000	DFW	14	31

The SAS System

85

Permanent Variable Attributes

Assign labels and formats in the DATA step.

```
libname ia 'SAS-data-library';
data ia.dfwlax;
   infile 'raw-data-file';
   input @1 Flight $3. @4 Date mmddyy8.
         @12 Dest $3. @15 FirstClass 3.
         @18 Economy 3.;
   format Date mmddyy10.;
   label Dest='Destination'
         FirstClass='First Class Passengers'
         Economy='Economy Passengers';
run;
```

86   c06s4d2

Examples of raw data file names:

z/OS (OS/390)	userid.prog1.rawdata(dfwlax)
Windows	c:\workshop\winsas\prog1\dfwlax.dat
UNIX	/users/userid/dfwlax.dat

Permanent Variable Attributes

Examine the descriptor portion of the **ia.dfwlax** data set.

```
proc contents data=ia.dfwlax;
run;
```

Partial Output

```
          Alphabetic List of Variables and Attributes

#   Variable     Type    Len    Format      Label

2   Date         Num      8     MMDDYY10.
3   Dest         Char     3                 Destination
5   Economy      Num      8                 Economy Passengers
4   FirstClass   Num      8                 First Class Passengers
1   Flight       Char     3
```

87   c06s4d2

Permanent Variable Attributes

```
proc print data=ia.dfwlax label
run;
```

```
                        The SAS System

                                       First
                                       Class    Economy
      Obs   Flight      Date  Destination Passengers Passengers

       1     439    12/11/2000    LAX        20       137
       2     921    12/11/2000    DFW        20       131
       3     114    12/12/2000    LAX        15       170
       4     982    12/12/2000    dfw         5        85
       5     439    12/13/2000    LAX        14       196
       6     982    12/13/2000    DFW        15       116
       7     431    12/14/2000    LaX        17       166
       8     982    12/14/2000    DFW         7        88
       9     114    12/15/2000    LAX         .       187
      10     982    12/15/2000    DFW        14        31
```

88   c06s4d2

Override Permanent Attributes

Use a FORMAT statement in a PROC step to temporarily override the format stored in the data set descriptor.

```
proc print data=ia.dfwlax label;
   format Date date9.;
run;
```

89   c06s4d3

Override Permanent Attributes

```
                        The SAS System

                                       First
                                       Class    Economy
      Obs   Flight      Date  Destination Passengers Passengers

       1     439    11DEC2000    LAX        20       137
       2     921    11DEC2000    DFW        20       131
       3     114    12DEC2000    LAX        15       170
       4     982    12DEC2000    dfw         5        85
       5     439    13DEC2000    LAX        14       196
       6     982    13DEC2000    DFW        15       116
       7     431    14DEC2000    LaX        17       166
       8     982    14DEC2000    DFW         7        88
       9     114    15DEC2000    LAX         .       187
      10     982    15DEC2000    DFW        14        31
```

90

 **Exercises**

6. Assigning Variable Attributes

a. In the formatted input workshop, you wrote a program and stored it in a file. (The program creates a SAS data set named **work.sanfran**, prints the data set, and shows the contents of the descriptor portion of the data set.) Retrieve the program and submit it.

1) View the PROC PRINT output. The **Date** values are displayed in the form **12/01/2000**. Labels should be used for all column headings except for the variable **Destination**.

Partial SAS Output (First 5 of 52 Observations)

```
                         The SAS System


                                                        Total
          Flight  Route                        Departure Passenger
    Obs      ID     ID    Destination  Aircraft Model      Date   Capacity


      1  IA11200 0000112     HND    JetCruise LF8100 12/01/2000    255
      2  IA01804 0000018     SEA    JetCruise SF1000 12/01/2000    150
      3  IA02901 0000029     HNL    JetCruise LF5200 12/02/2000    207
      4  IA03100 0000031     ANC    JetCruise LF8100 12/02/2000    255
      5  IA02901 0000029     HNL    JetCruise LF5200 12/03/2000    207
```

2) View the PROC CONTENTS output. Are the labels permanently stored in the data set descriptor? Is the DATE format stored in the descriptor for the variable **Date**?

Partial SAS Log

```
          Alphabetic List of Variables and Attributes


             #      Variable      Type      Len


             5      Date          Num        8
             3      Destination   Char       3
             1      FlightID      Char       7
             4      Model         Char      20
             2      RouteID       Char       7
             6      TotPassCap    Num        8
```

b. Alter your program so the labels and the DATE format are stored in the descriptor portion of the data set. Submit the program again.

1) View the PROC PRINT output. Are the labels still displayed? Are the values of **Date** still formatted correctly?

Partial SAS Output (First 5 of 52 Observations)

```
                                 The SAS System

                                                                 Total
              Flight  Route                             Departure Passenger
         Obs    ID     ID    Destination  Aircraft Model    Date   Capacity

          1 IA11200 0000112     HND       JetCruise LF8100 12/01/2000   255
          2 IA01804 0000018     SEA       JetCruise SF1000 12/01/2000   150
          3 IA02901 0000029     HNL       JetCruise LF5200 12/02/2000   207
          4 IA03100 0000031     ANC       JetCruise LF8100 12/02/2000   255
          5 IA02901 0000029     HNL       JetCruise LF5200 12/03/2000   207
```

2) View the PROC CONTENTS output. Are the labels permanently stored in the data set descriptor? Is the DATE format stored in the descriptor for the variable **Date**?

Partial SAS Log

```
           Alphabetic List of Variables and Attributes

     #   Variable      Type    Len   Format      Label

     5   Date          Num      8    MMDDYY10.   Departure Date
     3   Destination   Char     3
     1   FlightID      Char     7                Flight ID
     4   Model         Char    20                Aircraft Model
     2   RouteID       Char     7                Route ID
     6   TotPassCap    Num      8                Total Passenger Capacity
```

6.5   Changing Variable Attributes (Self-Study)

Objectives

- Use features in the windowing environment to change variable attributes.
- Use programming statements to change variable attributes.

93

Changing Variable Attributes under Windows

Change the name of the variable **Dest** to **Destination**.

1. If the Explorer window is not active, select **View** ⇨ **Contents Only**.

2. Double-click on **Libraries** to view a list of currently defined libraries.

The functionality of the SAS Explorer is similar to explorers for Windows-based systems. In addition to this view, you can view a list of folders and files, or you can specify a tree view.

3. Double-click on the **ia** library to show all members of that library.

4. Right-click on the **dfwlax** data set and select <u>**View Columns**</u>.

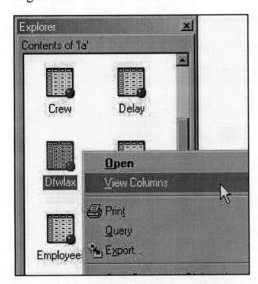

5. Right-click on the **Dest** variable and select <u>**Modify**</u>.

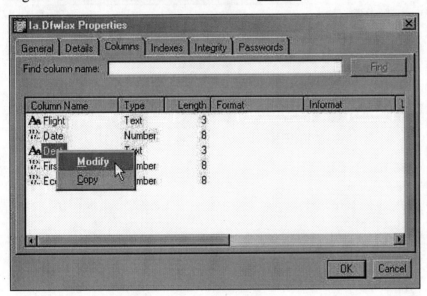

6. Type the new name, **Destination**, over the old name and select **OK**.

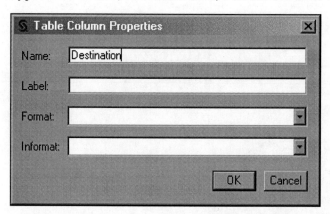

7. The new name is displayed for the variable.

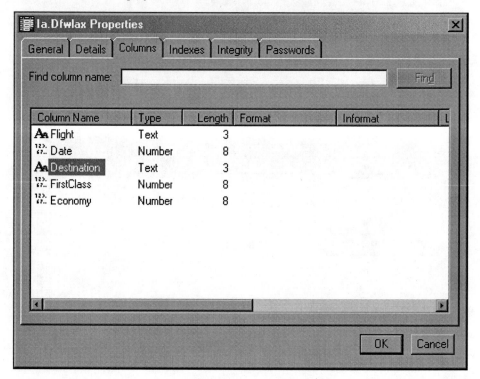

Changing Variable Attributes under UNIX

Change the name of the variable **Dest** to **Destination**.

1. If the Explorer window is not active, select **View** ⇨ **Contents Only**.

2. Double-click on **Libraries** to view a list of currently defined libraries.

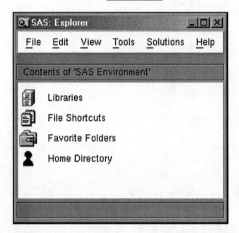

3. Double-click on the **ia** library to show all members of that library.

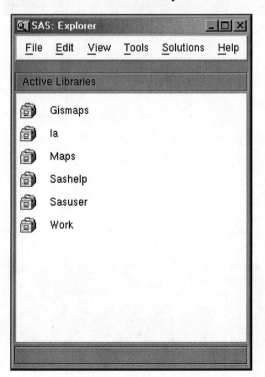

4. Right-click on the **dfwlax** data set and select <u>View Columns</u>.

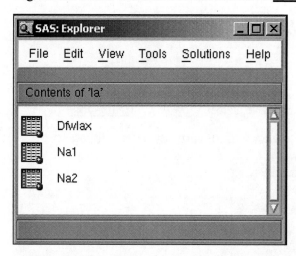

5. Right-click on the **Dest** variable and select <u>Modify</u>.

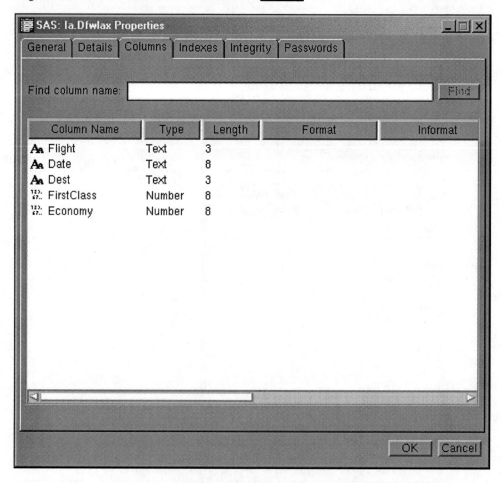

6. Type the new name, **Destination**, over the old name and select **OK**.

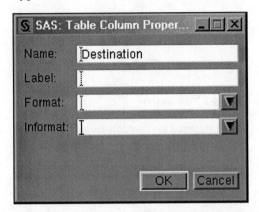

7. The new name is displayed for the variable.

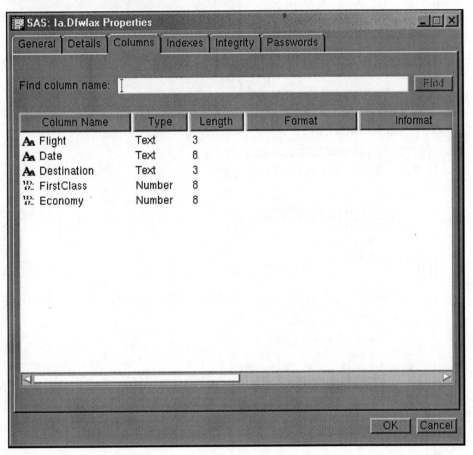

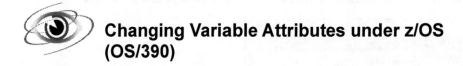

Changing Variable Attributes under z/OS (OS/390)

Change the name of the variable **Dest** to **Destination**.

1. If the Explorer window is not active, type **pmenu** on the command line and press Enter.

2. Select <u>**View**</u> ⇨ <u>**Contents Only**</u>.

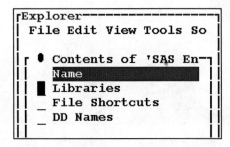

3. Type **s** beside the **ia** library and press Enter to display all currently active SAS data libraries.

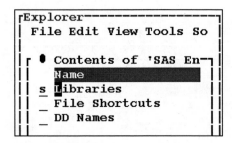

4. Type **s** beside the **ia** library and press Enter to show all members of that library.

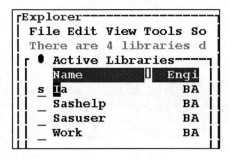

5. Type **s** beside the **dfwlax** data set and press Enter to display the attributes of
    the variables in the **dfwlax** data set.

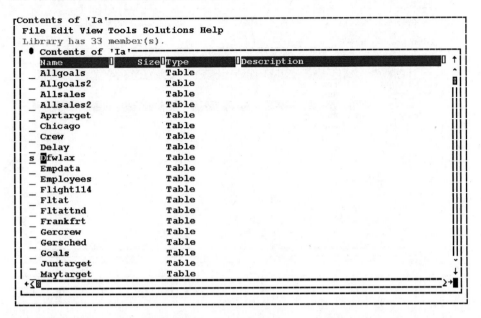

6. Type **?** beside the **Dest** variable and press Enter.

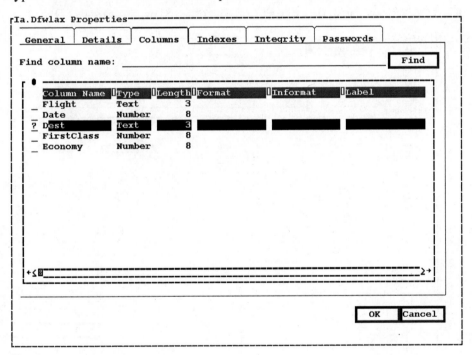

7. Select **Modify** to rename the variable.

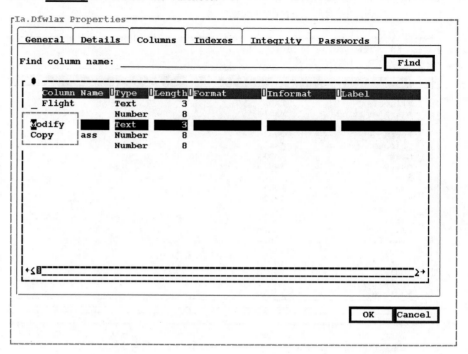

8. Type the new name, **Destination**, over the old name and select **OK**.

9. The new name is displayed for the variable.

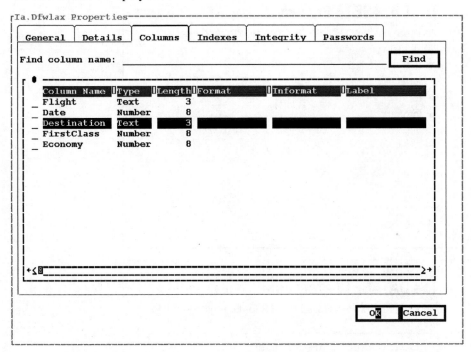

The DATASETS Procedure

You can use the DATASETS procedure to modify a variable's

- name
- label
- format
- informat.

95

The DATASETS Procedure

General form of PROC DATASETS for changing variable attributes:

```
PROC DATASETS LIBRARY=libref ;
    MODIFY SAS-data-set ;
    RENAME old-name-1=new-name-1
            <. . . old-name-n=new-name-n>;
    LABEL variable-1='label-1'
            <. . . variable-n='label-n'>;
    FORMAT variable-list-1 format-1
            <. . . variable-list-n format-n>;
    INFORMAT variable-list-1 informat-1
            <. . . variable-list-n informat-n>;
RUN;
```

96

Data Set Contents

Use the DATASETS procedure to change the name of the variable **Dest** to **Destination**.

Look at the attributes of the variables in the **ia.dfwlax** data set.

```
proc contents data=ia.dfwlax;
run;
```

```
        Alphabetic List of Variables and Attributes

        #     Variable     Type    Len

        2     Date         Num      8
        3     Dest         Char     3
        5     Economy      Num      8
        4     FirstClass   Num      8
        1     Flight       Char     3
```

97   c06s5d1

The DATASETS Procedure

Rename the variable **Dest** to **Destination**.

```
proc datasets library=ia;
   modify dfwlax;
   rename Dest=Destination;
run;
```

98   c06s5d1

Data Set Contents

Look at the attributes of the variables in the **ia.dfwlax** data set after running PROC DATASETS.

```
proc contents data=ia.dfwlax;
run;
```

```
        Alphabetic List of Variables and Attributes

        #     Variable      Type    Len

        2     Date          Num      8
        3     Destination   Char     3
        5     Economy       Num      8
        4     FirstClass    Num      8
        1     Flight        Char     3
```

99   c06s5d1

 **Exercises**

For these exercises, use the **passngrs** data set stored in a permanent SAS data library.

> Fill in the blank with the location of your SAS data library. **If you have started a new SAS session since the previous lab,** submit the LIBNAME statement to assign the libref **ia** to the SAS data library.
>
> `libname ia '_____';`

7. **Changing Variable Attributes**

    a. Use the SAS windowing environment to change the following attributes of the **FClass** variable.

        1) Rename the variable to **FirstClass**.

        2) Assign the label **First Class Passengers** to the variable.

        3) Run PROC CONTENTS to verify that the changes were made.

        Partial Output

```
              Alphabetic List of Variables and Attributes

        #    Variable     Type    Len    Label

        5    BClass       Num      8
        3    Depart       Num      8
        2    Dest         Char     3
        6    EClass       Num      8
        4    FirstClass   Num      8     First Class Passengers
        1    FlightID     Char     7
```

b. Use program statements to change the following attributes of the **Depart** variable:

1) Assign the DATE9. format to the variable.

2) Assign the label **Departure Date** to the variable.

3) Run PROC CONTENTS to verify that the changes were made.

Partial Output

```
          Alphabetic List of Variables and Attributes

     #    Variable     Type    Len    Format    Label

     5    BClass       Num      8
     3    Depart       Num      8     DATE9.    Departure Date
     2    Dest         Char     3
     6    EClass       Num      8
     4    FirstClass   Num      8               First Class Passengers
     1    FlightID     Char     7
```

6.6   Reading Excel Spreadsheets (Self-Study)

Objectives

- Create a SAS data set from an Excel spreadsheet using the Import Wizard.
- Create a SAS data set from an Excel spreadsheet using the IMPORT procedure.

102

Business Task

The flight data for Dallas and Los Angeles are in an Excel spreadsheet. Read the data into a SAS data set.

Excel Spreadsheet

	A	B	C	D	E
1	Flight	Date	Dest	FirstClass	Economy
2	439	12/11/00	LAX	20	137
3	921	12/11/00	DFW	20	131
4	114	12/12/00	LAX	15	170

SAS Data Set

Flight	Date	Dest	FirstClass	Economy
439	12/11/00	LAX	20	137
921	12/11/00	DFW	20	131
114	12/12/00	LAX	15	170

103

The Import Wizard

The *Import Wizard* is a point-and-click graphical interface that enables you to create a SAS data set from several types of external files including

- dBASE files (*.DBF)
- Excel spreadsheets (*.XLS)
- Microsoft Access tables (*.MDB)
- JMP data files (*.JMP)
- delimited files (*.*)
- comma-separated values (*.CSV).

104

The data sources available to you depend on the SAS/ACCESS products that you have licensed. If you do not have any SAS/ACCESS products licensed, the only types of data source files available to you are

- .CSV
- .TXT
- delimited files.

For most data sources, SAS attempts to generate SAS variable names from the column names in the input file's first row of data. If the column names are not valid SAS names, SAS uses default variable names. For example, for a delimited file, the default variable names are VAR1, VAR2, VAR3, and so on.

 If a column name contains special characters that are not valid in a SAS name, such as a blank, SAS converts the character to an underscore. For example, the column name **Occupancy Code** becomes the variable name **Occupancy_Code**.

Reading Raw Data with the Import Wizard

Use the Import Wizard to import the file **DallasLA.xls** into SAS. This is an Excel file that contains flight information. Name the resulting data set **work.dfwlax**.

1. Select **File** ⇨ **Import Data...**. The Import Wizard – Select import type window opens.

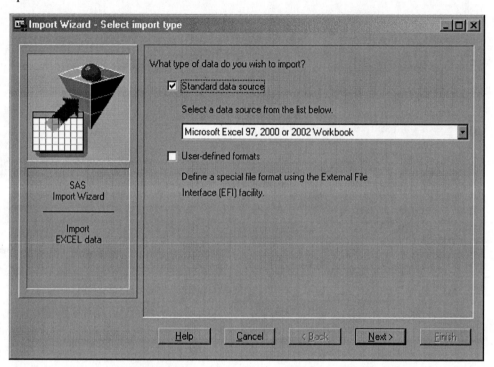

2. Select the drop-down button.

3. From the list box, select **Microsoft Excel 97, 2000 or 2002 Workbook**.

4. Select **Next >**. The Connect to MS Excel window opens.

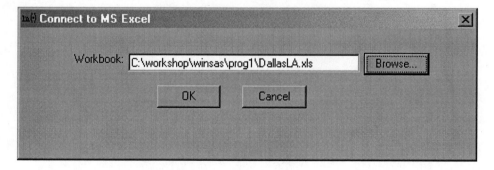

5. Type **DallasLA.xls**, the name of the workbook file to be imported.

    You can also select **Browse...** to specify a workbook file to import from the Open window. After you select the pathname, select **Open** to complete your selections and return to the Connect to MS Excel window.

6. Select **OK**. The Import Wizard – Select Table window opens.

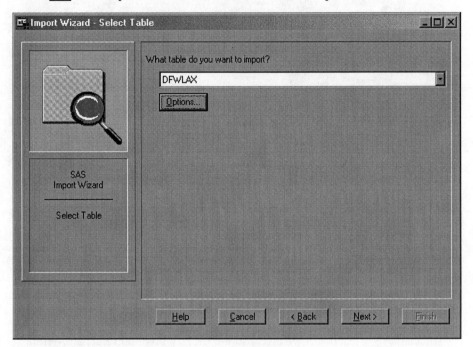

7. Select **DFWLAX**, the name of the worksheet (or named range) to be imported.

    ✎   You can select **Options...** to change default import settings through the SAS Import: Spreadsheet Options window.

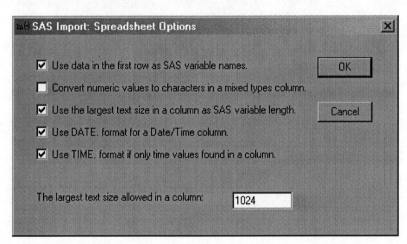

8. Select **Next >** to open the Import Wizard – Select library and member window, where you specify the storage location for the imported file.

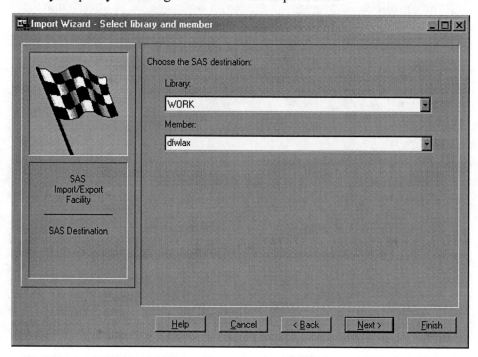

9. In the Library box on the left, leave the library as **WORK**. In the Member box on the right, type **dfwlax**.

   You can also select the down arrow in the Library box and select a different library. You can select the down arrow in the Member box to select an existing data set. If you select an existing data set, you will be asked later to verify that you want to replace it.

10. Select **Next >** to move to the next window or **Finish** to create the SAS data set from the Excel spreadsheet.

    If you select **Finish** and you select the name of an existing SAS data set for the name of your new SAS data set (in the Import Wizard – Select library and member window), you are prompted to determine whether or not you want to replace the existing data set. Select **OK** or **Cancel**.

    If you select **Next >**, you are taken to the Import Wizard – Create SAS Statements window.

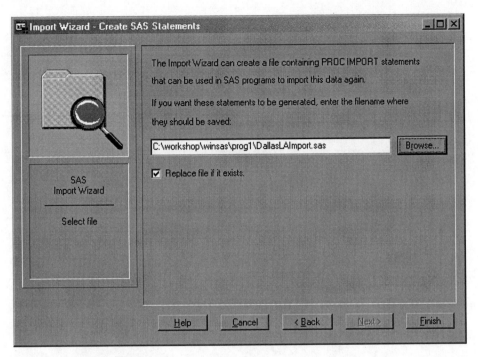

11. Type **DallasLAImport.sas**, which is the name of the location where you want to store the SAS code.

    You can also select **Browse...** to specify a location from the Save As window. After you select the pathname, select **Save** to complete your selections and return to the Import Wizard – Create SAS Statements window.

    If the file already exists, you are prompted to replace the existing file, append to the existing file, or cancel the save.

12. Select **Finish**.

13. Check the log to see that the SAS data set is successfully created.

```
NOTE: WORK.DFWLAX was successfully created.
```

14. Go to the Program Editor window and write SAS code to print the data set.

File: c06s6d1.sas

```
proc print data=work.dfwlax;
run;
```

SAS Output

```
                            The SAS System

                                            First
             Obs   Flight    Date     Dest  Class    Economy

              1     439    12/11/00   LAX    20        137
              2     921    12/11/00   DFW    20        131
              3     114    12/12/00   LAX    15        170
              4     982    12/12/00   dfw     5         85
              5     439    12/13/00   LAX    14        196
              6     982    12/13/00   DFW    15        116
              7     431    12/14/00   LaX    17        166
              8     982    12/14/00   DFW     7         88
              9     114    12/15/00   LAX     .        187
             10     982    12/15/00   DFW    14         31
```

15. Go to the Program Editor window and open the SAS code created by the Import Wizard.

```
PROC IMPORT OUT=WORK.dfwlax
        DATAFILE="C:\workshop\winsas\prog1\DallasLA.xls"
            DBMS=EXCEL REPLACE;
        SHEET="DFWLAX";
        GETNAMES=YES;
        MIXED=NO;
        SCANTEXT=YES;
        USEDATE=YES;
        SCANTIME=YES;
RUN;
```

For additional documentation related to statements used when reading Microsoft Excel files with the IMPORT procedure, see *Base SAS® 9.1 Procedures Guide, Volumes 1,2, and 3* (order # 58943) and *SAS/ACCESS® 9.1 Interface to PC Files: Reference* (order # 58974).

The IMPORT Procedure

General form of the IMPORT procedure:

```
PROC IMPORT OUT=SAS-data-set
            DATAFILE='external-file-name'
            < DBMS=file-type > <REPLACE>;
RUN;
```

REPLACE
        overwrites an existing SAS data set.

106

Available DBMS Specifications

Identifier	Input Data Source	Extension
ACCESS	Microsoft Access table	.MDB
CSV	delimited file (comma-separated values)	.CSV
DBF	dBASE 5.0, IV, III+, and II files	.DBF
DLM	delimited file (default delimiter is a blank)	.*
EXCEL	Microsoft Excel spreadsheet	.XLS
JMP	JMP table	.JMP
TAB	delimited file (tab-delimited values)	.TXT
WK1	Lotus 1-2-3 Release 2 spreadsheet	.WK1
WK3	Lotus 1-2-3 Release 3 spreadsheet	.WK3
WK4	Lotus 1-2-3 Release 4 or 5 spreadsheet	.WK4

If *external-file-name* contains a valid extension so that PROC IMPORT can recognize the type of data, you may omit the DBMS= option.

If you specify DBMS=ACCESS to import a Microsoft Access table, PROC IMPORT can distinguish whether the table is in Access 97, 2000, or 2002 format.

If you specify DBMS=EXCEL to import a Microsoft Excel spreadsheet, PROC IMPORT can distinguish between Excel 2002, 2000, 97, 5.0 and 4.0 spreadsheets.

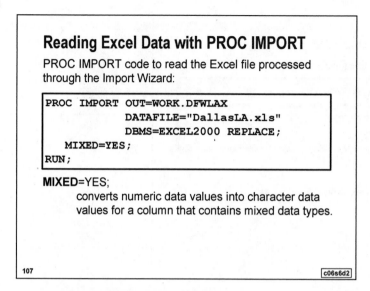

The default is MIXED=NO, which means that numeric data will be imported as missing values in a character column. The MIXED= option is available only when reading Excel data.

When using the Import Wizard, the MIXED=YES option can be set by selecting **Convert numeric values to characters in a mixed types column** in the SAS Import: Spreadsheet Options window.

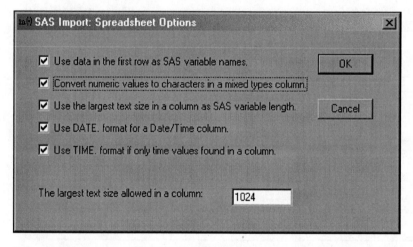

Other commonly used PROC IMPORT data source statements include

GETNAMES=NO;

> Do not attempt to generate SAS variable names from the column names in the input file's first row of data.

SHEET="*spreadsheet-name*";

> Read a particular spreadsheet from a file that contains multiple spreadsheets.

Reading Tab-Delimited Data

What if the data in the previous example were stored in a tab-delimited file?

Change the PROC IMPORT code to read the tab-delimited file.

```
PROC IMPORT OUT= WORK.DFWLAX
            DATAFILE= "DallasLA.txt"
            DBMS=TAB REPLACE;
RUN;
```

108   c06s6d3

Excel SAS/ACCESS LIBNAME Engine

If you wish to access Excel data without making a copy as a SAS data set, use the Excel LIBNAME statement.

General form of an Excel LIBNAME statement:

LIBNAME *libref* '*location-of-Excel-workbook*' *<options>*;

Example:

```
libname myxls 'c:\temp\sales.xls';
```

109

The Excel SAS/ACCESS LIBNAME engine is available in SAS 9.1.

    Due to the .xls extension, SAS recognizes the library path as an Excel workbook. Unlike other SAS/ACCESS interfaces, the Excel engine need not be specified in the LIBNAME statement.

Excel SAS/ACCESS LIBNAME Engine

The entire Excel workbook is treated like a SAS library. Individual worksheets and named ranges are considered equivalent to SAS data sets.

Use PROC PRINT to display data from the DFWLAX worksheet in the Excel workbook named DallasLA.xls:

```
libname xlsdata 'DallasLA.xls';

proc print data=xlsdata.dfwlax;
run;
```

110   c06s6d4

The MIXED=YES and GETNAMES=NO options are supported by the LIBNAME statement when using the Excel SAS/ACCESS engine.

 **Exercises**

(Applicable Only for Windows Users)

8. Reading an Excel Spreadsheet

    a. The Excel spreadsheet **sfosch.xls** contains information about International Airlines flights originating in San Francisco.

        Use the Import Wizard to create a SAS data set named **work.sfoexcel** from the Excel spreadsheet.

        Save the PROC IMPORT code that is generated to a file named **ImportSFO.sas**.

        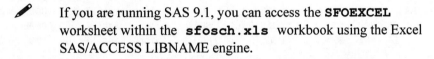 If you are running SAS 9.1, you can access the **SFOEXCEL** worksheet within the **sfosch.xls** workbook using the Excel SAS/ACCESS LIBNAME engine.

    b. Use PROC PRINT to display the data portion of the SAS data set **work.sfoexcel**. Do not display the date and time the SAS session started. Do not display page numbers. Set the linesize to 72.

Partial SAS Output (First 15 of 52 Observations)

```
                                  The SAS System


      Flight
 Obs  ID       RouteID   Origin   Destination   Model           Date

   1  IA11200  0000112   0000112   HND          JetCruise LF8100  01DEC2000
   2  IA01804  0000018   0000018   SEA          JetCruise SF1000  01DEC2000
   3  IA02901  0000029   0000029   HNL          JetCruise LF5200  02DEC2000
   4  IA03100  0000031   0000031   ANC          JetCruise LF8100  02DEC2000
   5  IA02901  0000029   0000029   HNL          JetCruise LF5200  03DEC2000
   6  IA03100  0000031   0000031   ANC          JetCruise MF4000  03DEC2000
   7  IA00800  0000008   0000008   RDU          JetCruise MF4000  04DEC2000
   8  IA01805  0000018   0000018   SEA          JetCruise SF1000  04DEC2000
   9  IA01804  0000018   0000018   SEA          JetCruise LF5100  06DEC2000
  10  IA03101  0000031   0000031   ANC          JetCruise LF8100  06DEC2000
  11  IA01802  0000018   0000018   SEA          JetCruise SF1000  07DEC2000
  12  IA11200  0000112   0000112   HND          JetCruise LF8100  08DEC2000
  13  IA03101  0000031   0000031   ANC          JetCruise LF8100  08DEC2000
  14  IA01804  0000018   0000018   SEA          JetCruise SF1000  08DEC2000
  15  IA11201  0000112   0000112   HND          JetCruise LF8100  09DEC2000


                                                    Tot
      Depart   FClass   BClass   EClass    Pass    Cargo   Cargo
 Obs  Day      Pass     Pass     Pass      Cap     Wt      Rev

   1   6        19       31       171       255    61300   79077
   2   6        10        .       123       150    10300   13287
   3   7        13       24       138       207    47400   61146
   4   7        13       22       250       255    24800   31992
   5   1        14       25       132       207    48200   62178
   6   1        16        .       243       267    25600   33024
   7   2        16        .       243       267    25600   33024
   8   2        11        .       123       150    10100   13029
   9   4        11       12       111       165    12500   16125
  10   4        14       26       233       255    28000   36120
  11   5        10        .       132       150     8500   10965
  12   6        17       33       194       255    56700   73143
  13   6        13       17       242       255    26400   34056
  14   6        12        .       119       150    10700   13803
  15   7        15       32       175       255    61100   78819
```

   c. Use PROC CONTENTS to display the descriptor portion of the
work.sfoexcel data set.

Partial SAS Output

```
          -----Alphabetic List of Variables and Attributes-----

  #    Variable      Type   Len   Pos   Format   Informat   Label
-----------------------------------------------------------------------
  9    BClassPass    Num     8    16                         BClassPass
 13    CargoRev      Num     8    48                         CargoRev
 12    CargoWt       Num     8    40                         CargoWt
  6    Date          Char    9    96    $9.      $9.         Date
  7    DepartDay     Num     8     0                         DepartDay
  4    Destination   Char    3    77    $3.      $3.         Destination
 10    EClassPass    Num     8    24                         EClassPass
  8    FClassPass    Num     8     8                         FClassPass
  1    FlightID      Char    7    56    $7.      $7.         FlightID
  5    Model         Char   16    80    $16.     $16.        Model
  3    Origin        Char    7    70    $7.      $7.         Origin
  2    RouteID       Char    7    63    $7.      $7.         RouteID
 11    TotPassCap    Num     8    32                         TotPassCap
```

9. **Reading a Comma-delimited File**

   a. The file named **sfosch.csv** (delimited file with comma-separated values)
contains the same information about International Airlines flights as the
Excel spreadsheet named **sfosch.xls**.

     Include the program in the file named **ImportSFO.sas** that you saved in
the previous exercise. Alter the PROC IMPORT statement so it creates a SAS
data set named **work.sfocsv** from the comma-delimited file.

   b. Use PROC PRINT to display the data portion of the **work.sfocsv** data
set. Do not display the date and time the SAS session started. Do not display
page numbers. Set the linesize to 72.

Partial SAS Output (First 9 of 52 Observations)

```
                              The SAS System

      Flight
Obs   ID          RouteID        Origin   Destination   Model

  1   IA11200         112           112      HND         JetCruise LF8100
  2   IA01804          18            18      SEA         JetCruise SF1000
  3   IA02901          29            29      HNL         JetCruise LF5200
  4   IA03100          31            31      ANC         JetCruise LF8100
  5   IA02901          29            29      HNL         JetCruise LF5200
  6   IA03100          31            31      ANC         JetCruise MF4000
  7   IA00800           8             8      RDU         JetCruise MF4000
  8   IA01805          18            18      SEA         JetCruise SF1000
  9   IA01804          18            18      SEA         JetCruise LF5100


Obs   Date        DepartDay   FClassPass    BClassPass     EClassPass

  1   01DEC2000        6          19            31            171
  2   01DEC2000        6          10             .            123
  3   02DEC2000        7          13            24            138
  4   02DEC2000        7          13            22            250
  5   03DEC2000        1          14            25            132
  6   03DEC2000        1          16             .            243
  7   04DEC2000        2          16             .            243
  8   04DEC2000        2          11             .            123
  9   06DEC2000        4          11            12            111


Obs     TotPassCap       CargoWt        CargoRev

  1         255           61300          79077
  2         150           10300          13287
  3         207           47400          61146
  4         255           24800          31992
  5         207           48200          62178
  6         267           25600          33024
  7         267           25600          33024
  8         150           10100          13029
  9         165           12500          16125
```

6.7 Solutions to Exercises

1. **Reading Raw Data Using Column Input**

   a.

   ```
   data work.sanfran;
       infile 'raw-data-file';
       input FlightID $ 1-7 RouteID $ 8-14
             Destination $ 18-20 Model $ 21-40
             DepartDay 51 TotPassCap 65-67;
   run;
   ```

   b.

   1) 52 records were read.

   2) 52 observations were stored in the SAS data set.

   3) 6 variables were stored in the SAS data set.

   c.

   ```
   options nodate nonumber ls=72;
   proc print data=work.sanfran;
   run;
   ```

   d.

   ```
   proc contents data=work.sanfran;
   run;
   ```

2. **Reading Raw Data Using Column Input (Optional)**

```
data work.emps;
   infile 'raw-data-filename';
   input EmpID       $ 31-35
         LastName    $  1-20
         FirstName   $ 21-30
         JobCode     $ 36-43
         Salary        54-59;
run;

proc print data=work.emps noobs;
   title 'Salary Information for Pilots and Mechanics';
run;
```

3. Reading Raw Data Using Formatted Input

a.

```
data work.sanfran;
   infile 'raw-data-file';
   input @1 FlightID $7. @8 RouteID $7.
         @18 Destination $3. @21 Model $20.
         @41 Date date9. @65 TotPassCap 3.;
run;
```

b.

```
proc print data=work.sanfran label;
   format Date mmddyy10.;
   label FlightID='Flight ID'
         RouteID='Route ID'
         Model='Aircraft Model'
         Date='Departure Date'
         TotPassCap='Total Passenger Capacity';
run;
```

c.

```
proc contents data=work.sanfran;
run;
```

d. Use the FILE command or select **Save As** from the **File** pull-down menu.

4. Reading Raw Data Using Formatted Input (Optional)

```
data work.dfwlax;
   infile 'raw-data-filename';
   input @1  FlightNum  $3.
         @4  FlightDate  mmddyy8.
         @12 Dest       $3.
         @18 Economy     3.
         @15 FirstClass  3.;
run;

options nodate nonumber;
proc print data=work.dfwlax noobs;
   title 'Passenger Counts for Flights to LAX and DFW';
   sum Economy FirstClass;
   format Economy FirstClass comma9. FlightDate date9.;
run;
```

5. Examining Data Errors

a.

```
data work.passngrs;
    infile 'raw-data-file';
    input @1 FlightID $7. @18 Destination $3.
          @41 Date date9. @53 FClassPass 3.
          @57 BClassPass 3. @61 EClassPass 3.;
run;
```

b.

1) 52 records were read.

2) 52 observations are in the resulting data set.

3) 6 variables are in the resulting data set.

4) There is invalid data for **BClassPass** in record numbers 11 and 26.

c.

```
options ls=72 nodate nonumber;
proc print data=work.passngrs;
    format Date date9.;
run;
```

6. Assigning Variable Attributes

a.

```
data work.sanfran;
    infile 'raw-data-file';
    input @1 FlightID $7. @8 RouteID $7.
          @18 Destination $3. @21 Model $20.
          @41 Date date9. @65 TotPassCap 3.;
run;
proc print data=work.sanfran label;
    format Date mmddyy10.;
    label FlightID='Flight ID'
          RouteID='Route ID'
          Model='Aircraft Model'
          Date='Departure Date'
          TotPassCap='Total Passenger Capacity';
run;
proc contents data=work.sanfran;
run;
```

1) **Date** values are formatted properly. Labels are displayed.

2) Labels are not in the descriptor. The DATE format is not in the descriptor.

b.

```
data work.sanfran;
   infile 'raw-data-file';
   input @1 FlightID $7. @8 RouteID $7.
         @18 Destination $3. @21 Model $20.
         @41 Date date9. @65 TotPassCap 3.;
   format Date mmddyy10.;
   label FlightID='Flight ID'
         RouteID='Route ID'
         Model='Aircraft Model'
         Date='Departure Date'
         TotPassCap='Total Passenger Capacity';
run;
proc print data=work.sanfran label;
run;
proc contents data=work.sanfran;
run;
```

1) Yes, the labels are displayed. Yes, the **Date** values are formatted correctly.
2) Yes, the labels are in the descriptor. Yes, the DATE format is in the descriptor.

7. Changing Variable Attributes

a.

1) Use the demo for your operating system shown in the lecture portion of this section for changing the name of a variable.

2) You can type in the variable label on the same window where you rename the variable.

3)

```
libname ia 'SAS-data-library';
proc contents data=ia.passngrs;
run;
```

b.

```
proc datasets library=ia;
   modify passngrs;
   format Depart date9.;
   label Depart='Departure Date';
run;
proc contents data=ia.passngrs;
run;
```

8. Reading an Excel Spreadsheet

a.

1) Select **Import Data** from the **File** pull-down menu.

2) Select *Excel 97, 2000 or 2002 Workbook* as the data source and select **Next>**.

3) Select **Browse** to locate the spreadsheet **sfosch.xls** and select **OK**.

4) Select the worksheet named **SFOEXCEL**, then select **Next>**.

5) Leave **WORK** as the library. Type **sfoexcel** in the Member field and select **Next>**.

6) Select **Browse** to locate the directory where you want to store the program and name the program **ImportSFO.sas**.

7) Select **Save** ⇨ **Finish**.

b.

```
options ls=72 nodate nonumber;
proc print data=work.sfoexcel;
run;
```

c.

```
proc contents data=work.sfoexcel;
run;
```

✎   Alternate solution using the Excel LIBNAME engine:

```
libname sfoxls 'sfosch.xls';
options ls=72 nodate nonumber;
proc print data=sfoxls.sfoexcel;
run;
proc contents data=sfoxls.sfoexcel;
run;
```

9. Reading a Comma-delimited File

a.

```
PROC IMPORT OUT= WORK.sfocsv
            DATAFILE= "sfosch.csv"
            DBMS=csv REPLACE;
RUN;
```

b.

```
options ls=72 nodate nonumber;
proc print data=work.sfocsv;
run;
```

Chapter 7   DATA Step Programming

7.1 Reading SAS Data Sets and Creating Variables

Objectives

- Create a SAS data set using another SAS data set as input.
- Create SAS variables.
- Use operators and SAS functions to manipulate data values.
- Control which variables are included in a SAS data set.

3

Reading a SAS Data Set

Create a temporary SAS data set named **onboard** from the permanent SAS data named **ia.dfwlax** and create a variable that represents the total passengers on board.

Sum **FirstClass** and **Economy** values to compute **Total**.

SAS date values

ia.dfwlax

New Variable

Flight	Date	Dest	FirstClass	Economy	Total
439	14955	LAX	20	137	157
921	14955	DFW	20	131	151
114	14956	LAX	15	170	185

4

Reading a SAS Data Set

To create a SAS data set using a SAS data set as input, you must use a

- DATA statement to start a DATA step and name the SAS data set being created (output data set: **onboard)**
- SET statement to identify the SAS data set being read (input data set: **ia.dfwlax**).

To create a variable, you must use an

- assignment statement to add the values of the variables **FirstClass** and **Economy** and assign the sum to the variable **Total.**

5

You **cannot** use INFILE and INPUT statements to read SAS data sets. They can only be used to read raw data files.

You **cannot** use a SET statement to read raw data files. It can only be used to read SAS data sets.

Reading a SAS Data Set

General form of a DATA step:

```
DATA output-SAS-data-set;
    SET input-SAS-data-set;
    additional SAS statements
RUN;
```

By default, the SET statement reads all of the

- observations from the input SAS data set
- variables from the input SAS data set.

6

Assignment Statements

An assignment statement
- evaluates an expression
- assigns the resulting value to a variable.

General form of an assignment statement:

> *variable=expression;*

7

SAS Expressions

An *expression* contains operands and operators that form a set of instructions that produce a value.

Operands are	Operators are
• variable names • constants.	• symbols that request arithmetic calculations • SAS functions.

8

Using Operators

Selected operators for basic arithmetic calculations in an assignment statement:

Operator	Action	Example	Priority
+	Addition	Sum=x+y;	III
-	Subtraction	Diff=x-y;	III
*	Multiplication	Mult=x*y;	II
/	Division	Divide=x/y;	II
**	Exponentiation	Raise=x**y;	I
-	Negative prefix	Negative=-x;	I

9

Rules for Operators

- Operations of priority I are performed before operations of priority II, and so on.
- Consecutive operations with the same priority are performed
    - from right to left within priority I
    - from left to right within priority II and III.
- Parentheses can be used to control the order of operations.

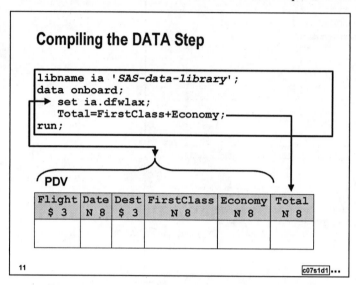

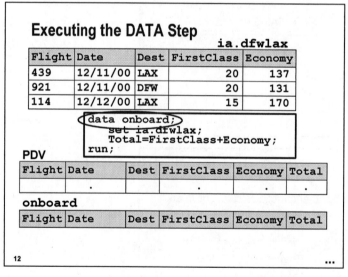

Executing the DATA Step

ia.dfwlax

Flight	Date	Dest	FirstClass	Economy
439	12/11/00	LAX	20	137
921	12/11/00	DFW	20	131
114	12/12/00	LAX	15	170

```
data onboard;
   set ia.dfwlax;
      Total=FirstClass+Economy;
run;
```

PDV

Flight	Date	Dest	FirstClass	Economy	Total
439	12/11/00	LAX	20	137	.

onboard

Flight	Date	Dest	FirstClass	Economy	Total

13   ...

Executing the DATA Step

ia.dfwlax

Flight	Date	Dest	FirstClass	Economy
439	12/11/00	LAX	20	137
921	12/11/00	DFW	20	131
114	12/12/00	LAX	15	170

```
data onboard;
   set ia.dfwlax;
      Total=FirstClass+Economy;
run;
```

PDV

Flight	Date	Dest	FirstClass	Economy	Total
439	12/11/00	LAX	20	137	157

onboard

Flight	Date	Dest	FirstClass	Economy	Total

14   ...

Executing the DATA Step

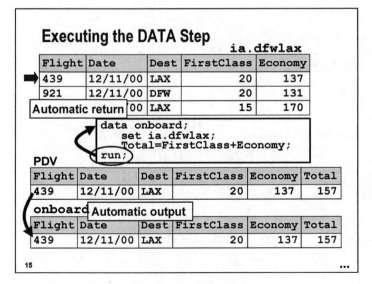

ia.dfwlax

Flight	Date	Dest	FirstClass	Economy
439	12/11/00	LAX	20	137
921	12/11/00	DFW	20	131
Automatic return 00	LAX		15	170

```
data onboard;
   set ia.dfwlax;
      Total=FirstClass+Economy;
run;
```

PDV

Flight	Date	Dest	FirstClass	Economy	Total
439	12/11/00	LAX	20	137	157

onboard Automatic output

Flight	Date	Dest	FirstClass	Economy	Total
439	12/11/00	LAX	20	137	157

15   ...

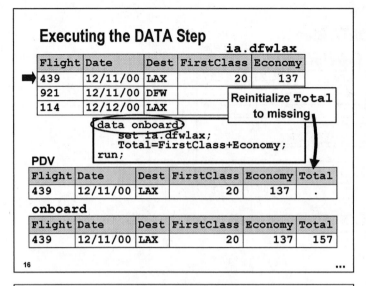

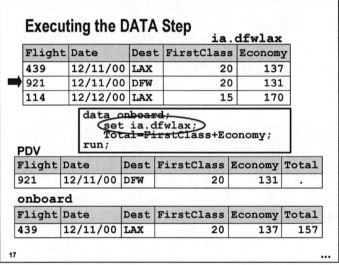

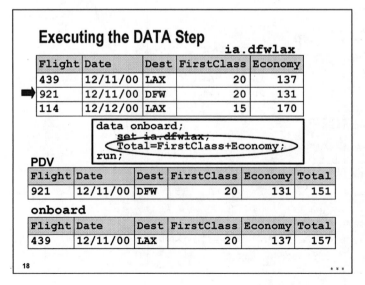

Executing the DATA Step

ia.dfwlax

Flight	Date	Dest	FirstClass	Economy
439	12/11/00	LAX	20	137
→ 921	12/11/00	DFW	20	131
Automatic return 00		LAX	15	170

```
data onboard;
   set ia.dfwlax;
      Total=FirstClass+Economy;
   run;
```

PDV

Flight	Date	Dest	FirstClass	Economy	Total
921	12/11/00	DFW	20	131	151

onboard Automatic output

Flight	Date	Dest	FirstClass	Economy	Total
439	12/11/00	LAX	20	137	157
921	12/11/00	DFW	20	131	151

19

...

Executing the DATA Step

ia.dfwlax

Flight	Date	Dest	FirstClass	Economy
439	12/11/00	LAX	20	137
921	12/11/00	DFW	20	131
114	12/12/00	LAX	15	170

```
data onboard;
   set ia.dfwlax;
      Total=FirstClass+Economy;
run;
```

PDV

Flight	Date	Dest	FirstClass	Economy	Total
114	12/12/00	LAX	15	170	185

onboard

Flight	Date	Dest	FirstClass	Economy	Total
439	12/11/00	LAX	20	137	157
921	12/11/00	DFW	20	131	151
114	12/12/00	LAX	15	170	185

20

Assignment Statements

```
proc print data=onboard;
   format Date date9.;
run;
```

```
                        The SAS System

                                     First
 Obs    Flight       Date     Dest   Class    Economy    Total

   1      439     11DEC2000   LAX      20       137       157
   2      921     11DEC2000   DFW      20       131       151
   3      114     12DEC2000   LAX      15       170       185
   4      982     12DEC2000   dfw       5        85        90
   5      439     13DEC2000   LAX      14       196       210
   6      982     13DEC2000   DFW      15       116       131
   7      431     14DEC2000   LaX      17       166       183
   8      982     14DEC2000   DFW       7        88        95
   9      114     15DEC2000   LAX       .       187         .
  10      982     15DEC2000   DFW      14        31        45
```

Why is **Total** missing in observation 9?

21

c07s1d1

Using SAS Functions

A SAS function is a routine that returns a value that is determined from specified arguments.

General form of a SAS function:

> *function-name(argument1,argument2, . . .)*

Example

```
Total=sum(FirstClass,Economy);
```

22

Using SAS Functions

SAS functions

- perform arithmetic operations
- compute sample statistics (for example: sum, mean, and standard deviation)
- manipulate SAS dates and process character values
- perform many other tasks.

Sample statistics functions ignore missing values.

23

Using the SUM Function

```
data onboard;
   set ia.dfwlax;
   Total=sum(FirstClass,Economy);
run;
```

24   c07s1d2

Using the SUM Function

```
proc print data=onboard;
   format Date date9.;
run;
```

```
                        The SAS System

                                    First
    Obs    Flight      Date    Dest  Class   Economy   Total

     1      439     11DEC2000   LAX    20       137      157
     2      921     11DEC2000   DFW    20       131      151
     3      114     12DEC2000   LAX    15       170      185
     4      982     12DEC2000   dfw     5        85       90
     5      439     13DEC2000   LAX    14       196      210
     6      982     13DEC2000   DFW    15       116      131
     7      431     14DEC2000   LaX    17       166      183
     8      982     14DEC2000   DFW     7        88       95
     9      114     15DEC2000   LAX     .       187      187
    10      982     15DEC2000   DFW    14        31       45
```

25   c07s1d2

Using Date Functions

You can use SAS date functions to

- create SAS date values
- extract information from SAS date values.

26

Date Functions: Create SAS Dates

TODAY()	obtains the date value from the system clock.
MDY(*month*,*day*,*year*)	uses numeric *month*, *day*, and *year* values to return the corresponding SAS date value.

27

Date Functions: Extracting Information

YEAR(*SAS-date*)	extracts the year from a SAS date and returns a four-digit value for year.
QTR(*SAS-date*)	extracts the quarter from a SAS date and returns a number from 1 to 4.
MONTH(*SAS-date*)	extracts the month from a SAS date and returns a number from 1 to 12.
WEEKDAY(*SAS-date*)	extracts the day of the week from a SAS date and returns a number from 1 to 7, where 1 represents Sunday, and so on.

28

Using the WEEKDAY Function

Add an assignment statement to the DATA step to create a variable that shows the day of the week that the flight occurred.

```
data onboard;
   set ia.dfwlax;
   Total=sum(FirstClass,Economy);
   DayOfWeek=weekday(Date);
run;
```

Print the data set, but do not display the variables **FirstClass** and **Economy**.

29   c07s1d3

Using the WEEKDAY Function

```
proc print data=onboard;
   var Flight Dest Total DayOfWeek Date;
   format Date weekdate.;
run;
```

```
                        The SAS System

                                 Day
                                  Of
    Obs  Flight  Dest  Total     Week              Date

     1    439    LAX    157       2      Monday, December 11, 2000
     2    921    DFW    151       2      Monday, December 11, 2000
     3    114    LAX    185       3      Tuesday, December 12, 2000
     4    982    dfw     90       3      Tuesday, December 12, 2000
     5    439    LAX    210       4      Wednesday, December 13, 2000
     6    982    DFW    131       4      Wednesday, December 13, 2000
     7    431    LaX    183       5      Thursday, December 14, 2000
     8    982    DFW     95       5      Thursday, December 14, 2000
     9    114    LAX    187       6      Friday, December 15, 2000
    10    982    DFW     45       6      Friday, December 15, 2000
```

What if you do not want the variables **FirstClass** and
30 **Economy** in the data set?   c07s1d3

Selecting Variables

You can use a DROP or KEEP statement in a DATA
step to control what variables are **written to** the new SAS
data set.

General form of DROP and KEEP statements:

> **DROP** *variables;*
>
> **KEEP** *variables;*

31

Selecting Variables

Do not store the variables **FirstClass** and **Economy**
in the data set.

Equivalent

```
data onboard;
   set ia.dfwlax;
   drop FirstClass Economy;
   Total=FirstClass+Economy;
run;
```

```
   keep Flight Date Dest Total;
```

PDV

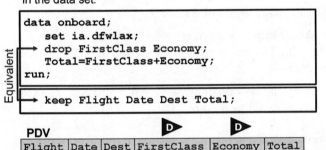

Flight	Date	Dest	FirstClass	Economy	Total
	.		.	.	.

32   c07s1d4

Selecting Variables

```
proc print data=onboard;
   format Date date9.;
run;
```

The SAS System

Obs	Flight	Date	Dest	Total
1	439	11DEC2000	LAX	157
2	921	11DEC2000	DFW	151
3	114	12DEC2000	LAX	185
4	982	12DEC2000	dfw	90
5	439	13DEC2000	LAX	210
6	982	13DEC2000	DFW	131
7	431	14DEC2000	LaX	183
8	982	14DEC2000	DFW	95
9	114	15DEC2000	LAX	.
10	982	15DEC2000	DFW	45

33   c07s1d4

 **Exercises**

For these exercises, use SAS data sets stored in a permanent SAS data library.

> Fill in the blank with the location of your SAS data library. **If you have started a new SAS session since the previous lab**, submit the LIBNAME statement to assign the libref **ia** to the SAS data library.
>
> `libname ia '`_____`' ;`

1. **Reading SAS Data Sets and Creating Variables**

   a. Use the **ia.fltattnd** data set to create a temporary SAS data set named **bonus**.

      - Create a variable named **BonusAmt** that contains an annual bonus amount for each employee calculated as 8% of **Salary**.

      - Create a variable named **AnnivMo** that contains the employment month for each employee. Hint: Determine the month portion of the employee's date of hire (**HireDate**).

      - The **bonus** data set should contain only the variables **EmpID**, **Salary**, **BonusAmt**, **HireDate**, and **AnnivMo**.

   b. Use the PRINT procedure to display the data portion of the **bonus** data set. Display the values of **Salary** and **BonusAmt** with dollar signs, commas, and no decimal places.

      SAS Output

Obs	HireDate	EmpID	Salary	BonusAmt	Anniv Mo
1	23MAY1982	E01483	$30,000	$2,400	5
2	19MAY1986	E01384	$38,000	$3,040	5
3	02JUN1983	E00223	$18,000	$1,440	6
4	09OCT1981	E00632	$40,000	$3,200	10
5	22NOV1991	E03884	$38,000	$3,040	11
6	02AUG1984	E00034	$28,000	$2,240	8
7	14JAN1980	E03591	$43,000	$3,440	1
8	18FEB1980	E04064	$37,000	$2,960	2
9	06DEC1984	E01996	$20,000	$1,600	12
10	12MAY1992	E04356	$34,000	$2,720	5
11	25SEP1980	E01447	$35,000	$2,800	9
12	02JAN1981	E02679	$31,000	$2,480	1
13	09JAN1981	E02606	$26,000	$2,080	1
14	10DEC1987	E03323	$22,000	$1,760	12

2. Reading SAS Data Sets and Creating Variables (Optional)

    a. Write a DATA step to read a SAS data set and create a new variable.

- Use the **ia.weekrev** SAS data set to create a temporary SAS data set named **temprev**.

- Create a variable named **TotalRev** by adding **CargoRev** and **PasRev**.

- Add a statement, which drops **CargoRev** and **PasRev** from the **temprev** data set.

    b. Write a PROC PRINT step to view the **temprev** data set.

- Suppress the observation column.

- Display the values of **TotalRev** with dollar signs, commas, and no decimal places.

- Add a grand total for **TotalRev**.

- Display only the variables **FlightID**, **Origin**, **Date**, and **TotalRev**.

Partial SAS Output

```
                    Revenue Data for
                  Flights to San Francisco

       Flight
         ID      Origin       Date        TotalRev

       IA02402    DFW      01DEC2000      $13,552
       IA02403    DFW      01DEC2000      $13,647
       IA02400    JFK      01DEC2000      $13,710
       IA02401    JFK      01DEC2000      $13,632
       IA02406    JFK      01DEC2000      $12,941
       IA02402    DFW      02DEC2000      $13,715
       IA02403    DFW      02DEC2000      $13,359
       IA02400    JFK      02DEC2000      $13,607
                    .
                    .
                    .
       IA02405    YYZ      05DEC2000      $13,389
       IA02402    DFW      06DEC2000      $13,547
       IA02403    DFW      06DEC2000      $13,439
       IA02400    JFK      06DEC2000      $13,429
       IA02401    JFK      06DEC2000      $13,625
       IA02400    JFK      07DEC2000      $13,710
       IA02401    JFK      07DEC2000      $13,394
       IA02404    YYZ      07DEC2000      $13,364
       IA02405    YYZ      07DEC2000      $13,509
                                       ============
                                         $462,544
```

7.2   Conditional Processing

Objectives

- Execute statements conditionally using IF-THEN logic.
- Control the length of character variables explicitly with the LENGTH statement.
- Select rows to include in a SAS data set.
- Use SAS date constants.

36

Conditional Execution

International Airlines wants to compute revenue for Los Angeles and Dallas flights based on the prices in the table below.

DESTINATION	CLASS	AIRFARE
LAX	First	2000
	Economy	1200
DFW	First	1500
	Economy	900

37

Conditional Execution

General form of IF-THEN and ELSE statements:

```
IF expression THEN statement;
ELSE statement;
```

Expression contains operands and operators that form a set of instructions that produce a value.

Operands are	Operators are

▪ variable names
▪ constants.
	▪ symbols that request
	   – a comparison
	   – a logical operation
	   – an arithmetic calculation
	▪ SAS functions.

Only one executable statement is allowed on an IF-THEN or ELSE statement.

38

Conditional Execution

Compute revenue figures based on flight destination.

DESTINATION	CLASS	AIRFARE
LAX	First	2000
	Economy	1200
DFW	First	1500
	Economy	900

```
data flightrev;
   set ia.dfwlax;
   Total=sum(FirstClass,Economy);
   if Dest='LAX' then
      Revenue=sum(2000*FirstClass,1200*Economy);
   else if Dest='DFW' then
      Revenue=sum(1500*FirstClass,900*Economy);
run;
```

39   c07s2d1

Conditional Execution

```
proc print data=flightrev;
   format Date date9.;
run;
```

```
                        The SAS System

                              First
Obs   Flight      Date   Dest  Class  Economy  Total  Revenue

  1    439    11DEC2000  LAX    20     137     157    204400
  2    921    11DEC2000  DFW    20     131     151    147900
  3    114    12DEC2000  LAX    15     170     185    234000
  4    982    12DEC2000  dfw     5      85      90        .
  5    439    13DEC2000  LAX    14     196     210    263200
  6    982    13DEC2000  DFW    15     116     131    126900
  7    431    14DEC2000  LaX    17     166     183        .
  8    982    14DEC2000  DFW     7      88      95     89700
  9    114    15DEC2000  LAX     .     187     187    224400
 10    982    15DEC2000  DFW    14      31      45     48900
```

Why are two **Revenue** values missing?

46   c07s2d1

The UPCASE Function

You can use the UPCASE function to convert letters from lowercase to uppercase.

General form of the UPCASE function:

> **UPCASE** *(argument)*

47

Conditional Execution

Use the UPCASE function to convert the **Dest** values to uppercase for the comparison.

```
data flightrev;
   set ia.dfwlax;
   Total=sum(FirstClass,Economy);
   if upcase(Dest)='LAX' then
      Revenue=sum(2000*FirstClass,1200*Economy);
   else if upcase(Dest)='DFW' then
      Revenue=sum(1500*FirstClass,900*Economy);
run;
```

48   c07s2d2

Conditional Execution

```
proc print data=flightrev;
   format Date date9.;
run;
```

```
                        The SAS System

                                First
Obs  Flight      Date  Dest     Class  Economy  Total  Revenue

  1    439  11DEC2000  LAX        20      137     157   204400
  2    921  11DEC2000  DFW        20      131     151   147900
  3    114  12DEC2000  LAX        15      170     185   234000
  4    982  12DEC2000  dfw         5       85      90    84000
  5    439  13DEC2000  LAX        14      196     210   263200
  6    982  13DEC2000  DFW        15      116     131   126900
  7    431  14DEC2000  LaX        17      166     183   233200
  8    982  14DEC2000  DFW         7       88      95    89700
  9    114  15DEC2000  LAX         .      187     187   224400
 10    982  15DEC2000  DFW        14       31      45    48900
```

52   c07s2d2

(handwritten margin note: "if must have do, end have")

Conditional Execution

You can use the DO and END statements to execute a
group of statements based on a condition.

General form of the DO and END statements:

```
IF expression THEN DO;
    executable statements
END;
ELSE DO;
    executable statements
END;
```

53

Conditional Execution

Use DO and END statements to execute a group of
statements based on a condition.

```
data flightrev;
   set ia.dfwlax;
   Total=sum(FirstClass,Economy);
   if upcase(Dest)='DFW' then do;
      Revenue=sum(1500*FirstClass,900*Economy);
      City='Dallas';
   end;
   else if upcase(Dest)='LAX' then do;
      Revenue=sum(2000*FirstClass,1200*Economy);
      City='Los Angeles';
   end;
run;
```

54   c07s2d3

Conditional Execution

```
proc print data=flightrev;
   var Dest City Flight Date Revenue;
   format Date date9.;
run;
```

```
                      The SAS System

    Obs   Dest    City     Flight       Date      Revenue

     1    LAX     Los An    439      11DEC2000     204400
     2    DFW     Dallas    921      11DEC2000     147900
     3    LAX     Los An    114      12DEC2000     234000
     4    dfw     Dallas    982      12DEC2000      84000
     5    LAX     Los An    439      13DEC2000     263200
     6    DFW     Dallas    982      13DEC2000     126900
     7    LaX     Los An    431      14DEC2000     233200
     8    DFW     Dallas    982      14DEC2000      89700
     9    LAX     Los An    114      15DEC2000     224400
    10    DFW     Dallas    982      15DEC2000      48900
```

Why are City values truncated?

55   c07s2d3

(handwritten left margin) when creating a variable conditionally want to use length statement

(handwritten right margin) DON'T USE ON NUMERIC VARIABLES. IF DO SET TO $8.

Variable Lengths

At compile time, the length of a variable is determined the first time the variable is encountered.

```
data flightrev;
   set ia.dfwlax;
   Total=sum(FirstClass,Economy);
   if upcase(Dest)='DFW' then do;
      Revenue=sum(1500*FirstClass,900*Economy);
      City='Dallas';
   end;
   else if upcase(Dest)='LAX' then do;
      Revenue=sum(2000*FirstClass,1200*Economy);
      City='Los Angeles';
   end;
run;
```

6 characters between the quotes: Length=6

56

(handwritten left margin) allows you to control order in PDV

The LENGTH Statement

You can use the LENGTH statement to define the length of a variable explicitly.

General form of the LENGTH statement:

LENGTH *variable(s)* $ *length*;

Example:

```
length City $ 11;
```

57

The LENGTH Statement

```
data flightrev;
   set ia.dfwlax;
   length City $ 11;
   Total=sum(FirstClass,Economy);
   if upcase(Dest)='DFW' then do;
      Revenue=sum(1500*FirstClass,900*Economy);
      City='Dallas';
   end;
   else if upcase(Dest)='LAX' then do;
      Revenue=sum(2000*FirstClass,1200*Economy);
      City='Los Angeles';
   end;
run;
```

58

c07s2d4

The LENGTH Statement

```
proc print data=flightrev;
    var Dest City Flight Date Revenue;
    format Date date9.;
run;
```

```
                         The SAS System

  Obs    Dest    City          Flight      Date      Revenue

   1     LAX     Los Angeles     439     11DEC2000    204400
   2     DFW     Dallas          921     11DEC2000    147900
   3     LAX     Los Angeles     114     12DEC2000    234000
   4     dfw     Dallas          982     12DEC2000     84000
   5     LAX     Los Angeles     439     13DEC2000    263200
   6     DFW     Dallas          982     13DEC2000    126900
   7     LaX     Los Angeles     431     14DEC2000    233200
   8     DFW     Dallas          982     14DEC2000     89700
   9     LAX     Los Angeles     114     15DEC2000    224400
  10     DFW     Dallas          982     15DEC2000     48900
```

59   c07s2d4

Subsetting Rows

In a DATA step, you can subset the rows (observations) in a SAS data set with a

- WHERE statement
- DELETE statement
- subsetting IF statement.

The WHERE statement in a DATA step is the same as the WHERE statement you saw in a PROC step.

60

Deleting Rows

You can use a DELETE statement to control which rows are written to the SAS data set.

General form of the DELETE statement:

> IF *expression* **THEN DELETE**;

The *expression* can be any SAS expression.

61

Deleting Rows

Delete rows that have a **Total** value that is less than or equal to 175.

```
data over175;
   set ia.dfwlax;
   length City $ 11;
   Total=sum(FirstClass,Economy);
   if Total le 175 then delete;
   if upcase(Dest)='DFW' then do;
      Revenue=sum(1500*FirstClass,900*Economy);
      City='Dallas';
   end;
   else if upcase(Dest)='LAX' then do;
      Revenue=sum(2000*FirstClass,1200*Economy);
      City='Los Angeles';
   end;
run;
```

62   c07s2d5

Deleting Rows

```
proc print data=over175;
   var Dest City Flight Date Total Revenue;
   format Date date9.;
run;
```

The SAS System

Obs	Dest	City	Flight	Date	Total	Revenue
1	LAX	Los Angeles	114	12DEC2000	185	234000
2	LAX	Los Angeles	439	13DEC2000	210	263200
3	LaX	Los Angeles	431	14DEC2000	183	233200
4	LAX	Los Angeles	114	15DEC2000	187	224400

63   c07s2d5

Selecting Rows

You can use a subsetting IF statement to control which rows are written to the SAS data set.

General form of the subsetting IF statement:

> **IF** *expression*;

The *expression* can be any SAS expression.

The subsetting IF statement is valid only in a DATA step.

If w/o then is subsetting

64

Process Flow of a Subsetting IF

Subsetting IF:

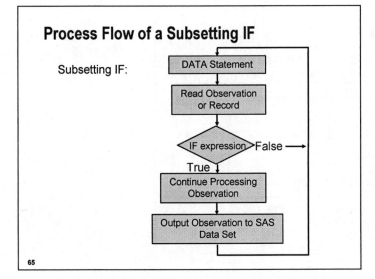

65

Selecting Rows

Select rows that have a **Total** value that is greater than 175.

```
data over175;
   set ia.dfwlax;
   length City $ 11;
   Total=sum(FirstClass,Economy);
   if Total gt 175;
   if upcase(Dest)='DFW' then do;
      Revenue=sum(1500*FirstClass,900*Economy);
      City='Dallas';
   end;
   else if upcase(Dest)='LAX' then do;
      Revenue=sum(2000*FirstClass,1200*Economy);
      City='Los Angeles';
   end;
run;
```

Subset example (handwritten)

67   c07s2d6

Selecting Rows

```
proc print data=over175;
   var Dest City Flight Date Total Revenue;
   format Date date9.;
run;
```

```
                        The SAS System

Obs   Dest    City        Flight      Date      Total   Revenue

 1    LAX     Los Angeles   114    12DEC2000     185     234000
 2    LAX     Los Angeles   439    13DEC2000     210     263200
 3    LaX     Los Angeles   431    14DEC2000     183     233200
 4    LAX     Los Angeles   114    15DEC2000     187     224400
```

68   c07s2d6

Selecting Rows

The variable **Date** in the **ia.dfwlax** data set contains SAS date values (numeric values).

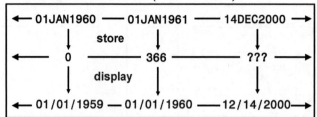

What if you only wanted flights that were before a specific date, such as **14DEC2000**?

69

Using SAS Date Constants

The constant **'ddMMMyyyy'd** (example: '14dec2000'd) creates a SAS date value from the date enclosed in quotes.

dd	is a one- or two-digit value for the day.
MMM	is a three-letter abbreviation for the month (JAN, FEB, MAR, and so on).
yyyy	is a two- or four-digit value for the year.
d	is required to convert the quoted string to a SAS date.

70

allows you to put date in normal format Converts to SAS date form.

have to use this date format

Using SAS Date Constants

```
data over175;
   set ia.dfwlax;
   length City $ 11;
   Total=sum(FirstClass,Economy);
   if Total gt 175 and Date lt '14dec2000'd;
   if upcase(Dest)='DFW' then do;
      Revenue=sum(1500*FirstClass,900*Economy);
      City='Dallas';
   end;
   else if upcase(Dest)='LAX' then do;
      Revenue=sum(2000*FirstClass,1200*Economy);
      City='Los Angeles';
   end;
run;
```

71   c07s2d7

Using SAS Date Constants

```
proc print data=over175;
   var Dest City Flight Date Total Revenue;
   format Date date9.;
run;
```

```
                         The SAS System

Obs   Dest      City       Flight       Date    Total    Revenue

 1    LAX    Los Angeles     114     12DEC2000    185     234000
 2    LAX    Los Angeles     439     13DEC2000    210     263200
```

72   c07s2d7

Subsetting Data

What if the data were in a raw data file instead of a
SAS data set?

```
data over175;
   infile 'raw-data-file';
   input @1 Flight $3. @4 Date mmddyy8.
         @12 Dest $3. @15 FirstClass 3.
         @18 Economy 3.;
   length City $ 11;
   Total=sum(FirstClass,Economy);
   if Total gt 175 and Date lt '14dec2000'd;
   if upcase(Dest)='DFW' then do;
      Revenue=sum(1500*FirstClass,900*Economy);
      City='Dallas';
   end;
   else if upcase(Dest)='LAX' then do;
      Revenue=sum(2000*FirstClass,1200*Economy);
      City='Los Angeles';
   end;
run;
```

73   c07s2d8

✎   You can use the $UPCASE informat in the INPUT statement to translate the
    Dest values to uppercase as they are read from the raw data file.

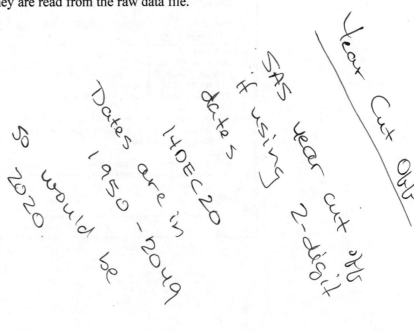

Year Cut Off

SAS year cut off
if using 2-digit
dates

14DEC20

Dates are in
1950 - 2049

So would be
2020.

Subsetting Data

```
proc print data=over175;
   var Dest City Flight Date Total Revenue;
   format Date date9.;
run;
```

```
                         The SAS System

Obs   Dest     City        Flight       Date    Total   Revenue

 1    LAX    Los Angeles     114     12DEC2000    185    234000
 2    LAX    Los Angeles     439     13DEC2000    210    263200
```

74   c07s2d8

WHERE or Subsetting IF?

Step and Usage	WHERE	IF
PROC step	Yes	No
DATA step (source of variable)		
INPUT statement	No	Yes
Assignment statement	No	Yes
SET statement (single data set)	Yes	Yes
SET/MERGE (multiple data sets)		
Variable in ALL data sets	Yes	Yes
Variable not in ALL data sets	No	Yes

75

Can't use if in proc step

WHERE or Subsetting IF?

Use a WHERE statement and a subsetting IF statement in the same step.

```
data over175;
   set ia.dfwlax;
   where Date lt '14dec2000'd;
   length City $ 11;
   Total=sum(FirstClass,Economy);
   if Total gt 175;
   if upcase(Dest)='DFW' then do;
      Revenue=sum(1500*FirstClass,900*Economy);
      City='Dallas';
   end;
   else if upcase(Dest)='LAX' then do;
      Revenue=sum(2000*FirstClass,1200*Economy);
      City='Los Angeles';
   end;
run;
```

76   c07s2d9

WHERE or Subsetting IF?

```
proc print data=over175;
    var Dest City Flight Date Total Revenue;
    format Date date9.;
run;
```

		The SAS System				
Obs	Dest	City	Flight	Date	Total	Revenue
1	LAX	Los Angeles	114	12DEC2000	185	234000
2	LAX	Los Angeles	439	13DEC2000	210	263200

77

c07s2d9

 **Exercises**

For these exercises, use SAS data sets stored in a permanent SAS data library.

Fill in the blank with the location of your SAS data library. **If you have started a new SAS session since the previous lab**, submit the LIBNAME statement to assign the libref **ia** to the SAS data library.

```
libname ia '_____';
```

3. **Creating Variables Using Conditional Execution**

    a. Use the **ia.fltattnd** data set to create a temporary SAS data set named **raises**.

        - Create a variable named **Increase** that contains an annual salary increase amount for each employee. Calculate the **Increase** values as

            – 10% of **Salary** when **JobCode='FLTAT1'**

            – 8% of **Salary** when **JobCode='FLTAT2'**

            – 6% of **Salary** when **JobCode='FLTAT3'**.

        - Create a variable named **NewSal** that contains the new annual salary for each employee by adding the raise to the original salary.

        - The **raises** data set should contain only the variables **EmpID**, **Salary**, **Increase**, and **NewSal**.

b. Use the PRINT procedure to display the data portion of the **raises** data set. Display the values of **Salary**, **Increase**, and **NewSal** with dollar signs, commas, and no decimal places.

SAS Output

```
                        The SAS System

       Obs     EmpID      Salary    Increase      NewSal

        1      E01483    $30,000     $2,400      $32,400
        2      E01384    $38,000     $2,280      $40,280
        3      E00223    $18,000     $1,080      $19,080
        4      E00632    $40,000     $2,400      $42,400
        5      E03884    $38,000     $3,040      $41,040
        6      E00034    $28,000     $1,680      $29,680
        7      E03591    $43,000     $4,300      $47,300
        8      E04064    $37,000     $2,220      $39,220
        9      E01996    $20,000     $1,200      $21,200
       10      E04356    $34,000     $2,720      $36,720
       11      E01447    $35,000     $3,500      $38,500
       12      E02679    $31,000     $3,100      $34,100
       13      E02606    $26,000     $2,600      $28,600
       14      E03323    $22,000     $1,760      $23,760
```

4. Selecting Rows

a. Alter the DATA step you wrote in the previous exercise by creating another variable named **BonusAmt** that contains an annual bonus for each employee based on the employee's current salary (before the increase). Calculate the **BonusAmt** as

- 15% of **Salary** when **JobCode='FLTAT1'**
- 12% of **Salary** when **JobCode='FLTAT2'**
- 10% of **Salary** when **JobCode='FLTAT3'**.

Hint: Remember that there is a way to execute more than one statement based on the result of an IF expression.

Include only observations (rows) that have a **BonusAmt** value that exceeds 2000 dollars. The **raises** data set should contain only the variables **EmpID**, **Salary**, **Increase**, **NewSal**, and **BonusAmt**.

b. Use the PRINT procedure to display the data portion of the **raises** data set. Display the values of **Salary**, **Increase**, **NewSal**, and **BonusAmt** with dollar signs, commas, and no decimal places.

SAS Output

			The SAS System		
Obs	EmpID	Salary	Increase	BonusAmt	NewSal
1	E01483	$30,000	$2,400	$3,600	$32,400
2	E01384	$38,000	$2,280	$3,800	$40,280
3	E00632	$40,000	$2,400	$4,000	$42,400
4	E03884	$38,000	$3,040	$4,560	$41,040
5	E00034	$28,000	$1,680	$2,800	$29,680
6	E03591	$43,000	$4,300	$6,450	$47,300
7	E04064	$37,000	$2,220	$3,700	$39,220
8	E04356	$34,000	$2,720	$4,080	$36,720
9	E01447	$35,000	$3,500	$5,250	$38,500
10	E02679	$31,000	$3,100	$4,650	$34,100
11	E02606	$26,000	$2,600	$3,900	$28,600
12	E03323	$22,000	$1,760	$2,640	$23,760

5. Creating Variables Using Conditional Execution

a. Alter the DATA step you wrote in the previous exercise **3.a** by creating a character variable named **JobTitle** that contains the value

- **Flight Attendant I**, when **JobCode='FLTAT1'**
- **Flight Attendant II**, when **JobCode='FLTAT2'**
- **Senior Flight Attendant** when **JobCode='FLTAT3'**.

Remember to include the new variable **JobTitle** in your data set.

b. Use the PRINT procedure to display the data portion of the **raises** data set. Display the values of **Salary**, **Increase**, **NewSal**, and **BonusAmt** with dollar signs, commas, and no decimal places. Verify that the values of the variable **JobTitle** are not truncated.

SAS Output

```
                           The SAS System

 Obs EmpID    Salary        JobTitle          Increase BonusAmt   NewSal

   1 E01483  $30,000 Flight Attendant II        $2,400   $3,600  $32,400
   2 E01384  $38,000 Senior Flight Attendant    $2,280   $3,800  $40,280
   3 E00632  $40,000 Senior Flight Attendant    $2,400   $4,000  $42,400
   4 E03884  $38,000 Flight Attendant II        $3,040   $4,560  $41,040
   5 E00034  $28,000 Senior Flight Attendant    $1,680   $2,800  $29,680
   6 E03591  $43,000 Flight Attendant I         $4,300   $6,450  $47,300
   7 E04064  $37,000 Senior Flight Attendant    $2,220   $3,700  $39,220
   8 E04356  $34,000 Flight Attendant II        $2,720   $4,080  $36,720
   9 E01447  $35,000 Flight Attendant I         $3,500   $5,250  $38,500
  10 E02679  $31,000 Flight Attendant I         $3,100   $4,650  $34,100
  11 E02606  $26,000 Flight Attendant I         $2,600   $3,900  $28,600
  12 E03323  $22,000 Flight Attendant II        $1,760   $2,640  $23,760
```

7.3 Dropping and Keeping Variables (Self-Study)

Objectives

- Compare DROP and KEEP statements to DROP= and KEEP= data set options.

80

Selecting Variables

You can use a DROP= or KEEP= data set option in a DATA statement to control what variables are **written to** the new SAS data set.

General form of the DROP= and KEEP= data set options:

> *SAS-data-set*(**DROP=***variables*)
> or
> *SAS-data-set*(**KEEP=***variables*)

81

Selecting Variables

Do not store the variables **FirstClass** and **Economy** in the data set.

```
data onboard(drop=FirstClass Economy);
   set ia.dfwlax;
   Total=FirstClass+Economy;
run;
```

Equivalent

```
data onboard(keep=Flight Date Dest Total);
```

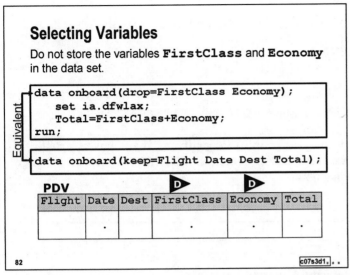

PDV

Flight	Date	Dest	FirstClass	Economy	Total
	.		.	.	.

82   c07s3d1

Selecting Variables

```
proc print data=onboard;
   format Date date9.;
run;
```

```
                    The SAS System

        Obs    Flight      Date      Dest    Total

         1      439     11DEC2000    LAX     157
         2      921     11DEC2000    DFW     151
         3      114     12DEC2000    LAX     185
         4      982     12DEC2000    dfw      90
         5      439     13DEC2000    LAX     210
         6      982     13DEC2000    DFW     131
         7      431     14DEC2000    LaX     183
         8      982     14DEC2000    DFW      95
         9      114     15DEC2000    LAX       .
        10      982     15DEC2000    DFW      45
```

83   c07s3d1

Selecting Variables

DROP= and KEEP= data set options in a DATA statement are similar to DROP and KEEP statements.

Equivalent

```
data onboard(drop=FirstClass Economy);
   set ia.dfwlax;
   Total=FirstClass+Economy;
run;
```

```
data onboard(keep=Flight Date Dest Total);
```

Equivalent Steps

Equivalent

```
data onboard;
   drop FirstClass Economy;
   set ia.dfwlax;
   Total=FirstClass+Economy;
run;
```

```
   keep Flight Date Dest Total;
```

84   c07s3d2

 **Exercises**

For these exercises, use SAS data sets stored in a permanent SAS data library.

Fill in the blank with the location of your SAS data library. **If you have started a new SAS session since the previous lab**, submit the LIBNAME statement to assign the libref **ia** to the SAS data library.

```
libname ia '_____' ;
```

6. Reading SAS Data Sets and Creating Variables

a. Use the **ia.fltattnd** data set to create a data set named **bonus**.

- Create a variable named **BonusAmt** that contains an annual bonus amount for each employee calculated as 8% of **Salary.**

- Create a variable named **AnnivMo** that contains the employment month for each employee. Hint: Determine the month portion of the employee's date of hire (**HireDate**).

- The **bonus** data set should contain only the variables **EmpID**, **Salary**, **BonusAmt**, **HireDate**, and **AnnivMo**. Use a DROP= or KEEP= data set option instead of a DROP or KEEP statement.

b. Use the PRINT procedure to display the data portion of the **bonus** data set. Display the values of **Salary** and **BonusAmt** with dollar signs, commas, and no decimal places.

SAS Output

```
                        The SAS System

                                                      Anniv
    Obs     HireDate      EmpID      Salary     BonusAmt    Mo

      1     23MAY1982     E01483     $30,000     $2,400      5
      2     19MAY1986     E01384     $38,000     $3,040      5
      3     02JUN1983     E00223     $18,000     $1,440      6
      4     09OCT1981     E00632     $40,000     $3,200     10
      5     22NOV1991     E03884     $38,000     $3,040     11
      6     02AUG1984     E00034     $28,000     $2,240      8
      7     14JAN1980     E03591     $43,000     $3,440      1
      8     18FEB1980     E04064     $37,000     $2,960      2
      9     06DEC1984     E01996     $20,000     $1,600     12
     10     12MAY1992     E04356     $34,000     $2,720      5
     11     25SEP1980     E01447     $35,000     $2,800      9
     12     02JAN1981     E02679     $31,000     $2,480      1
     13     09JAN1981     E02606     $26,000     $2,080      1
     14     10DEC1987     E03323     $22,000     $1,760     12
```

7.4 Reading Excel Spreadsheets Containing Date Fields (Self-Study)

Objectives

- Create a SAS data set from an Excel spreadsheet that contains date fields.
- Create a SAS data set from an Excel spreadsheet that contains datetime fields.

87

Business Task

The flight data for Dallas and Los Angeles are in an Excel spreadsheet. The departure date is stored as a date field in the spreadsheet.

Excel Spreadsheet

	A	B	C	D	E	F
A1			= 'Flight			
1	Flight	Date	Dest	FirstClass	Economy	
2	439	12/11/00	LAX	20	137	
3	921	12/11/00	DFW	20	131	
4	114	12/12/00	LAX	15	170	

SAS Data Set

Flight	Date	Dest	FirstClass	Economy
439	12/11/00	LAX	20	137
921	12/11/00	DFW	20	131
114	12/12/00	LAX	15	170

88

Importing Date Fields

Use the IMPORT procedure to create a SAS data set from the spreadsheet containing date fields.

```
proc import out=work.dfwlaxdates
            datafile='datefields.xls'
            dbms=excel2000 replace;
run;

proc print data=work.dfwlaxdates;
run;
```

89   c07s4d1

Importing Date Fields

PROC IMPORT automatically converts the spreadsheet date fields to SAS date values and assigns the DATE9. format.

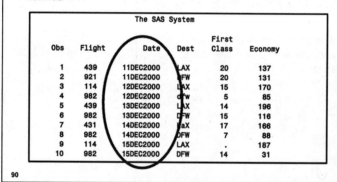

90

The Import Wizard and the Excel LIBNAME statement engine also convert spreadsheet dates to SAS date values and assign the DATE9. format.

Importing Date-Time Fields

PROC IMPORT also converts spreadsheet fields that contain date-time information into SAS date values and assigns the DATE9. format.

Excel Spreadsheet

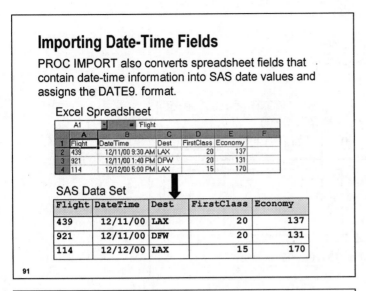

SAS Data Set

Flight	DateTime	Dest	FirstClass	Economy
439	12/11/00	LAX	20	137
921	12/11/00	DFW	20	131
114	12/12/00	LAX	15	170

91

Importing Date-Time Fields

To import datetime fields as SAS datetime values, add the USEDATE=NO statement to the PROC IMPORT step.

```
proc import out=work.dfwlaxdatetimes
            datafile='datetimefields.xls'
            dbms=excel2000 replace;
   usedate=no;
run;

proc print data=work.dfwlaxdatetimes;
run;
```

92   c07s4d2

The LIBNAME statement supports the USEDATE=NO option with the Excel SAS/ACCESS engine.

To read datetime fields as SAS datetime values using the Import Wizard, de-select **Use DATE. format for a Date/Time column** in the SAS Import: Spreadsheet Options window.

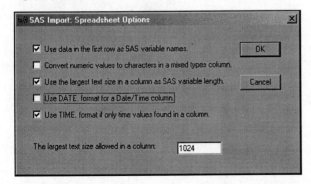

SAS Datetime Values

A *SAS datetime value* is interpreted as the number of seconds between midnight, January 1, 1960, and a specific date and time.

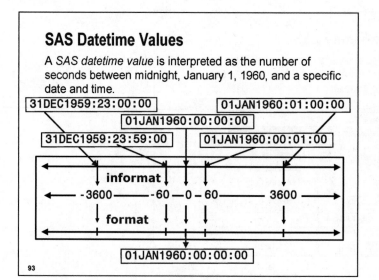

93

Importing Date-Time Fields

The DATETIME19. format is assigned to the SAS datetime values.

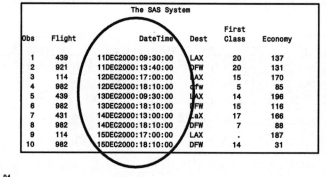

```
                        The SAS System

                                          First
Obs    Flight            DateTime   Dest   Class   Economy

  1      439    11DEC2000:09:30:00   LAX     20       137
  2      921    11DEC2000:13:40:00   DFW     20       131
  3      114    12DEC2000:17:00:00   LAX     15       170
  4      982    12DEC2000:18:10:00   dfw      5        85
  5      439    13DEC2000:09:30:00   LAX     14       196
  6      982    13DEC2000:18:10:00   DFW     15       116
  7      431    14DEC2000:13:00:00   LaX     17       166
  8      982    14DEC2000:18:10:00   DFW      7        88
  9      114    15DEC2000:17:00:00   LAX      .       187
 10      982    15DEC2000:18:10:00   DFW     14        31
```

94

Exercises

(Applicable Only to Windows Users)

7. **Reading an Excel Spreadsheet Containing Date Fields**

   a. The Excel spreadsheet **sfoschdates.xls** contains information about International Airlines flights originating in San Francisco.

      Use the Import Wizard or PROC IMPORT to create a SAS data set named **work.sfodatetime** from the Excel spreadsheet.

   b. Use PROC PRINT to display the data portion of the SAS data set **work.sfodatetime**. Do not display the date and time the SAS session started. Do not display page numbers. Set the line size to 72.

      📝 If you use the Excel LIBNAME engine, you can display the data directly from the Excel worksheet named **SFODATA** found in **sfoschdates.xls**.

Partial SAS Output (First 8 of 52 Observations)

```
                              The SAS System


      Flight
Obs   ID        RouteID   Origin   Destination   Model                Date

  1   IA11200   0000112   0000112      HND        JetCruise LF8100   01DEC2000
  2   IA01804   0000018   0000018      SEA        JetCruise SF1000   01DEC2000
  3   IA02901   0000029   0000029      HNL        JetCruise LF5200   02DEC2000
  4   IA03100   0000031   0000031      ANC        JetCruise LF8100   02DEC2000
  5   IA02901   0000029   0000029      HNL        JetCruise LF5200   03DEC2000
  6   IA03100   0000031   0000031      ANC        JetCruise MF4000   03DEC2000
  7   IA00800   0000008   0000008      RDU        JetCruise MF4000   04DEC2000
  8   IA01805   0000018   0000018      SEA        JetCruise SF1000   04DEC2000

                                              Tot
      Depart    FClass    BClass   EClass     Pass     Cargo    Cargo
Obs   Day       Pass      Pass     Pass       Cap      Wt       Rev

  1   6         19        31       171        255      61300    79077
  2   6         10         .       123        150      10300    13287
  3   7         13        24       138        207      47400    61146
  4   7         13        22       250        255      24800    31992
  5   1         14        25       132        207      48200    62178
  6   1         16         .       243        267      25600    33024
  7   2         16         .       243        267      25600    33024
  8   2         11         .       123        150      10100    13029
```

7.5 Solutions to Exercises

1. **Reading SAS Data Sets and Creating Variables**

    a.

    ```
    data bonus;
       set ia.fltattnd;
       keep EmpID Salary BonusAmt HireDate AnnivMo;
       BonusAmt=.08*Salary;
       AnnivMo=month(HireDate);
    run;
    ```

    b.

    ```
    proc print data=bonus;
       format Salary BonusAmt dollar8.0;
    run;
    ```

2. **Reading SAS Data Sets and Creating Variables (Optional)**

    a.

    ```
    data work.temprev;
       set ia.weekrev;
       TotalRev=CargoRev+PasRev;
       drop CargoRev PasRev;
    run;
    ```

    b.

    ```
    proc print data=work.temprev noobs;
       title1 'Revenue Data for';
       title2 'Flights to San Francisco';
       var FlightID Origin Date TotalRev;
       sum TotalRev;
       format TotalRev dollar12.;
    run;
    ```

3. Creating Variables Using Conditional Execution

a.

```
data raises;
   set ia.fltattnd;
   keep EmpID Salary Increase NewSal;
   if JobCode='FLTAT1' then Increase=.10*Salary;
   else if JobCode='FLTAT2' then Increase=.08*Salary;
   else if JobCode='FLTAT3' then Increase=.06*Salary;
   NewSal=sum(Salary,Increase);
run;
```

b.

```
proc print data=raises;
   format Salary Increase NewSal dollar8.0;
run;
```

4. Selecting Rows

a.

```
data raises;
   set ia.fltattnd;
   keep EmpID Salary Increase NewSal BonusAmt;
   if JobCode='FLTAT1' then do;
      Increase=.10*Salary;
      BonusAmt=.15*Salary;
   end;
   else if JobCode='FLTAT2' then do;
      Increase=.08*Salary;
      BonusAmt=.12*Salary;
   end;
   else if JobCode='FLTAT3' then do;
      Increase=.06*Salary;
      BonusAmt=.10*Salary;
   end;
   if BonusAmt gt 2000;
   NewSal=sum(Salary,Increase);
run;
```

b.

```
proc print data=raises;
   format Salary Increase NewSal BonusAmt dollar8.0;
run;
```

5. Creating Variables Using Conditional Execution

a.

```
data raises;
   set ia.fltattnd;
   keep EmpID Salary Increase NewSal BonusAmt
JobTitle;
   length JobTitle $ 23;
   if JobCode='FLTAT1' then do;
      Increase=.10*Salary;
      BonusAmt=.15*Salary;
      Jobtitle='Flight Attendant I';
   end;
   else if JobCode='FLTAT2' then do;
      Increase=.08*Salary;
      BonusAmt=.12*Salary;
      Jobtitle='Flight Attendant II';
   end;
   else if JobCode='FLTAT3' then do;
      Increase=.06*Salary;
      BonusAmt=.10*Salary;
      Jobtitle='Senior Flight Attendant';
   end;
   if BonusAmt gt 2000;
   NewSal=sum(Salary,Increase);
run;
```

b.

```
proc print data=raises;
   format Salary Increase NewSal BonusAmt dollar8.0;
run;
```

6. Reading SAS Data Sets and Creating Variables

a.

```
data bonus(keep=EmpID Salary BonusAmt HireDate
AnnivMo);
   set ia.fltattnd;
   BonusAmt=.08*Salary;
   AnnivMo=month(HireDate);
run;
```

b.

```
proc print data=bonus;
   format Salary BonusAmt dollar8.0;
run;
```

7.   Reading an Excel Spreadsheet Containing Date Fields

a.

```
proc import out=work.sfodatetime
            datafile='sfoschdates.xls'
            dbms=excel2000;
run;
```

b.

```
options ls=72 nodate nonumber;
proc print data=work.sfodatetime;
run;
```

Using the Excel LIBNAME engine:

```
libname sfoxls 'sfoschdates.xls';
options ls=72 nodate nonumber;
proc print data=sfoxls.sfodata;
run;
```

Chapter 8 Combining SAS® Data Sets

8.1 Concatenating SAS Data Sets

Objectives

- Define concatenation.
- Use the SET statement in a DATA step to concatenate two or more SAS data sets.
- Use the RENAME= data set option to change the names of variables.
- Use the SET and BY statements in a DATA step to interleave two or more SAS data sets.

3

Concatenating SAS Data Sets

Use the SET statement in a DATA step to concatenate SAS data sets.

General form of a DATA step concatenation:

```
DATA SAS-data-set ;
    SET SAS-data-set1 SAS-data-set2 . . . ;
    <other SAS statements>
RUN;
```

4

Concatenating SAS Data Sets

You can read any number of SAS data sets with a single SET statement.

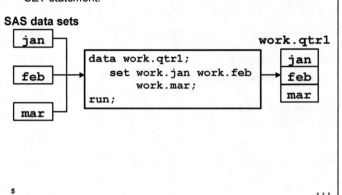

SAS data sets

```
data work.qtr1;
    set work.jan work.feb
        work.mar;
run;
```

work.qtr1

5

Business Task

Two SAS data sets, **na1** and **na2**, contain data for newly hired navigators. Concatenate the data sets into a new data set named **newhires**.

na1

Name	Gender	JobCode
TORRES	M	NA1
LANG	F	NA1
SMITH	F	NA1

na2

Name	Gender	JobCode
LISTER	M	NA2
TORRES	F	NA2

The data sets contain the same variables.

6

Concatenating SAS Data Sets: Compilation

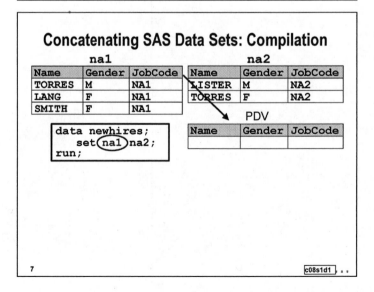

na1

Name	Gender	JobCode
TORRES	M	NA1
LANG	F	NA1
SMITH	F	NA1

na2

Name	Gender	JobCode
LISTER	M	NA2
TORRES	F	NA2

```
data newhires;
    set na1 na2;
run;
```

PDV

Name	Gender	JobCode

7   c08s1d1

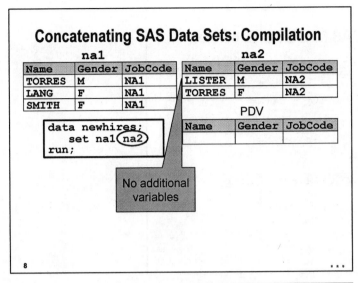

Concatenating SAS Data Sets: Compilation

na1

Name	Gender	JobCode
TORRES	M	NA1
LANG	F	NA1
SMITH	F	NA1

na2

Name	Gender	JobCode
LISTER	M	NA2
TORRES	F	NA2

PDV

Name	Gender	JobCode

```
data newhires;
   set na1 na2;
run;
```

No additional variables

8

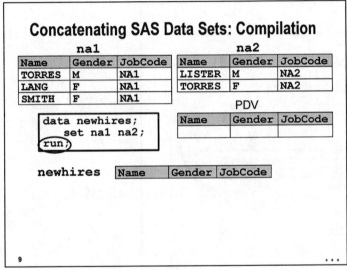

Concatenating SAS Data Sets: Compilation

na1

Name	Gender	JobCode
TORRES	M	NA1
LANG	F	NA1
SMITH	F	NA1

na2

Name	Gender	JobCode
LISTER	M	NA2
TORRES	F	NA2

PDV

Name	Gender	JobCode

```
data newhires;
   set na1 na2;
run;
```

newhires | Name | Gender | JobCode |

9

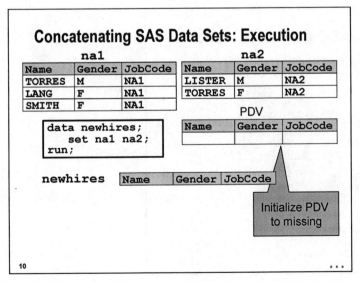

Concatenating SAS Data Sets: Execution

na1

Name	Gender	JobCode
TORRES	M	NA1
LANG	F	NA1
SMITH	F	NA1

na2

Name	Gender	JobCode
LISTER	M	NA2
TORRES	F	NA2

PDV

Name	Gender	JobCode

```
data newhires;
   set na1 na2;
run;
```

newhires | Name | Gender | JobCode |

Initialize PDV to missing

10

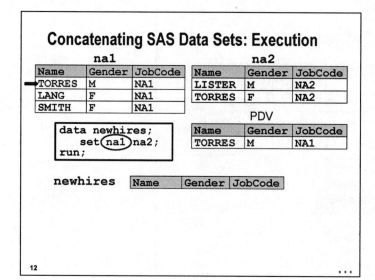

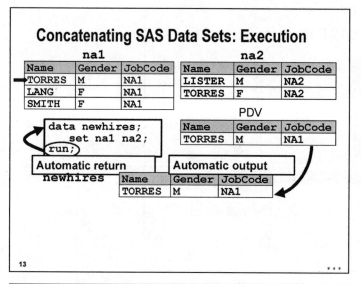

Concatenating SAS Data Sets: Execution

When SAS reaches end-of-file on the last data set, DATA step execution ends.

newhires

Name	Gender	JobCode
TORRES	M	NA1
LANG	F	NA1
SMITH	F	NA1
LISTER	M	NA2
TORRES	F	NA2

21

Business Task

Two SAS data sets, **fa1** and **fa2**, contain data for newly hired flight attendants. Concatenate the data sets into a new data set named **newfa**.

fa1

Name	Gender	JobCode
KENT	F	FA1
PATEL	M	FA1
JONES	F	FA1

fa2

Name	JCode	Gender
LOPEZ	FA2	F
GRANT	FA2	F

The data sets contain similar data, but the variable names are different (**JobCode** versus **JCode**).

22

Concatenating SAS Data Sets: Compilation

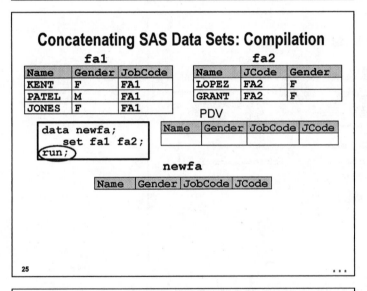

25

Concatenating SAS Data Sets: Execution

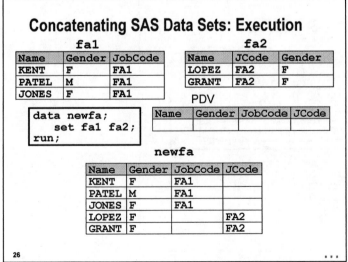

26

The RENAME= Data Set Option

You can use a RENAME= data set option to change the name of a variable.

General form of the RENAME= data set option:

> *SAS-data-set*(**RENAME=**(*old-name-1=new-name-1*
> *old-name-2=new-name-2*
> .
> .
> .
> *old-name-n=new-name-n*))

27

The RENAME= Data Set Option

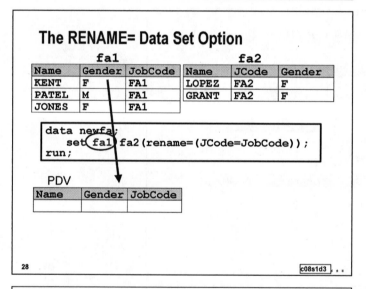

28   c08s1d3 * * *

The RENAME= Data Set Option

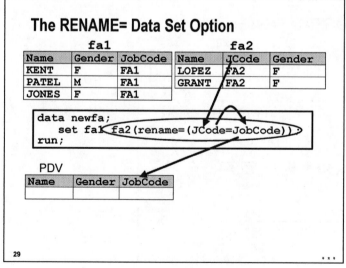

29   * * *

The RENAME= Data Set Option

fa1

Name	Gender	JobCode
KENT	F	FA1
PATEL	M	FA1
JONES	F	FA1

fa2

Name	JCode	Gender
LOPEZ	FA2	F
GRANT	FA2	F

```
data newfa;
    set fa1 fa2(rename=(JCode=JobCode));
run;
```

PDV

Name	Gender	JobCode

newfa

Name	Gender	JobCode
KENT	F	FA1
PATEL	M	FA1
JONES	F	FA1
LOPEZ	F	FA2
GRANT	F	FA2

30

Interleaving SAS Data Sets

Use the SET statement with a BY statement in a DATA step to interleave SAS data sets.

General form of a DATA step interleave:

```
DATA SAS-data-set;
    SET SAS-data-set1 SAS-data-set2 . . . ;
    BY BY-variable;
    <other SAS statements>
RUN;
```

31

Interleaving SAS Data Sets

Interleaving SAS data sets simply concatenates SAS data sets so the observations in the resulting data set are in order.

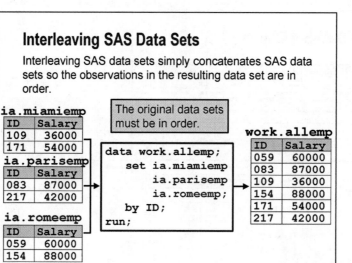

ia.miamiemp

ID	Salary
109	36000
171	54000

ia.parisemp

ID	Salary
083	87000
217	42000

ia.romeemp

ID	Salary
059	60000
154	88000

The original data sets must be in order.

```
data work.allemp;
   set ia.miamiemp
       ia.parisemp
       ia.romeemp;
   by ID;
run;
```

work.allemp

ID	Salary
059	60000
083	87000
109	36000
154	88000
171	54000
217	42000

32   c08s1d4 , . .

Interleaving SAS Data Sets

Interleave the **fa1** and **fa2** data sets by **Name**.

fa1

Name	Gender	JobCode
KENT	F	FA1
PATEL	M	FA1
JONES	F	FA1

fa2

Name	JCode	Gender
LOPEZ	FA2	F
GRANT	FA2	F

The data sets must be sorted first.

```
proc sort data=fa1;
   by name;
run;
```

```
proc sort data=fa2;
   by name;
run;
```

fa1

Name	Gender	JobCode
JONES	F	FA1
KENT	F	FA1
PATEL	M	FA1

fa2

Name	JCode	Gender
GRANT	FA2	F
LOPEZ	FA2	F

33   c08s1d5 , . .

Interleaving SAS Data Sets

fa1

Name	Gender	JobCode
JONES	F	FA1
KENT	F	FA1
PATEL	F	FA1

fa2

Name	JCode	Gender
GRANT	FA2	F
LOPEZ	FA2	F

```
data newfa;
   set fa1 fa2(rename=(JCode=JobCode));
   by Name;
run;
```

PDV

Name	Gender	JobCode

newfa

Name	Gender	JobCode
GRANT	F	FA2
JONES	F	FA1
KENT	F	FA1
LOPEZ	F	FA2
PATEL	M	FA1

36   . . .

In the case where the data values are equal, the observation is always read from the first data set listed in the SET statement. For example,

fa1

Name	Gender	JobCode
JONES	F	FA1
LOPEZ	F	FA1
PATEL	M	FA1

fa2

Name	Gender	JobCode
GRANT	F	FA2
LOPEZ	M	FA2

```
data newfa;
   set fa1 fa2;
   by Name;
run;
```

Results in:

newfa

Name	Gender	JobCode
GRANT	F	FA2
JONES	F	FA1
LOPEZ	F	FA1
LOPEZ	M	FA2
PATEL	M	FA1

 **Exercises**

1. **Concatenating SAS Data Sets**

   The goal is to create a second-quarter data set for International Airlines' Vienna hub.

   Combine target information for April, May, and June into one data set. This data is currently stored in separate data sets by month as follows:

   - `ia.aprtarget`
   - `ia.maytarget`
   - `ia.juntarget`

   a. As a first step, browse the descriptor portion of each data set to determine the number of observations, as well as the number of variables and their attributes.

      How many observations does each data set contain?
      `ia.aprtarget` 120
      `ia.maytarget` 67
      `ia.juntarget` 120

      What are the names of the variables in each data set?

`ia.aprtarget`	Date Destination EClass Tar	ERev FClass Tar FRev	Flight
`ia.maytarget`	Date Destination ERev ETarget	FRev FTarget Flight ID	
`ia.juntarget`	Date Destination ERev ETarget	FRev FTarget Flight ID	

   b. Concatenate the three data sets and create a new data set called `work.q2vienna`. Rename any variables necessary.

   c. Browse the SAS log. There should be no warning or error messages.
      - How many observations are written to the new data set?
      - How many variables does the new data set contain?

d. Submit a PROC PRINT step to verify the data.

Partial Output (First 9 of 307 observations)

```
                                 The SAS System

                  D
                  e
                  s
            F     t
            l     i              F   E
            i     n              T   T
            g     a              a   a
            h     t        D     r   r              F                E
     O      t     i        a     g   g              R                R
     b      I     o        t     e   e              e                e
     s      D     n        e     t   t              v                v

     1   IA06100  CDG   01APR2000  8   85      $3,328.00       $11,730.00
     2   IA05900  CDG   01APR2000  8   85      $2,392.00        $8,415.00
     3   IA07200  FRA   01APR2000 10   97      $1,720.00        $5,432.00
     4   IA04700  LHR   01APR2000 14  120      $2,576.00        $7,320.00
     5   IA06100  CDG   02APR2000  8   85      $3,328.00       $11,730.00
     6   IA05900  CDG   02APR2000  8   85      $2,392.00        $8,415.00
     7   IA07200  FRA   02APR2000 10   97      $1,720.00        $5,432.00
     8   IA04700  LHR   02APR2000 14  120      $2,576.00        $7,320.00
     9   IA06100  CDG   03APR2000  8   85      $3,328.00       $11,730.00
```

e. Recall the DATA step and modify it to create two new variables: **TotTar** and **TotRev**.

- **TotTar** is the total targeted number of economy and first class passengers.

- **TotRev** is the total revenue expected from economy and first class passengers.

Keep only the variables **FlightID**, **Destination**, **Date**, **TotTar**, and **TotRev**.

f. Submit a PROC PRINT step to verify the data.

Partial Output (First 9 of 307 observations)

```
                        The SAS System

            Flight                          Tot    Tot
     Obs      ID      Destination    Date    Tar    Rev

      1    IA06100       CDG      01APR2000   93   15058
      2    IA05900       CDG      01APR2000   93   10807
      3    IA07200       FRA      01APR2000  107    7152
      4    IA04700       LHR      01APR2000  134    9896
      5    IA06100       CDG      02APR2000   93   15058
      6    IA05900       CDG      02APR2000   93   10807
      7    IA07200       FRA      02APR2000  107    7152
      8    IA04700       LHR      02APR2000  134    9896
      9    IA06100       CDG      03APR2000   93   15058
```

8.2   Merging SAS Data Sets

Objectives

- Prepare data for merging using the SORT procedure and data set options.
- Merge SAS data sets on a single common variable.

39

Merging SAS Data Sets

Use the MERGE statement in a DATA step to join corresponding observations from two or more SAS data sets.

General form of a DATA step match-merge:

```
DATA SAS-data-set;
    MERGE SAS-data-sets;
    BY BY-variable(s);
    <other SAS statements>
RUN;
```

40

Merging SAS Data Sets

You can read any number of SAS data sets with a single MERGE statement.

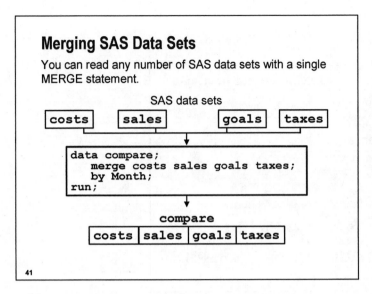

SAS data sets

```
data compare;
   merge costs sales goals taxes;
   by Month;
run;
```

compare

| costs | sales | goals | taxes |

41

✎ Merging combines data sets horizontally by a common variable.

Business Task

International Airlines is comparing monthly sales performance to monthly sales goals.

The sales and goals data are stored in separate SAS data sets.

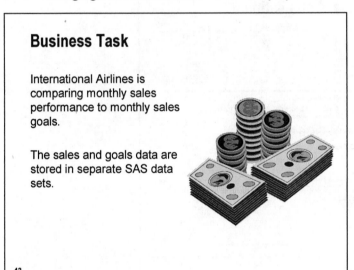

42

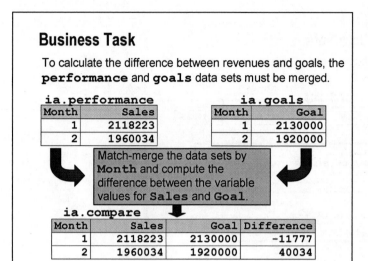

Business Task

To calculate the difference between revenues and goals, the **performance** and **goals** data sets must be merged.

ia.performance

Month	Sales
1	2118223
2	1960034

ia.goals

Month	Goal
1	2130000
2	1920000

Match-merge the data sets by **Month** and compute the difference between the variable values for **Sales** and **Goal**.

ia.compare

Month	Sales	Goal	Difference
1	2118223	2130000	-11777
2	1960034	1920000	40034

43

Merging SAS Data: Compilation

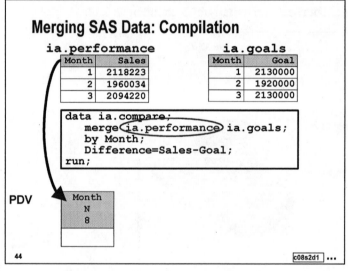

ia.performance

Month	Sales
1	2118223
2	1960034
3	2094220

ia.goals

Month	Goal
1	2130000
2	1920000
3	2130000

```
data ia.compare;
   merge ia.performance ia.goals;
   by Month;
   Difference=Sales-Goal;
run;
```

PDV

Month
N
8

44   c08s2d1 ...

Merging SAS Data: Compilation

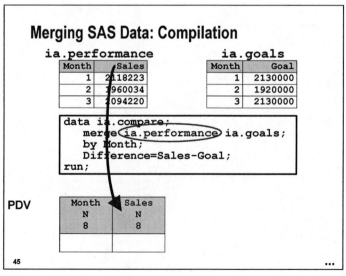

ia.performance

Month	Sales
1	2118223
2	1960034
3	2094220

ia.goals

Month	Goal
1	2130000
2	1920000
3	2130000

```
data ia.compare;
   merge ia.performance ia.goals;
   by Month;
   Difference=Sales-Goal;
run;
```

PDV

Month	Sales
N	N
8	8

45   ...

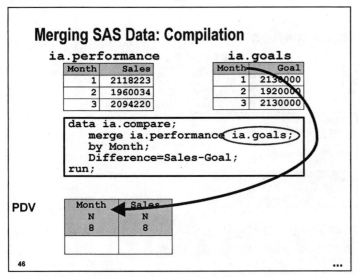

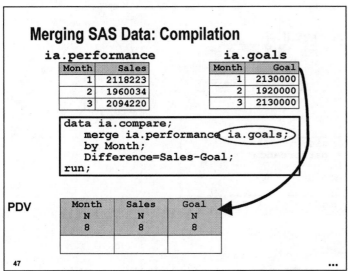

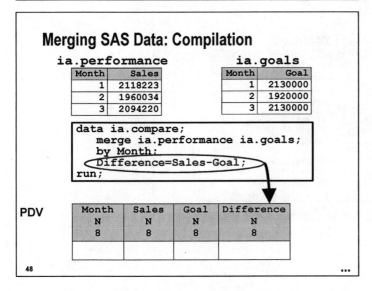

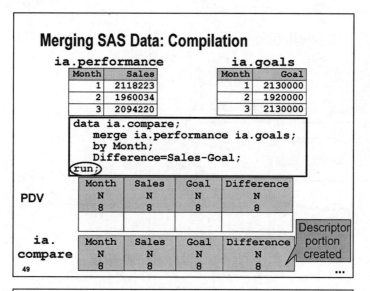

data must be sorted

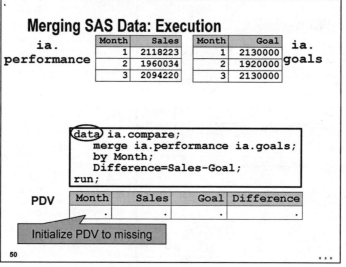

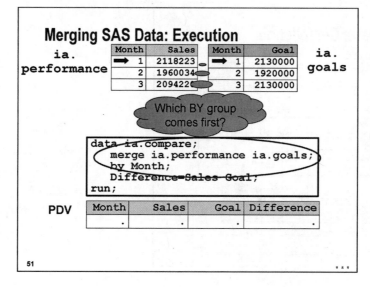

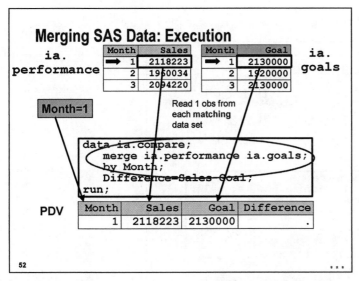

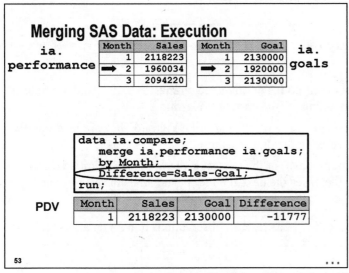

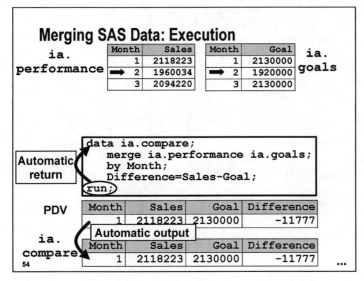

By default, SAS outputs all variables from the PDV to the SAS data set.

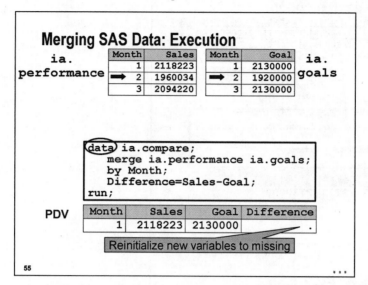

SAS reinitializes variables created in the DATA step to missing at the start of every DATA step iteration.

Before reading additional observations during a match-merge, SAS first determines if there are observations remaining for the current BY group.

- If there are observations remaining for the current BY group, they are read into the PDV, processed, and written to the output data set.

- If there are no more observations for the current BY group, SAS reinitializes the remainder of the PDV, identifies the next BY group, and reads the corresponding observations.

This process is repeated until SAS has read all observations in both data sets.

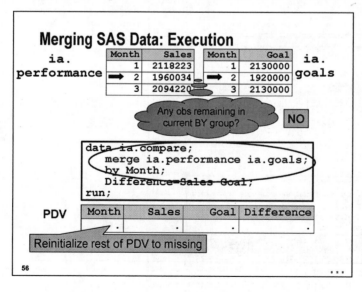

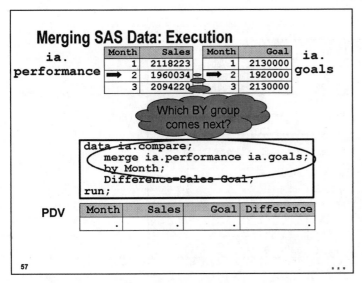

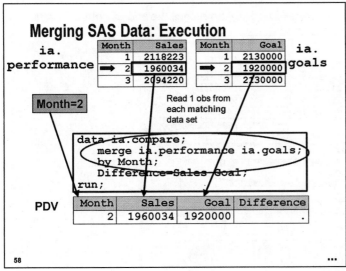

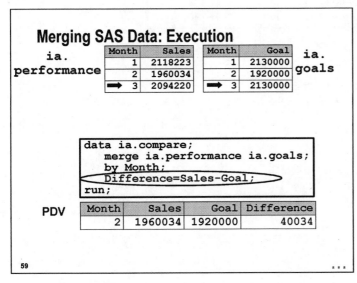

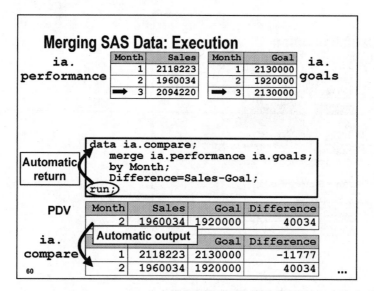

The same process is repeated until SAS reaches the end of both data sets.

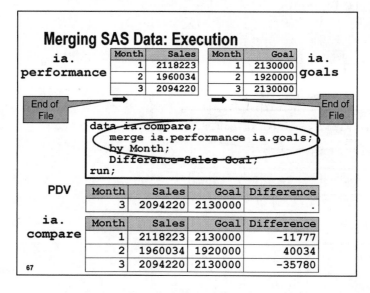

Business Task

Merge two data sets to acquire the names of the German crew who are scheduled to fly next week.

ia.gercrew

EmpID	LastName
E00632	STRAUSS
E01483	SCHELL-HAUNGS
E01996	WELLHAEUSSER
E04064	WASCHK

ia.gersched

EmpID	FlightNum
E04064	5105
E00632	5250
E01996	5501

To match-merge the data sets by **EmpID**, the data sets must be ordered by **EmpID**.

```
proc sort data=ia.gersched
          out=work.gersched;
  by EmpID;
run;
```

68
c08s2d2

Merging SAS Data: Execution

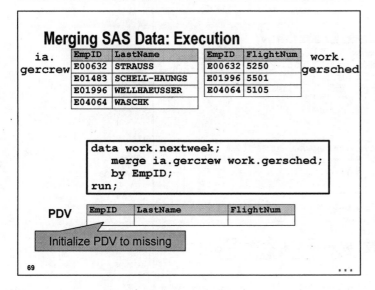

ia.gercrew

EmpID	LastName
E00632	STRAUSS
E01483	SCHELL-HAUNGS
E01996	WELLHAEUSSER
E04064	WASCHK

EmpID	FlightNum
E00632	5250
E01996	5501
E04064	5105

work.gersched

```
data work.nextweek;
  merge ia.gercrew work.gersched;
  by EmpID;
run;
```

PDV

EmpID	LastName	FlightNum

Initialize PDV to missing

69
. . .

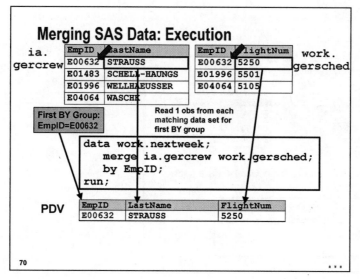

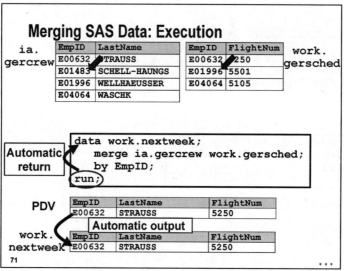

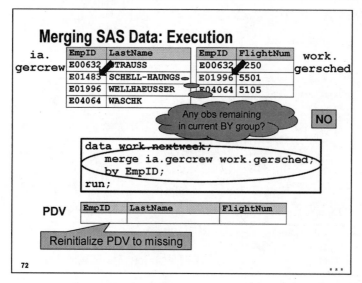

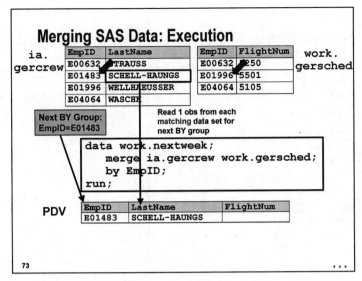

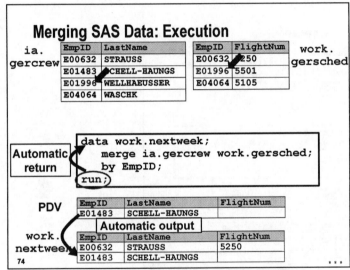

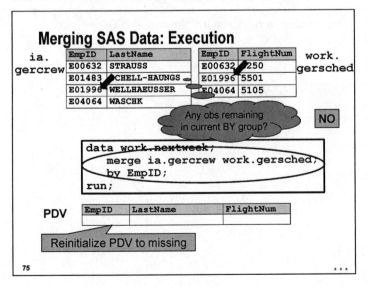

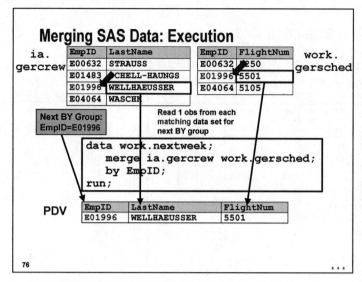

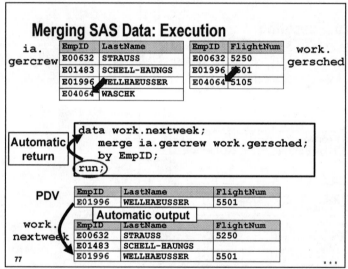

🖉   The same process repeated until SAS reaches the end of both data sets.

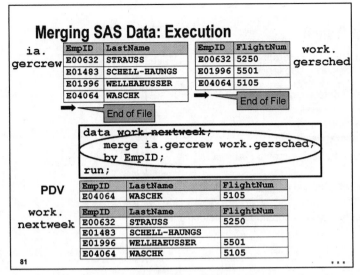

Merging SAS Data: Execution

ia.gercrew

EmpID	LastName
E00632	STRAUSS
E01483	SCHELL-HAUNGS
E01996	WELLHAEUSSER
E04064	WASCHK

work.gersched

EmpID	FlightNum
E00632	5250
E01996	5501
E04064	5105

End of File

End of File

```
data work.nextweek;
   merge ia.gercrew work.gersched;
   by EmpID;
run;
```

PDV

EmpID	LastName	FlightNum
E04064	WASCHK	5105

work.nextweek

EmpID	LastName	FlightNum
E00632	STRAUSS	5250
E01483	SCHELL-HAUNGS	
E01996	WELLHAEUSSER	5501
E04064	WASCHK	5105

81

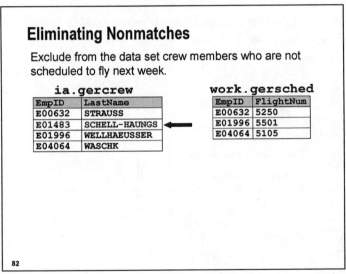

Eliminating Nonmatches

Exclude from the data set crew members who are not scheduled to fly next week.

ia.gercrew

EmpID	LastName
E00632	STRAUSS
E01483	SCHELL-HAUNGS
E01996	WELLHAEUSSER
E04064	WASCHK

work.gersched

EmpID	FlightNum
E00632	5250
E01996	5501
E04064	5105

82

The data set **work.gersched** contains only employees who are scheduled to fly next week

The IN= Data Set Option

Use the IN= data set option to determine which data set(s) contributed to the current observation.

General form of the IN= data set option:

> SAS-data-set(**IN**=*variable*)

variable is a temporary numeric variable that has two possible values:

0 indicates that the data set did not contribute to the current observation.

1 indicates that the data set did contribute to the current observation.

83

✎ The variable created with the IN= data set option is only available during execution and is not written to the SAS data set.

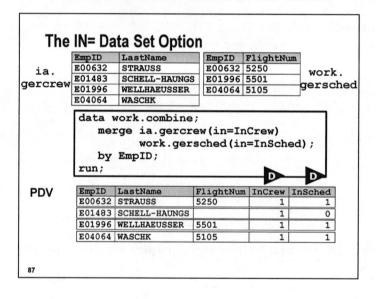

The IN= Data Set Option

ia.
gercrew

EmpID	LastName
E00632	STRAUSS
E01483	SCHELL-HAUNGS
E01996	WELLHAEUSSER
E04064	WASCHK

EmpID	FlightNum
E00632	5250
E01996	5501
E04064	5105

work.
gersched

```
data work.combine;
   merge ia.gercrew(in=InCrew)
         work.gersched(in=InSched);
   by EmpID;
run;
```

PDV

EmpID	LastName	FlightNum	InCrew	InSched
E00632	STRAUSS	5250	1	1
E01483	SCHELL-HAUNGS		1	0
E01996	WELLHAEUSSER	5501	1	1
E04064	WASCHK	5105	1	1

87

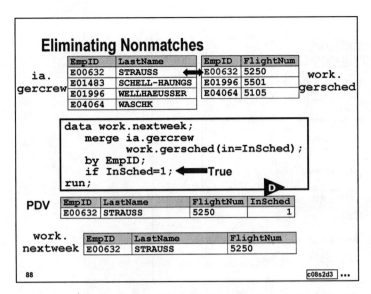

The subsetting IF controls what observations are written to the SAS data set. If the condition evaluates to **true**, the observation is written to the SAS data set. If the condition is evaluated to **false**, the observation is not written to the SAS data set.

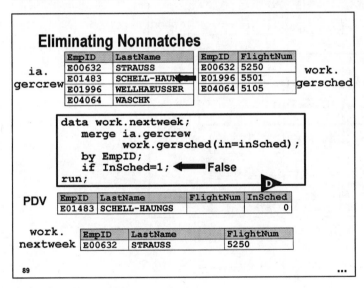

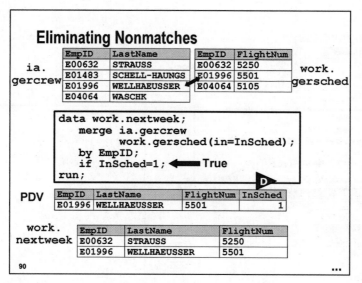

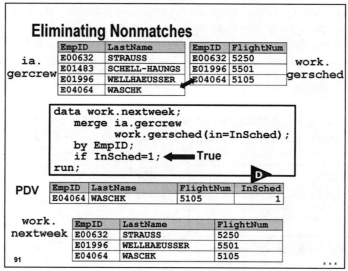

 **Exercises**

2. **Merging SAS Data Sets**

The weather in Birmingham, Alabama on December 15, 1999, might have caused some customers to alter their shipping plans. Investigate how much cargo revenue was lost on all flights out of Birmingham by comparing the targeted revenue with the actual revenue.

a. Sort the data set **ia.target121999** into a temporary data set called **sortb**. Sort by the variable **FlightID**. Use the WHERE statement to create a subset for Birmingham on December 15, 1999.

    where Date='15dec1999'd and Origin='BHM';

b. Sort the data set **ia.sales121999** into a temporary data set called **sorts**. Sort by the variable **FlightID**. Use the WHERE statement to create a subset for Birmingham on December 15,1999.

    where Date='15dec1999'd and Origin='BHM';

c. Create a new temporary data set called **compare** by merging the **sortb** and **sorts** data sets by the variable **FlightID**. Subtract **CargoRev** from **CargoTarRev** to create a new variable called **LostCargoRev**.

d. Print the data set **compare** (print only the variables **CargoTarRev**, **CargoRev**, and **LostCargoRev**) and label the **LostCargoRev** variable. Format the **LostCargoRev** variable with a dollar sign and two decimal digits.

SAS Output

```
                              The SAS System

              Target Revenue      Revenue from       Lost Cargo
     Obs         from Cargo           Cargo            Revenue

      1          $3,441.00         $3,751.00         $-310.00
      2          $3,441.00         $3,441.00            $0.00
      3          $3,441.00         $2,821.00          $620.00
      4          $3,441.00         $3,751.00         $-310.00
      5          $3,441.00         $2,883.00          $558.00
      6          $3,441.00         $2,945.00          $496.00
```

3. Identifying Data Set Contributors (Optional)

The **ia.frankfrt** data set contains information about flights to Frankfurt. The data set contains the variables **Flight** (the flight number), **Date** (the date of the flight), and **IDNo** (the ID number of the pilot who is assigned to the flight).

The **ia.pilots** data set contains pilot information and includes the variable **IDNum** (the ID number of each pilot).

a. Merge the **ia.pilots** and **ia.frankfrt** data sets by ID number to create a temporary data set named **schedule** that contains a work schedule for the pilots. Note that the ID number of each pilot does not have the same variable name in each data set. The **schedule** data set should contain only the variables **IDNum**, **LName**, **FName**, **Date**, and **Flight**.

- Check the log to ensure no errors occurred.
- Use PROC PRINT to verify that the data sets were merged properly. Note that some pilots did not fly to Frankfurt.

SAS Output

```
                          The SAS System

        Obs     IDNum     LName          FName          Date       Flight

          1     1076      VENTER         RANDALL        04MAR00      821
          2     1076      VENTER         RANDALL        05MAR00      821
          3     1106      MARSHBURN      JASPER            .
          4     1107      THOMPSON       WAYNE             .
          5     1118      DENNIS         ROGER          06MAR00      821
          6     1333      BLAIR          JUSTIN         02MAR00      821
          7     1404      CARTER         DONALD         01MAR00      219
          8     1404      CARTER         DONALD         02MAR00      219
          9     1407      GRANT          DANIEL         01MAR00      821
         10     1410      HARRIS         CHARLES        06MAR00      219
         11     1428      BRADY          CHRISTINE         .
         12     1439      HARRISON       FELICIA        03MAR00      821
         13     1442      NEWKIRK        SANDRA            .
         14     1478      NEWTON         JAMES          03MAR00      219
         15     1545      HUNTER         CLYDE             .
         16     1556      PENNINGTON     MICHAEL           .
         17     1739      BOYCE          JONATHAN       05MAR00      219
         18     1777      LUFKIN         ROY               .
         19     1830      TRIPP          KATHY          04MAR00      219
         20     1830      TRIPP          KATHY          07MAR00      219
         21     1890      STEPHENSON     ROBERT            .
         22     1905      GRAHAM         ALVIN             .
         23     1928      UPCHURCH       LARRY             .
```

b. Alter the DATA step to create a temporary data set named **schedule** that contains only pilots who had Frankfurt assignments.

- Use PROC PRINT to verify that the data sets were merged properly.

SAS Output

```
                        The SAS System

     Obs     IDNum    LName      FName       Date     Flight

       1     1076     VENTER     RANDALL     04MAR00    821
       2     1076     VENTER     RANDALL     05MAR00    821
       3     1118     DENNIS     ROGER       06MAR00    821
       4     1333     BLAIR      JUSTIN      02MAR00    821
       5     1404     CARTER     DONALD      01MAR00    219
       6     1404     CARTER     DONALD      02MAR00    219
       7     1407     GRANT      DANIEL      01MAR00    821
       8     1410     HARRIS     CHARLES     06MAR00    219
       9     1439     HARRISON   FELICIA     03MAR00    821
      10     1478     NEWTON     JAMES       03MAR00    219
      11     1739     BOYCE      JONATHAN    05MAR00    219
      12     1830     TRIPP      KATHY       04MAR00    219
      13     1830     TRIPP      KATHY       07MAR00    219
```

c. Alter the DATA step to create a temporary data set named **nofrank** that contains only pilots who did **not** have Frankfurt assignments.

- Use a KEEP statement to restrict the **nofrank** data set to contain only the variables **IDNum**, **LName**, and **FName**.

- Use PROC PRINT to verify that the data sets were merged properly.

SAS Output

```
                     The SAS System

        Obs     IDNum    LName         FName

          1     1106     MARSHBURN     JASPER
          2     1107     THOMPSON      WAYNE
          3     1428     BRADY         CHRISTINE
          4     1442     NEWKIRK       SANDRA
          5     1545     HUNTER        CLYDE
          6     1556     PENNINGTON    MICHAEL
          7     1777     LUFKIN        ROY
          8     1890     STEPHENSON    ROBERT
          9     1905     GRAHAM        ALVIN
         10     1928     UPCHURCH      LARRY
```

8.3   Combining SAS Data Sets: Additional Features (Self-Study)

Objectives

- Define types of DATA step merges.
- Illustrate how the DATA step handles different types of merges.

94

Other Merges

In addition to one-to-one merges, the DATA step merge works with many other kinds of data combinations:

one-to-many	unique BY values are in one data set and duplicate matching BY values are in the other data set.
many-to-many	duplicate matching BY values are in both data sets.

95

One-to-Many Merging

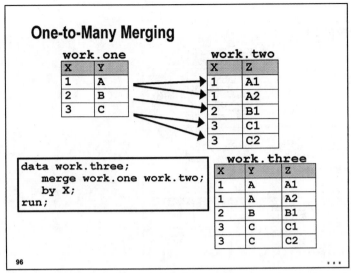

work.one

X	Y
1	A
2	B
3	C

work.two

X	Z
1	A1
1	A2
2	B1
3	C1
3	C2

```
data work.three;
   merge work.one work.two;
   by X;
run;
```

work.three

X	Y	Z
1	A	A1
1	A	A2
2	B	B1
3	C	C1
3	C	C2

96   ...

One-to-Many Merging

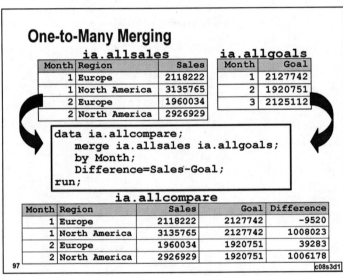

ia.allsales

Month	Region	Sales
1	Europe	2118222
1	North America	3135765
2	Europe	1960034
2	North America	2926929

ia.allgoals

Month	Goal
1	2127742
2	1920751
3	2125112

```
data ia.allcompare;
   merge ia.allsales ia.allgoals;
   by Month;
   Difference=Sales-Goal;
run;
```

ia.allcompare

Month	Region	Sales	Goal	Difference
1	Europe	2118222	2127742	-9520
1	North America	3135765	2127742	1008023
2	Europe	1960034	1920751	39283
2	North America	2926929	1920751	1006178

97   c08s3d1

Many-to-Many Merging

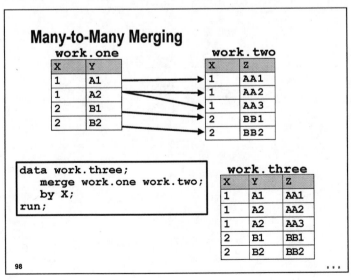

work.one

X	Y
1	A1
1	A2
2	B1
2	B2

work.two

X	Z
1	AA1
1	AA2
1	AA3
2	BB1
2	BB2

```
data work.three;
   merge work.one work.two;
   by X;
run;
```

work.three

X	Y	Z
1	A1	AA1
1	A2	AA2
1	A2	AA3
2	B1	BB1
2	B2	BB2

98   ...

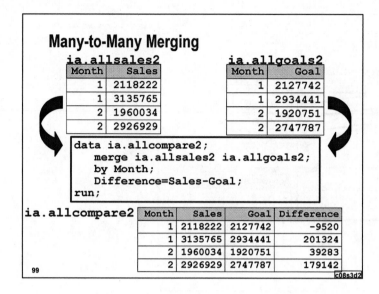

Many-to-Many Merging

ia.allsales2

Month	Sales
1	2118222
1	3135765
2	1960034
2	2926929

ia.allgoals2

Month	Goal
1	2127742
1	2934441
2	1920751
2	2747787

```
data ia.allcompare2;
   merge ia.allsales2 ia.allgoals2;
   by Month;
   Difference=Sales-Goal;
run;
```

ia.allcompare2

Month	Sales	Goal	Difference
1	2118222	2127742	-9520
1	3135765	2934441	201324
2	1960034	1920751	39283
2	2926929	2747787	179142

99

c08s3d2

8.4 Solutions to Exercises

1. **Concatenating SAS Data Sets**

   a.

   Each data set contains these observations:

`ia.aprtarget`	<u>120</u>
`ia.maytarget`	<u>67</u>
`ia.juntarget`	<u>120</u>

   The variable names in each data set are:

   ```
   ia.aprtarget  Flight, Destination, Date, FClassTar,
                 EClassTar, FRev, ERev


   ia.maytarget  FlightID, Destination, Date, FTarget,
                 ETarget, FRev, ERev


   ia.juntarget  FlightID, Destination, Date, FTarget,
                 ETarget, FRev, ERev
   ```

   b.

   ```
   data work.q2vienna;
     set ia.aprtarget(rename=(Flight=FlightID
                              FClassTar=FTarget
                              EClassTar=ETarget))
         ia.maytarget ia.juntarget;
   run;
   ```

   c.

   - There are <u>307</u> observations written to the new data set.
   - There are <u>7</u> variables in the new data set.

   d.

   ```
   proc print data=work.q2vienna;
   run;
   ```

e.

```
data work.q2vienna;
   keep FlightID Destination Date TotTar TotRev;
   set ia.aprtarget(rename=(Flight=FlightID
                            FClassTar=FTarget
                            EClassTar=ETarget))
       ia.maytarget ia.juntarget;
   TotTar=sum(FTarget,ETarget);
   TotRev=sum(FRev,ERev);
run;
```

f.

```
proc print data=work.q2vienna;
run;
```

2. Merging SAS Data Sets

You must sort both SAS data sets prior to merging. Within the PROC SORT, you can add a WHERE statement to subset the observations written to the new SAS data sets created with the OUT= option.

When using a WHERE statement in PROC SORT, be sure to specify an OUT= option. Otherwise, you permanently subset the data.

```
proc sort data=ia.target121999 out=sortb;
   by FlightID;
   where Date='15dec1999'd and Origin='BHM';
run;
proc sort data=ia.sales121999 out=sorts;
   by FlightID;
   where Date='15dec1999'd and Origin='BHM';
run;
data compare;
   merge sortb sorts;
   by FlightID;
   LostCargoRev=CargoTarRev-CargoRev;
run;
proc print data=compare label;
   format LostCargoRev dollar12.2;
   var CargoTarRev CargoRev LostCargoRev;
   label LostCargoRev='Lost Cargo Revenue';
run;
```

3. Identifying Data Set Contributors (Optional)

a.

```
proc sort data=ia.pilots out=pilots;
   by IDNum;
run;
proc sort data=ia.frankfrt out=frankfrt;
   by IDNo;
run;
data schedule;
   keep IDNum LName FName Date Flight;
   merge pilots frankfrt(rename=(IDNo=IDNum));
   by IDNum;
run;
proc print data=schedule;
run;
```

b.

```
data schedule;
   keep IDNum LName FName Date Flight;
   merge pilots frankfrt(in=inFrank rename=(IDNo=IDNum));
   by IDNum;
   if inFrank=1;
run;
proc print data=schedule;
run;
```

c.

```
data nofrank;
   keep IDNum LName FName;
   merge pilots frankfrt(in=inFrank rename=(IDNo=IDNum));
   by IDNum;
   if inFrank=0;
run;
proc print data=nofrank;
run;
```

Chapter 9 Producing Summary Reports

9.1 Introduction to Summary Reports

Objectives

- Identify the different report writing procedures.

3

Summary Reports

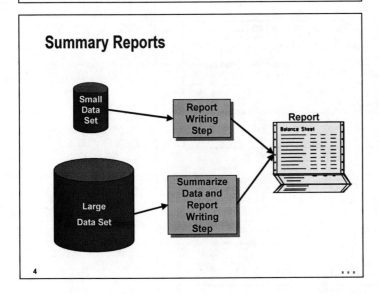

4

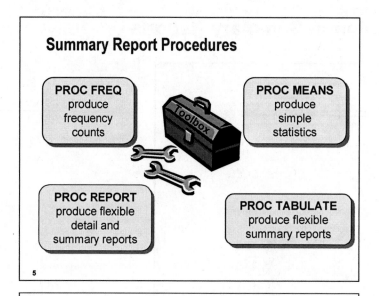

PROC FREQ Output

```
                Distribution of Job Code Values

                     The FREQ Procedure

   Job                               Cumulative    Cumulative
   Code     Frequency     Percent     Frequency      Percent

   FLTAT1        14        20.29           14         20.29
   FLTAT2        18        26.09           32         46.38
   FLTAT3        12        17.39           44         63.77
   PILOT1         8        11.59           52         75.36
   PILOT2         9        13.04           61         88.41
   PILOT3         8        11.59           69        100.00
```

PROC MEANS Output

```
                     Salary by Job Code

                     The MEANS Procedure

                  Analysis Variable : Salary

   Job      N
   Code    Obs    N        Mean      Std Dev     Minimum      Maximum

   FLTAT1   14   14    25642.86     2951.07    21000.00     30000.00

   FLTAT2   18   18    35111.11     1906.30    32000.00     38000.00

   FLTAT3   12   12    44250.00     2301.19    41000.00     48000.00

   PILOT1    8    8    69500.00     2976.10    65000.00     73000.00

   PILOT2    9    9    80111.11     3756.48    75000.00     86000.00

   PILOT3    8    8    99875.00     7623.98    92000.00    112000.00
```

PROC REPORT Output

```
                    Salary Analysis

        Job Code  Home Base        Salary


        FLTAT1    CARY           $131,000
                  FRANKFURT      $100,000
                  LONDON         $128,000
        FLTAT2    CARY           $245,000
                  FRANKFURT      $181,000
                  LONDON         $206,000
        FLTAT3    CARY           $217,000
                  FRANKFURT      $134,000
                  LONDON         $180,000
        PILOT1    CARY           $211,000
                  FRANKFURT      $135,000
                  LONDON         $210,000
        PILOT2    CARY           $323,000
                  FRANKFURT      $240,000
                  LONDON         $158,000
        PILOT3    CARY           $300,000
                  FRANKFURT      $205,000
                  LONDON         $294,000
                                ===========
                               $3,598,000
```

8

PROC TABULATE Output

Average Salary for Cary and Frankfurt

	Location		All
	CARY	FRANKFURT	
	Salary	Salary	Salary
	Mean	Mean	Mean
JobCode			
FLTAT1	$26,200	$25,000	$25,667
FLTAT2	$35,000	$36,200	$35,500
FLTAT3	$43,400	$44,667	$43,875
All	$34,882	$34,583	$34,759

9

9.2 Basic Summary Reports

Objectives

- Create one-way and two-way frequency tables using the FREQ procedure.
- Restrict the variables processed by the FREQ procedure.
- Generate simple descriptive statistics using the MEANS procedure.
- Group observations of a SAS data set for analysis using the CLASS statement in the MEANS procedure.

11

Goal Report 1

International Airlines wants to know how many employees are in each job code.

```
              Distribution of Job Code Values

                    The FREQ Procedure

   Job                                Cumulative    Cumulative
   Code      Frequency     Percent    Frequency      Percent

   FLTAT1        14         20.29         14          20.29
   FLTAT2        18         26.09         32          46.38
   FLTAT3        12         17.39         44          63.77
   PILOT1         8         11.59         52          75.36
   PILOT2         9         13.04         61          88.41
   PILOT3         8         11.59         69         100.00
```

12

Goal Report 2

Categorize job code and salary values to determine how many employees fall into each group.

```
                      Salary Distribution by Job Codes

                           The FREQ Procedure

                        Table of JobCode by Salary

     JobCode           Salary

     Frequency
     Percent
     Row Pct
     Col Pct        Less tha 25,000 t More tha   Total
                    n 25,000 o 50,000 n 50,000

     Flight Attendant       5       39        0      44
                         7.25    56.52     0.00   63.77
                        11.36    88.64     0.00
                       100.00   100.00     0.00

     Pilot                  0        0       25      25
                         0.00     0.00    36.23   36.23
                         0.00     0.00   100.00
                         0.00     0.00   100.00

     Total                  5       39       25      69
                         7.25    56.52    36.23  100.00
```

13

Creating a Frequency Report

PROC FREQ displays frequency counts of the data values in a SAS data set.

General form of a simple PROC FREQ step:

```
PROC FREQ DATA=SAS-data-set;
RUN;
```

Example:

```
proc freq data=ia.crew;
run;
```

14

Creating a Frequency Report

By default, PROC FREQ

- analyzes every variable in the SAS data set
- displays each distinct data value
- calculates the number of observations in which each data value appears (and the corresponding percentage)
- indicates for each variable how many observations have missing values.

15

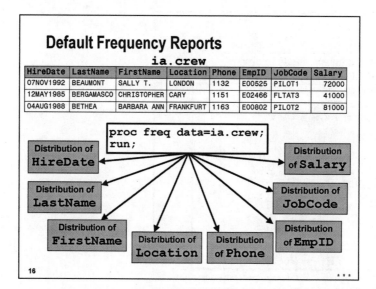

By default, PROC FREQ creates a report on every variable in the data set. For example, the **EmpID** report displays every unique value of **EmpID**, counts how many observations have each value, and provides percentages and cumulative statistics. This is not a useful report because each employee has his or her own unique employee ID.

You do not typically create frequency reports for variables with a large number of distinct values, such as **EmpID**, or for analysis variables, such as **Salary**. You usually create frequency reports for categorical variables, such as **JobCode**. You can group variables into categories by creating and applying formats.

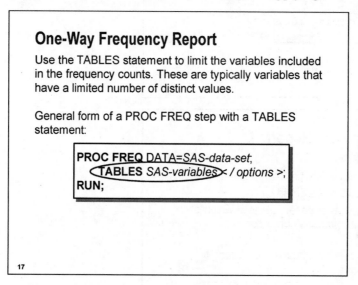

If you specify more than one variable in the TABLES statement, separate the variable names by a space. This creates one table for each variable. For example:

```
tables JobCode Location;
```

Creating a Frequency Report

```
proc freq data=ia.crew;
   tables JobCode;
   title 'Distribution of Job Code Values';
run;
```

```
                Distribution of Job Code Values

                      The FREQ Procedure

      Job                              Cumulative   Cumulative
      Code     Frequency    Percent    Frequency     Percent

      FLTAT1      14         20.29         14         20.29
      FLTAT2      18         26.09         32         46.38
      FLTAT3      12         17.39         44         63.77
      PILOT1       8         11.59         52         75.36
      PILOT2       9         13.04         61         88.41
      PILOT3       8         11.59         69        100.00
```

18   c09s2d1

Displaying the Number of Levels

Use the NLEVELS option in the PROC FREQ statement to display the number of levels for the variables included in the frequency counts.

```
proc freq data=ia.crew nlevels;
   tables Location;
   title 'Distribution of Location Values';
run;
```

19   c09s2d1a

Creating a Frequency Report

```
              Distribution of Location Values

                    The FREQ Procedure

                 Number of Variable Levels

                 Variable       Levels

                 Location          3


      Location   Frequency    Percent   Cumulative   Cumulative
                                        Frequency     Percent

      CARY          27         39.13        27         39.13
      FRANKFURT     19         27.54        46         66.67
      LONDON        23         33.33        69        100.00
```

20   c09s2d1a

To display the number of levels without displaying the frequency counts, add the NOPRINT option to the TABLES statement.

```
proc freq data=ia.crew nlevels;
   tables JobCode Location / noprint;
   title 'Number of Levels for Job Code and Location';
run;
```

To display the number of levels for all variables without displaying any frequency counts, use the _ALL_ keyword and the NOPRINT option in the TABLES statement.

```
proc freq data=ia.crew nlevels;
   tables _all_ / noprint;
   title 'Number of Levels for All Variables';
run;
```

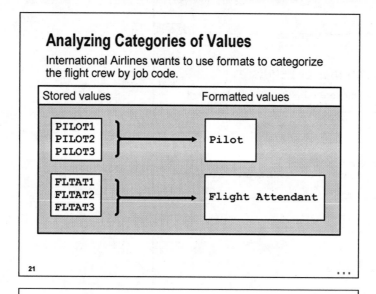

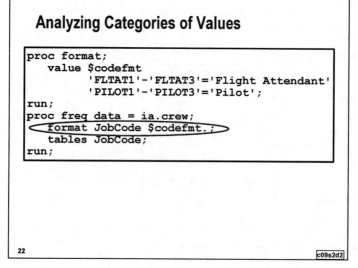

Analyzing Categories of Values

```
                 Distribution of Job Code Values

                      The FREQ Procedure

                                         Cumulative    Cumulative
   JobCode           Frequency   Percent  Frequency      Percent

   Flight Attendant      44       63.77       44         63.77
   Pilot                 25       36.23       69        100.00
```

23

✏️   PROC FREQ automatically groups the data by a variable's formatted value if
      a format is associated with that variable.

Crosstabular Frequency Reports

A two-way, or *crosstabular*, frequency report analyzes all
possible combinations of the distinct values of two
variables.

The asterisk (*) operator in the TABLES statement is used
to cross variables.

General form of the FREQ procedure to create a
crosstabular report:

```
PROC FREQ DATA=SAS-data-set;
   TABLES variable1*variable2;
RUN;
```

24

Crosstabular Frequency Reports

```
proc format;
   value $codefmt
         'FLTAT1'-'FLTAT3'='Flight Attendant'
         'PILOT1'-'PILOT3'='Pilot';
   value money
         low-<25000 ='Less than 25,000'
         25000-50000='25,000 to 50,000'
         50000<-high='More than 50,000';
run;
proc freq data=ia.crew;
   tables JobCode*Salary;
   format JobCode $codefmt. Salary money.;
   title 'Salary Distribution by Job Codes';
run;
```

25   c09s2d3

In a crosstabular report, the values of the first variable in the TABLES statement form the rows of the frequency table and the values of the second variable form the columns.

Crosstabular Frequency Reports

```
              Salary Distribution by Job Codes

                     The FREQ Procedure

                   Table of JobCode by Salary

      JobCode           Salary

      Frequency
      Percent
      Row Pct
      Col Pct          Less tha 25,000 t More tha   Total
                       n 25,000 o 50,000 n 50,000

      Flight Attendant      5       39        0         44
                         7.25    56.52     0.00      63.77
                        11.36    88.64     0.00
                       100.00   100.00     0.00

      Pilot                 0        0       25         25
                         0.00     0.00    36.23      36.23
                         0.00     0.00   100.00
                         0.00     0.00   100.00

      Total                 5       39       25         69
                         7.25    56.52    36.23     100.00
```

26

Crosstabular Frequency Reports

To display the crosstabulation results in a listing form,
add the CROSSLIST option to the TABLES statement.

```
proc freq data=ia.crew;
   tables JobCode*Location / crosslist;
   title 'Location Distribution for Job Codes';
run;
```

27   c09s2d3a

Crosstabular Frequency Reports

Partial Output

```
              Location Distribution for Job Codes

                     The FREQ Procedure

                 Table of JobCode by Location

Job                                         Row      Column
Code     Location    Frequency    Percent    Percent   Percent
-----------------------------------------------------------------
FLTAT1   CARY            5         7.25      35.71     18.52
         FRANKFURT       4         5.80      28.57     21.05
         LONDON          5         7.25      35.71     21.74

         Total          14        20.29     100.00
-----------------------------------------------------------------
FLTAT2   CARY            7        10.14      38.89     25.93
         FRANKFURT       5         7.25      27.78     26.32
         LONDON          6         8.70      33.33     26.09

         Total          18        26.09     100.00
-----------------------------------------------------------------
```

28

Business Task

International Airlines wants to determine the minimum,
maximum, and average salary for each job code.

29

Calculating Summary Statistics

The MEANS procedure displays simple descriptive
statistics for the numeric variables in a SAS data set.

General form of a simple PROC MEANS step:

PROC MEANS DATA=*SAS-data-set*;
RUN;

Example:

```
proc means data=ia.crew;
   title 'Salary Analysis';
run;
```

30   c09s2d4

Calculating Summary Statistics

		Salary Analysis			
		The MEANS Procedure			
Variable	N	Mean	Std Dev	Minimum	Maximum
HireDate	69	9812.78	1615.44	7318.00	12690.00
Salary	69	52144.93	25521.78	21000.00	112000.00

31

Calculating Summary Statistics

By default, PROC MEANS

- analyzes every numeric variable in the SAS data set
- prints the statistics N, MEAN, STD, MIN, and MAX
- excludes missing values before calculating statistics.

32

Default statistics are

N	number of rows with nonmissing values
MEAN	arithmetic mean (or average)
STD	standard deviation
MIN	minimum value
MAX	maximum value.

Other statistics include

RANGE	difference between lowest and highest values
MEDIAN	50th percentile value
SUM	total
NMISS	number of rows with missing values.

Selecting Variables

The VAR statement restricts the variables processed by PROC MEANS.

General form of the VAR statement:

> **VAR** *SAS-variable(s)*;

33

Selecting Variables

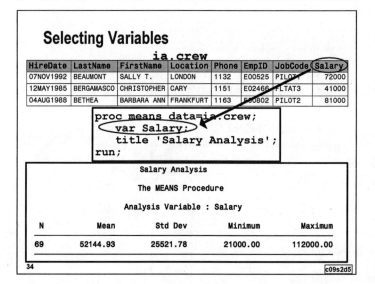

ia.crew

HireDate	LastName	FirstName	Location	Phone	EmpID	JobCode	Salary
07NOV1992	BEAUMONT	SALLY T.	LONDON	1132	E00525	PILOT	72000
12MAY1985	BERGAMASCO	CHRISTOPHER	CARY	1151	E02466	FLTAT3	41000
04AUG1988	BETHEA	BARBARA ANN	FRANKFURT	1163	E00802	PILOT2	81000

```
proc means data=ia.crew;
   var Salary;
   title 'Salary Analysis';
run;
```

```
                   Salary Analysis

                 The MEANS Procedure

             Analysis Variable : Salary

N        Mean        Std Dev       Minimum        Maximum

69     52144.93     25521.78      21000.00      112000.00
```

34   c09s2d5

Grouping Observations

The CLASS statement in the MEANS procedure groups the observations of the SAS data set for analysis.

General form of the CLASS statement:

> **CLASS** *SAS-variable(s)*;

35

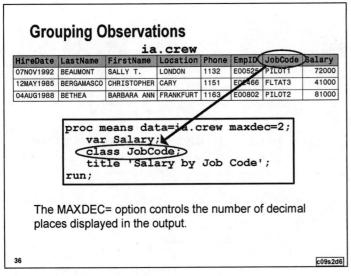

Grouping Observations

ia.crew

HireDate	LastName	FirstName	Location	Phone	EmpID	JobCode	Salary
07NOV1992	BEAUMONT	SALLY T.	LONDON	1132	E00525	PILOT1	72000
12MAY1985	BERGAMASCO	CHRISTOPHER	CARY	1151	E00466	FLTAT3	41000
04AUG1988	BETHEA	BARBARA ANN	FRANKFURT	1163	E00802	PILOT2	81000

```
proc means data=ia.crew maxdec=2;
   var Salary;
   class JobCode;
   title 'Salary by Job Code';
run;
```

The MAXDEC= option controls the number of decimal places displayed in the output.

36   c09s2d6

Grouping Observations

```
                   Salary by Job Code

                   The MEANS Procedure

                 Analysis Variable : Salary

Job       N
Code     Obs    N      Mean      Std Dev    Minimum     Maximum

FLTAT1   14    14    25642.86    2951.07    21000.00     30000.00

FLTAT2   18    18    35111.11    1906.30    32000.00     38000.00

FLTAT3   12    12    44250.00    2301.19    41000.00     48000.00

PILOT1    8     8    69500.00    2976.10    65000.00     73000.00

PILOT2    9     9    80111.11    3756.48    75000.00     86000.00

PILOT3    8     8    99875.00    7623.98    92000.00    112000.00
```

37

PROC MEANS may not always print two digits to the right of the decimal point. To control the maximum number of decimal places for PROC MEANS to use in printing results, use the MAXDEC= option in the PROC MEANS statement.

General form of the PROC MEANS statement with the MAXDEC= option:

> **PROC MEANS** DATA=*SAS-data-set* MAXDEC=*number*;
> **RUN;**

 **Exercises**

1. Creating Frequency Reports

   a. Use PROC FREQ to create a report using the **ia.sanfran** data set that displays the frequency count for each **DepartDay**. Add an appropriate title.

    SAS Output

```
              Flights from San Francisco by Day of Week

                        The FREQ Procedure

                                         Cumulative    Cumulative
    DepartDay    Frequency    Percent     Frequency      Percent
    ──────────────────────────────────────────────────────────────
        1            6         11.54          6          11.54
        2           13         25.00         19          36.54
        3            5          9.62         24          46.15
        4            7         13.46         31          59.62
        5            7         13.46         38          73.08
        6            8         15.38         46          88.46
        7            6         11.54         52         100.00
```

   b. Use PROC FREQ to create a report using the **ia.sanfran** data set that displays the frequency count for each **Destination**. Add an appropriate title.

    SAS Output

```
                      Flights from San Francisco

                        The FREQ Procedure

                                         Cumulative    Cumulative
    Destination    Frequency    Percent   Frequency      Percent
    ──────────────────────────────────────────────────────────────
    ANC               10        19.23        10          19.23
    HND                8        15.38        18          34.62
    HNL                3         5.77        21          40.38
    RDU                6        11.54        27          51.92
    SEA               25        48.08        52         100.00
```

c. **(Optional)** You can specify many options in the TABLES statement to control the calculations and appearance of a frequency table. The NOCUM option suppresses the printing of the cumulative frequencies and cumulative percentages. You can specify options in a TABLES statement in the following way:

> **tables *variable* / *options*;**

Recall your program from Exercise **1.b** and add the NOCUM option to the TABLES statement.

SAS Output

```
              Flights from San Francisco

                  The FREQ Procedure

        Destination    Frequency      Percent

        ANC                  10        19.23
        HND                   8        15.38
        HNL                   3         5.77
        RDU                   6        11.54
        SEA                  25        48.08
```

d. Use PROC FREQ to create a report using the `ia.sanfran` data set that displays the frequency count for each **Destination** by **DepartDay**.

Partial SAS Output

```
                    Flights from San Francisco

                        The FREQ Procedure

                  Table of Destination by DepartDay

         Destination
                   DepartDay

         Frequency
         Percent
         Row Pct
         Col Pct        1|       2|       3|       4|    Total
         ────────┼────────┼────────┼────────┼────────┼
         ANC             0        3        1        1       10
                      0.00     5.77     1.92     1.92    19.23
                      0.00    30.00    10.00    10.00
                      0.00    23.08    20.00    14.29
         ────────┼────────┼────────┼────────┼────────┼
         HND             1        2        1        3        8
                      1.92     3.85     1.92     5.77    15.38
                     12.50    25.00    12.50    37.50
                     16.67    15.38    20.00    42.86
         ────────┼────────┼────────┼────────┼────────┼
         HNL             0        0        0        0        3
                      0.00     0.00     0.00     0.00     5.77
                      0.00     0.00     0.00     0.00
                      0.00     0.00     0.00     0.00
         ────────┼────────┼────────┼────────┼────────┼
         RDU             2        1        1        0        6
                      3.85     1.92     1.92     0.00    11.54
                     33.33    16.67    16.67     0.00
                     33.33     7.69    20.00     0.00
         ────────┼────────┼────────┼────────┼────────┼
```

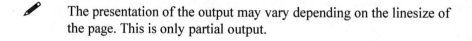 The presentation of the output may vary depending on the linesize of the page. This is only partial output.

2. Validating Data with PROC FREQ (Optional)

a. PROC FREQ is useful in checking the validity and completeness of data. Use PROC FREQ to check the validity of the variables **Gender** and **JobCode** in the **ia.mechanics** data set. What do you notice about the values of the variable **Gender**? What do you notice about the values of the variable **JobCode**?

SAS Output

```
                           The FREQ Procedure

                                       Cumulative    Cumulative
    Gender    Frequency     Percent     Frequency      Percent

    B               1        2.94            1          2.94
    F              17       50.00           18         52.94
    G               1        2.94           19         55.88
    M              15       44.12           34        100.00


    Job                                    Cumulative    Cumulative
    Code      Frequency     Percent     Frequency      Percent

    MECHO1          6       18.18            6         18.18
    MECHO2         12       36.36           18         54.55
    MECHO3         15       45.45           33        100.00

                      Frequency Missing = 1
```

b. Modify the previous report to display the frequency count for each **Gender** by **JobCode**. What are the **JobCode** values for the invalid values of **Gender**? (Output not shown since it provides the answer.)

3. Creating Basic Summary Reports

a. Generate a PROC MEANS report using the **ia.sanfran** data set as input to display statistics for the variables **CargoRev** and **TotPassCap** only. Remove any titles currently in effect.

SAS Output

The MEANS Procedure					
Variable	N	Mean	Std Dev	Minimum	Maximum
CargoRev	52	33433.50	23731.72	9417.00	84495.00
TotPassCap	52	203.8076923	52.4494298	150.0000000	267.0000000

b. Modify the previous report to display the data for each **Destination**. Limit the number of decimal places in the output to two. The output shown below is only partial output; all statistics should display in your report.

Partial SAS Output

The MEANS Procedure					
Destination	N Obs	Variable	N	Mean	Std Dev
ANC	10	CargoRev	10	35811.30	4458.74
		TotPassCap	10	257.60	11.69
HND	8	CargoRev	8	78625.50	3251.06
		TotPassCap	8	250.50	8.33
HNL	3	CargoRev	3	59684.00	3464.64
		TotPassCap	3	207.00	0.00
RDU	6	CargoRev	6	37840.00	4787.04
		TotPassCap	6	267.00	0.00
SEA	25	CargoRev	25	13813.32	2316.59
		TotPassCap	25	151.80	4.97

4. Requesting Specific Statistics through PROC MEANS (Optional)

You can request specific statistics by listing their names in a
PROC MEANS statement. For example, to request N (the frequency of non-missing values), and only N, use the following PROC MEANS step:

```
proc means data=SAS-data-set-name n;
run;
```

Modify the report from Exercise **3**, and alter the PROC MEANS statement to
request only the minimum (MIN), maximum (MAX), and mean (MEAN)
statistics.

SAS Output

```
                              The MEANS Procedure

                   N
Destination      Obs   Variable      Minimum      Maximum         Mean

ANC              10    CargoRev      31992.00     44643.00     35811.30
                       TotPassCap      238.00       267.00       257.60

HND               8    CargoRev      73143.00     84495.00     78625.50
                       TotPassCap      237.00       255.00       250.50

HNL               3    CargoRev      55728.00     62178.00     59684.00
                       TotPassCap      207.00       207.00       207.00

RDU               6    CargoRev      31734.00     43344.00     37840.00
                       TotPassCap      267.00       267.00       267.00

SEA              25    CargoRev       9417.00     17931.00     13813.32
                       TotPassCap      150.00       165.00       151.80
```

5. Creating HTML Output (Optional)

Modify the previous report by adding an ODS statement to create the output as HTML.

The MEANS Procedure

Destination	N Obs	Variable	Minimum	Maximum	Mean
ANC	10	CargoRev TotPassCap	31992.00 238.00	44643.00 267.00	35811.30 257.60
HND	8	CargoRev TotPassCap	73143.00 237.00	84495.00 255.00	78625.50 250.50
HNL	3	CargoRev TotPassCap	55728.00 207.00	62178.00 207.00	59684.00 207.00
RDU	6	CargoRev TotPassCap	31734.00 267.00	43344.00 267.00	37840.00 267.00
SEA	25	CargoRev TotPassCap	9417.00 150.00	17931.00 165.00	13813.32 151.80

9.3 The REPORT Procedure

Objectives

- Use the REPORT procedure to create a listing report.
- Apply the ORDER usage type to sort the data on a listing report.
- Apply the SUM and GROUP usage types to create a summary report.
- Use the RBREAK statement to produce a grand total.

40

REPORT Procedure Features

PROC REPORT enables you to

- create listing reports
- create summary reports
- enhance reports
- request separate subtotals and grand totals
- generate reports in an interactive point-and-click or programming environments.

41

PROC REPORT versus PROC PRINT

FEATURE	REPORT	PRINT
Detail Report	Yes	Yes
Summary Report	Yes	No
Crosstabular Report	Yes	No
Grand Totals	Yes	Yes
Subtotals	Yes	Yes, but not without Grand Total
Labels used automatically	Yes	No
Sort data for report	Yes	No

42

Creating a List Report

General form of a simple PROC REPORT step:

PROC REPORT DATA=*SAS-data-set <options>*;
RUN;

Selected options:

WINDOWS | WD   invokes the procedure in an interactive REPORT window (default).

NOWINDOWS | NOWD   displays the report in the OUTPUT window.

```
proc report data=ia.crew nowd;
run;
```

43

The REPORT Procedure

The default listing displays

- each data value as it is stored in the data set, or formatted value if a format is stored with the data
- variable names or labels as report column headings
- a default width for the report columns
- character values left-justified
- numeric values right-justified
- observations in the order in which they are stored in the data set.

44

Printing Selected Variables

You can use a COLUMN statement to
- select the variables to appear in the report
- order the variables in the report.

General form of the COLUMN statement:

COLUMN *SAS-variables*;

45

Sample Listing Report

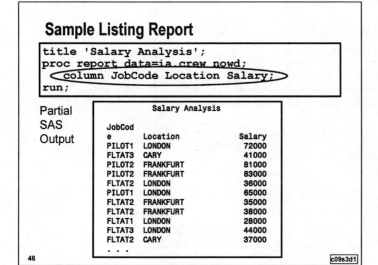

```
title 'Salary Analysis';
proc report data=ia.crew nowd;
  column JobCode Location Salary;
run;
```

Partial
SAS
Output

```
                  Salary Analysis

    JobCod
    e         Location          Salary
    PILOT1    LONDON             72000
    FLTAT3    CARY               41000
    PILOT2    FRANKFURT          81000
    PILOT2    FRANKFURT          83000
    FLTAT2    LONDON             36000
    PILOT1    LONDON             65000
    FLTAT2    FRANKFURT          35000
    FLTAT2    FRANKFURT          38000
    FLTAT1    LONDON             28000
    FLTAT3    LONDON             44000
    FLTAT2    CARY               37000
    . . .
```

46   c09s3d1

The DEFINE Statement

You can enhance the report by using DEFINE statements to

- define how each variable is used in the report
- assign formats to variables
- specify report column headers and column widths
- change the order of the rows in the report.

47

The DEFINE Statement

General form of the DEFINE statement:

DEFINE *variable* / *<usage> <attribute-list>*;

You can define options (usage and attributes) in the DEFINE statement in any order.

Variable Type	Default Usage	Report Produced
Character	Display	Listing
Numeric	Analysis	Summary

The ANALYSIS usage for numeric variables

- uses a default statistic of SUM
- has no effect when producing a listing report that contains character variables, so the original data value is displayed.

48

Character and Numeric Variables

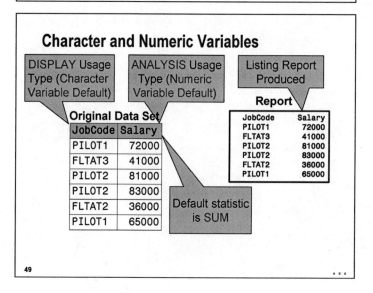

49

* * *

Numeric Variables Only

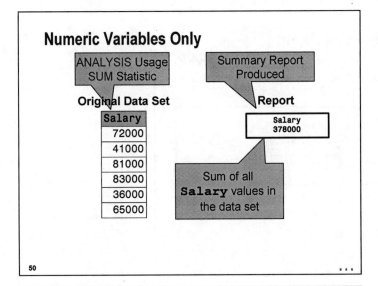

50

The DEFINE Statement

Selected attributes:

' *report-column-header* '	defines the report column header.

If there is a label stored in the descriptor portion of the data set, it is the default header.

51

The DEFINE Statement

Selected attributes:

FORMAT=	assigns a format to a variable.

If there is a format stored in the descriptor portion of the data set, it is the default format.

WIDTH=	controls the width of a report column.

The default width is
- the variable length for character variables
- 9 for numeric variables
- the format width if there is a format stored in the descriptor portion of the data set.

52

Enhancing the Listing Report

- Change column headings.
- Increase the column widths.
- Add a format to display **Salary** with dollar signs and commas.

```
proc report data=ia.crew nowd;
   column JobCode Location Salary;
   define JobCode  / width=8  'Job Code';
   define Location / 'Home Base';
   define Salary   / format=dollar10.;
run;
```

53   c09s3d2

Enhancing the Listing Report

Partial SAS Output

Job Code	Home Base	Salary
PILOT1	LONDON	$72,000
FLTAT3	CARY	$41,000
PILOT2	FRANKFURT	$81,000
PILOT2	FRANKFURT	$83,000
FLTAT2	LONDON	$36,000
PILOT1	LONDON	$65,000
FLTAT2	FRANKFURT	$35,000
FLTAT2	FRANKFURT	$38,000
FLTAT1	LONDON	$28,000

. . .

54

ORDER Usage Type

Selected attributes:

ORDER	orders the rows in the report.

- Orders the report in ascending order. Include the DESCENDING option in the DEFINE statement to force the order to be descending.
- Suppresses repetitious printing of values.
- Does **not** need data to be previously sorted.

55

ORDER Usage Type

Display the data in order by **JobCode**.

```
proc report data=ia.crew nowd;
   column JobCode Location Salary;
   define JobCode / order width=8 'Job Code';
   define Location / 'Home Base';
   define Salary / format=dollar10.;
run;
```

56   c09s3d3

ORDER Usage Type

Partial SAS Output

```
               Salary Analysis

     Job Code  Home Base        Salary
     FLTAT1    LONDON          $28,000
               FRANKFURT       $25,000
               CARY            $23,000

               . . .
               FRANKFURT       $27,000
               LONDON          $22,000
     FLTAT2    LONDON          $36,000
               FRANKFURT       $35,000

               . . .
               FRANKFURT       $33,000
               CARY            $38,000
```

57

Business Task

International Airlines wants to summarize **Salary** by
JobCode for each **Location**.

58

Desired Report

```
                          Salary Analysis

              Job Code  Home Base         Salary
              FLTAT1    CARY             $131,000
                        FRANKFURT        $100,000
                        LONDON           $128,000
              FLTAT2    CARY             $245,000
                        FRANKFURT        $181,000
                        LONDON           $206,000
              FLTAT3    CARY             $217,000
                        FRANKFURT        $134,000
                        LONDON           $180,000
              PILOT1    CARY             $211,000
                        FRANKFURT        $135,000
                        LONDON           $210,000
              PILOT2    CARY             $323,000
                        FRANKFURT        $240,000
                        LONDON           $158,000
              PILOT3    CARY             $300,000
                        FRANKFURT        $205,000
                        LONDON           $294,000
                                        ==========
                                        $3,598,000
```

59

Defining Group Variables

Use the REPORT procedure to create a summary report by defining variables as **group** variables.

All observations whose group variables have the same values are collapsed into a single row in the report.

60

Defining Group Variables

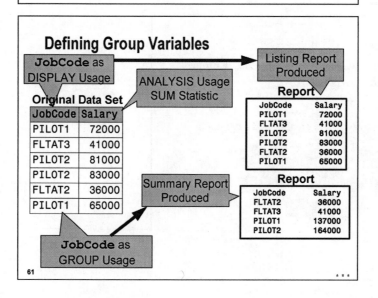

61

Defining Group Variables

You can define more than one variable as a group variable.

Nesting of group variables is determined by the order of the variables in the COLUMN statement.

62

Defining Group Variables

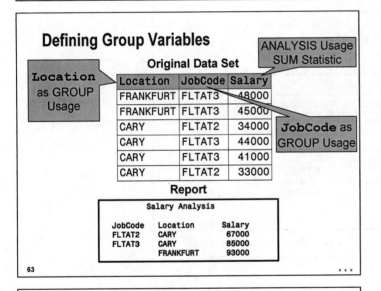

63

Defining Group Variables

If you have a group variable, there must be no display or order variables.

- Group variables produce summary reports (observations collapsed into groups).
- Display and order variables produce listing reports (one row for each observation).

64

Defining Analysis Variables

Default usage for numeric variables is ANALYSIS with a default statistic of SUM.

- If the report contains group variables, the report displays the sum of the numeric variables' values for each group.
- If the report contains at least one display or order variable and no group variables, the report lists all of the values of the numeric variable.
- If the report contains only numeric variables, the report displays grand totals for the numeric variables.

65

Defining Analysis Variables

Selected statistics include

SUM	sum (default)
N	number of nonmissing values
MEAN	average
MAX	maximum value
MIN	minimum value

To specify a statistic other than SUM, type the name of the statistic after the slash in the DEFINE statement.

Example:

```
define Salary / mean format=dollar10.;
```

66

Summarizing the Data

Use the GROUP usage in the DEFINE statement to specify the variables that define groups.

```
proc report data=ia.crew nowd;
   column JobCode Location Salary;
   define JobCode / group width=8 'Job Code';
   define Location / group 'Home Base';
   define Salary / format=dollar10.;
run;
```

67   c09s3d4

Summarizing the Data

Partial SAS Output

```
                          Salary Analysis

          Job Code    Home Base            Salary
          FLTAT1      CARY               $131,000
                      FRANKFURT          $100,000
                      LONDON             $128,000
          FLTAT2      CARY               $245,000
                      FRANKFURT          $181,000
                      LONDON             $206,000
          FLTAT3      CARY               $217,000
                      FRANKFURT          $134,000
                      LONDON             $180,000
          PILOT1      CARY               $211,000
                      FRANKFURT          $135,000
                      LONDON             $210,000
          PILOT2      CARY               $323,000
                      FRANKFURT          $240,000
                      LONDON             $158,000
          PILOT3      CARY               $300,000
                      FRANKFURT          $205,000
                      LONDON             $294,000
```

68

Printing Grand Totals

You can use an RBREAK statement to add a

- grand total to the top or bottom of the report
- line before the grand total
- line after the grand total.

General form of the RBREAK statement:

RBREAK BEFORE | AFTER </options>;

69

Printing Grand Totals

Selected options:

SUMMARIZE	Prints the total.
OL	Prints a single line above the total.
DOL	Prints a double line above the total.
UL	Prints a single line below the total.
DUL	Prints a double line below the total.

70

The RBREAK Statement

Use the RBREAK statement to display the grand total at the bottom of the report.

```
proc report data=ia.crew nowd;
   column JobCode Location Salary;
   define JobCode / group width=8 'Job Code';
   define Location / group 'Home Base';
   define Salary / format=dollar10.;
   rbreak after / summarize dol;
run;
```

71   c09s3d5

The RBREAK Statement

```
                    Salary Analysis

          Job Code  Home Base          Salary
          FLTAT1    CARY            $131,000
                    FRANKFURT       $100,000
                    LONDON          $128,000
          FLTAT2    CARY            $245,000
                    FRANKFURT       $181,000
                    LONDON          $206,000
          FLTAT3    CARY            $217,000
                    FRANKFURT       $134,000
                    LONDON          $180,000
          PILOT1    CARY            $211,000
                    FRANKFURT       $135,000
                    LONDON          $210,000
          PILOT2    CARY            $323,000
                    FRANKFURT       $240,000
                    LONDON          $158,000
          PILOT3    CARY            $300,000
                    FRANKFURT       $205,000
                    LONDON          $294,000
                                    ==========
                                  $3,598,000
```

72

Enhancing the Report

You can use the HEADLINE and HEADSKIP options in the PROC REPORT statement to make the report more readable.

```
proc report data=ia.crew nowd headline headskip;
   column JobCode Location Salary;
   define JobCode / group width=8 'Job Code';
   define Location / group 'Home Base';
   define Salary / format=dollar10.;
   rbreak after / summarize dol;
run;
```

73   c09s3d6

Enhancing the Report

```
                    Salary Analysis

        Job Code  Home Base         Salary


        FLTAT1    CARY            $131,000
                  FRANKFURT       $100,000
                  LONDON          $128,000
        FLTAT2    CARY            $245,000
                  FRANKFURT       $181,000
                  LONDON          $206,000
        FLTAT3    CARY            $217,000
                  FRANKFURT       $134,000
                  LONDON          $180,000
        PILOT1    CARY            $211,000
                  FRANKFURT       $135,000
                  LONDON          $210,000
        PILOT2    CARY            $323,000
                  FRANKFURT       $240,000
                  LONDON          $158,000
        PILOT3    CARY            $300,000
                  FRANKFURT       $205,000
                  LONDON          $294,000
                                ==========
                                $3,598,000
```

74

 **Exercises**

6. Creating a List Report

Use PROC REPORT and the **ia.employees** data set to produce a list report with the following characteristics:

- Output should be sent to the Output window.
- The report should display only the variables **Division**, **City**, and **Salary**.
- Each variable displayed should have a descriptive report column heading.
- Salary should be displayed with dollar signs, commas, and no decimals.
- The columns of the report should be wide enough so that individual data values are not truncated.
- The observations on the report should be ordered by the values of **Division**.
- The report should be titled **Employee Salary Data**.

Partial PROC REPORT Output

```
                     Employee Salary Data


    Division Name          City Based            Salary
    AIRPORT OPERATIONS     CARY                 $29,000
                           CARY                 $41,000
                           CARY                 $23,000
                           CARY                 $17,000
                           CARY                 $32,000
                           CARY                 $39,000
                           TORONTO              $29,000
                           CARY                 $33,000
```

7. Creating a Sorted List Report (Optional)

Modify the previous report so that both **Division** and **City** appear in sorted order.

Partial PROC REPORT Output

```
                     Employee Salary Data


    Division Name          City Based            Salary
    AIRPORT OPERATIONS     AUSTIN               $22,000
                                                $37,000
                                                $35,000
                           BRUSSELS             $16,000
                                                $38,000
                           CARY                 $29,000
                                                $41,000
```

8. Creating a Summary Report

Use PROC REPORT and the **ia.employees** data set to produce a summary report with the following characteristics:

- The report should display only the variables **Division**, **City**, and **Salary**.
- Each variable displayed should have a descriptive report column heading.
- Salary should be displayed with dollar signs, commas, and no decimals.
- The columns of the report should be wide enough so that individual data values are not truncated.
- The observations on the report should be summarized by the values of **City** for each **Division**.
- The report should be titled **Employee Salary Data by Division / City**.

Partial PROC REPORT Output

```
            Employee Salary Data by Division / City

     Division Name         City Based         Salary
     AIRPORT OPERATIONS     AUSTIN            $94,000
                            BRUSSELS          $54,000
                            CARY           $2,510,000
                            COPENHAGEN       $254,000
                            FRANKFURT        $285,000
                            GENEVA            $72,000
                            LONDON           $122,000
                            PARIS            $147,000
                            ROCKVILLE         $79,000
                            ROME             $112,000
                            SYDNEY           $108,000
                            TOKYO             $73,000
                            TORONTO          $137,000
     CORPORATE OPERATIONS   ATLANTA          $105,000
                            CARY             $210,000
```

9. Adding a Grand Total to the Report

Modify the previous report so that a grand total appears with a single line above the total and a double line below the total.

Partial PROC REPORT Output (Bottom of Report)

```
                    PITTSBURGH         $52,000
                    ROCKVILLE          $81,000
                    SAN FRANCISCO      $41,000
                    SAN JOSE           $21,000
                    SINGAPORE          $63,000
                    TOKYO             $101,000
                    TORONTO            $83,000
                                      _____
                                     $16,290,000
                                     ==============
```

9.4   The TABULATE Procedure (Self-Study)

Objectives

- Create one- and two-dimensional tabular reports using the TABULATE procedure.
- Produce totals for one dimension.
- Produce totals for both dimensions.

77

Introduction

The report writing features of PROC TABULATE include

- control of table construction
- differentiating between classification variables and analysis variables
- specifying statistics
- formatting of values
- labeling variables and statistics.

78

PROC TABULATE versus PROC REPORT

FEATURE	REPORT	TABULATE
Detail Report	Yes	No
Summary Report	Yes	Yes
Crosstabular Report	Yes	Yes
Grand Totals	Yes	Yes
Dividing Lines	Yes	Yes
Labels used automatically	Yes	Yes
Ability to create computed columns	Yes	No

79

PROC TABULATE Syntax

General form of a PROC TABULATE step:

```
PROC TABULATE DATA=SAS-data-set <options>;
    CLASS class-variables;
    VAR analysis-variables;
    TABLE page-expression,
          row-expression,
          column-expression </ option(s)>;
RUN;
```

80

A CLASS statement or a VAR statement must be specified, but both statements together are not required.

Specifying Classification Variables

A CLASS statement identifies variables to be used as classification, or grouping, variables.

```
PROC TABULATE DATA=SAS-data-set <options>;
   CLASS class-variables;
   VAR analysis-variables;
   TABLE page-expression,
         row-expression,
         column-expression </ option(s)>;
RUN;
```

Examples of class variables are **Location**, **Gender**, and **JobCode**.

81

Class variables

- can be numeric or character
- identify classes or categories on which calculations are done
- represent discrete categories if they are numeric (example, **Year**).

Specifying Analysis Variables

A VAR statement identifies variables to be used as analysis variables.

```
PROC TABULATE DATA=SAS-data-set <options>;
   CLASS class-variables;
   VAR analysis-variables;
   TABLE page-expression,
         row-expression,
         column-expression </ option(s)>;
RUN;
```

Examples of analysis variables are **Salary**, **CargoWt**, and **Revenue**.

82

Analysis variables

- are always numeric
- tend to be continuous
- are appropriate for calculating averages, sums, or other statistics.

Specifying Table Structure

A TABLE statement identifies table structure and format.

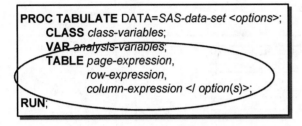

```
PROC TABULATE DATA=SAS-data-set <options>;
    CLASS class-variables;
    VAR analysis-variables;
    TABLE page-expression,
          row-expression,
          column-expression </ option(s)>;
RUN;
```

83

The TABLE Statement

You specify the table format and the desired statistics with expressions in the TABLE statement.

A simple expression consists of elements and operators.

Elements include
- variables
- statistics.

84

TABLE statement operators control the format of the table. These operators include

Operator	Action
Comma ,	Go to new table dimension.
Blank	Concatenate table information.
Asterisk *	Cross, nest, subgroup information.

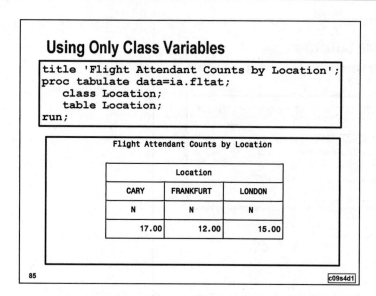

If there are only class variables in the TABLE statement, the default statistic is N, or number of non-missing values.

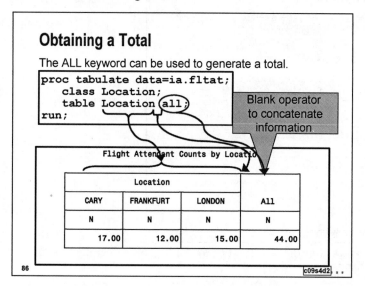

Two-Dimensional Tables

The comma (,) in the TABLE statement directs the table to move to a different dimension.

```
title2 'by JobCode';
proc tabulate data=ia.fltat;
   class Location JobCode;
   table JobCode, Location;
run;
```

Variables in the dimension closest to the column dimension are in the row dimension.

Comma operator moves to a new dimension.

Variable closest to semicolon is always in the column dimension.

87   c09s4d3 . .

Two-Dimensional Tables

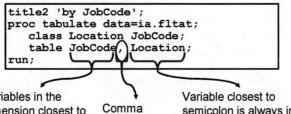

Row Dimension

Column Dimension

Flight Attendant Counts by Location by JobCode

JobCode	Location		
	CARY	FRANKFURT	LONDON
	N	N	N
FLTAT1	5.00	4.00	5.00
FLTAT2	7.00	5.00	6.00
FLTAT3	5.00	3.00	4.00

88   ...

Subsetting the Data

The WHERE statement can be used in PROC TABULATE to subset the data.

```
title 'Counts for Cary and Frankfurt';
proc tabulate data=ia.fltat;
   where Location in ('CARY', 'FRANKFURT');
   class Location JobCode;
   table JobCode, Location;
run;
```

89   c09s4d4

Subsetting the Data

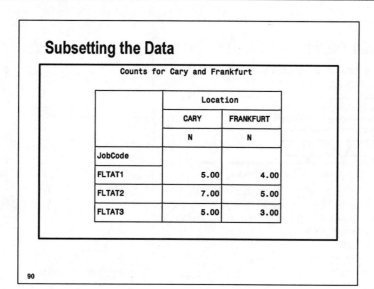

Counts for Cary and Frankfurt

	Location	
	CARY	FRANKFURT
	N	N
JobCode		
FLTAT1	5.00	4.00
FLTAT2	7.00	5.00
FLTAT3	5.00	3.00

90

Two-Dimensional Tables

The ALL keyword generates a total for the dimension in
which it is specified.

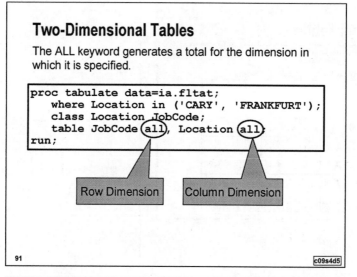

```
proc tabulate data=ia.fltat;
   where Location in ('CARY', 'FRANKFURT');
   class Location JobCode;
   table JobCode (all), Location (all)
run;
```

Row Dimension   Column Dimension

91   c09s4d5

Two-Dimensional Tables

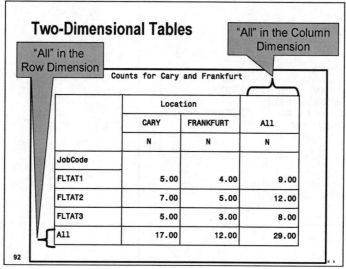

"All" in the Column Dimension

"All" in the
Row Dimension

Counts for Cary and Frankfurt

	Location		
	CARY	FRANKFURT	All
	N	N	N
JobCode			
FLTAT1	5.00	4.00	9.00
FLTAT2	7.00	5.00	12.00
FLTAT3	5.00	3.00	8.00
All	17.00	12.00	29.00

92

Using Analysis Variables

The asterisk (*) operator in the TABLE statement is used to nest information.

If there are analysis variables in the TABLE statement, the default statistic is SUM.

```
title 'Total Salary for Cary and Frankfurt';
proc tabulate data=ia.fltat;
    where Location in ('CARY', 'FRANKFURT');
    class Location JobCode;
    var Salary;
    table JobCode, Location*Salary;
run;
```

93   c09s4d6

Using Analysis Variables

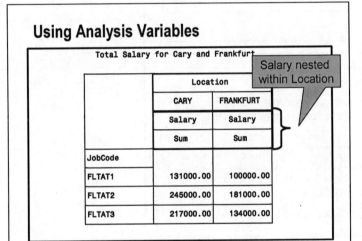

Total Salary for Cary and Frankfurt

Salary nested within Location

JobCode	Location	
	CARY	FRANKFURT
	Salary	Salary
	Sum	Sum
FLTAT1	131000.00	100000.00
FLTAT2	245000.00	181000.00
FLTAT3	217000.00	134000.00

94

Formatting the Statistic Data

To format the statistics in the cells, use the FORMAT= option in the PROC TABULATE statement.

```
proc tabulate data=ia.fltat format=dollar12.;
    where Location in ('CARY', 'FRANKFURT');
    class Location JobCode;
    var Salary;
    table JobCode, Location*Salary;
run;
```

95   c09s4d7

The FORMAT **statement** can be used to control data values in the exterior of the report (values of the class variables).

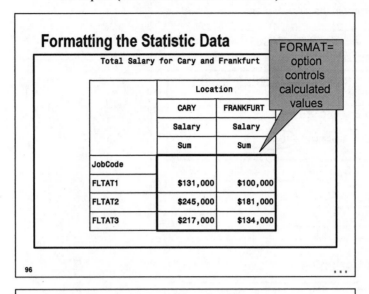

Specifying a Statistic

To specify a different statistic in the cells, follow the analysis variable with the asterisk operator and the desired statistic.

```
title 'Average Salary for Cary and Frankfurt';
proc tabulate data=ia.fltat format=dollar12.;
   where Location in ('CARY', 'FRANKFURT');
   class Location JobCode;
   var Salary;
   table JobCode, Location*Salary*mean;
run;
```

97   c09s4d8

Selected statistics in PROC TABULATE include

NMISS	number of missing observations
STD	standard deviation
MIN	minimum value
MAX	maximum value
RANGE	range of values
MEDIAN	middle value.

Specifying a Statistic

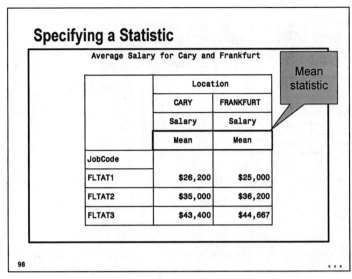

ALL with Analysis Variable

General form for generating overall information when using an analysis variable:

all**analysis-variable**statistic

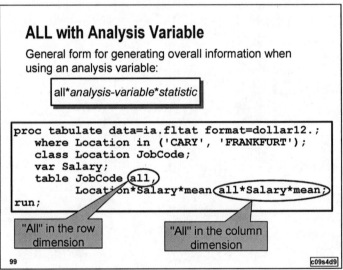

ALL with Analysis Variable

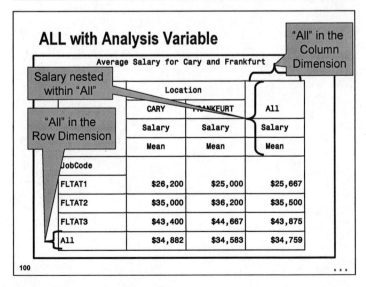

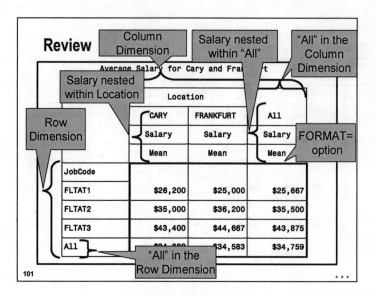

Exercises

10. Creating a One-Dimensional Frequency Report

Use PROC TABULATE and the **ia.employees** data set to produce a summary report that displays a frequency count for the variable **Division** with an appropriate title.

PROC TABULATE Output

Counts by Division				
Division				
AIRPORT OPERATIONS	CORPORATE OPERATIONS	CORPORATE PLANNING	FINANCE & IT	FLIGHT OPERATIONS
N	N	N	N	N
131.00	6.00	1.00	65.00	143.00

(Continued)

Counts by Division	
Division	
HUMAN RESOURCES	SALES & MARKETING
N	N
101.00	53.00

Depending on the width of your page, the report may span two separate pages, as shown in the output above.

11. Creating a Two-Dimensional Frequency Report

Modify the previous report to

- subset the data to only display divisions that have the word 'OPERATIONS' in the name
- display the variable **City** in the row dimension
- add row and column totals
- add an appropriate title.

PROC TABULATE Output

	Division			
	AIRPORT OPERATIONS	CORPORATE OPERATIONS	FLIGHT OPERATIONS	All
	N	N	N	N
City				
ATLANTA	.	1.00	.	1.00
AUSTIN	3.00	.	1.00	4.00
BRUSSELS	2.00	.	.	2.00
CARY	81.00	2.00	116.00	199.00
COPENHAGEN	8.00	.	.	8.00
FRANKFURT	10.00	.	13.00	23.00
GENEVA	2.00	.	.	2.00
LONDON	4.00	1.00	7.00	12.00
PARIS	5.00	.	.	5.00
PHOENIX	.	1.00	.	1.00
ROCKVILLE	3.00	.	.	3.00
ROME	3.00	.	.	3.00
SYDNEY	3.00	.	2.00	5.00
TOKYO	3.00	.	2.00	5.00
TORONTO	4.00	1.00	2.00	7.00
All	131.00	6.00	143.00	280.00

Counts for Operations Divisions

12. Creating a Report on an Analysis Variable

Modify the previous report to

- display the mean of the variable **Salary** in the column dimension
- display the overall mean of the variable salary in the column dimension
- display the data with dollar signs, commas, and no digits after the decimal point
- add an appropriate title.

PROC TABULATE Output

Average Salaries for Operations Divisions				
	Division			
	AIRPORT OPERATIONS	CORPORATE OPERATIONS	FLIGHT OPERATIONS	All
	Salary	Salary	Salary	Salary
	Mean	Mean	Mean	Mean
City				
ATLANTA	.	$105,000	.	$105,000
AUSTIN	$31,333	.	$22,000	$29,000
BRUSSELS	$27,000	.	.	$27,000
CARY	$30,988	$105,000	$32,224	$32,452
COPENHAGEN	$31,750	.	.	$31,750
FRANKFURT	$28,500	.	$34,000	$31,609
GENEVA	$36,000	.	.	$36,000
LONDON	$30,500	$125,000	$45,000	$46,833
PARIS	$29,400	.	.	$29,400
PHOENIX	.	$95,000	.	$95,000
ROCKVILLE	$26,333	.	.	$26,333
ROME	$37,333	.	.	$37,333
SYDNEY	$36,000	.	$28,500	$33,000
TOKYO	$24,333	.	$37,500	$29,600
TORONTO	$34,250	$85,000	$18,000	$36,857
All	$30,893	$103,333	$32,762	$33,400

13. Creating a Report Using HTML (Optional)

Modify the previous report to output the report to an HTML file.

PROC TABULATE Output

	Division			All
	AIRPORT OPERATIONS	**CORPORATE OPERATIONS**	**FLIGHT OPERATIONS**	
	Salary	Salary	Salary	Salary
	Mean	Mean	Mean	Mean
City				
ATLANTA	.	$105,000	.	$105,000
AUSTIN	$31,333	.	$22,000	$29,000
BRUSSELS	$27,000	.	.	$27,000
CARY	$30,988	$105,000	$32,224	$32,452
COPENHAGEN	$31,750	.	.	$31,750
FRANKFURT	$28,500	.	$34,000	$31,609
GENEVA	$36,000	.	.	$36,000
LONDON	$30,500	$125,000	$45,000	$46,833
PARIS	$29,400	.	.	$29,400
PHOENIX	.	$95,000	.	$95,000
ROCKVILLE	$26,333	.	.	$26,333
ROME	$37,333	.	.	$37,333
SYDNEY	$36,000	.	$28,500	$33,000
TOKYO	$24,333	.	$37,500	$29,600
TORONTO	$34,250	$85,000	$18,000	$36,857
All	$30,893	$103,333	$32,762	$33,400

The SAS System

9.5 Solutions to Exercises

1. Creating Frequency Reports

a.

```
proc freq data=ia.sanfran;
   tables DepartDay;
   title 'Flights from San Francisco by Day of Week';
run;
```

b.

```
proc freq data=ia.sanfran;
   tables Destination;
   title 'Flights from San Francisco';
run;
```

c. (Optional)

```
proc freq data=ia.sanfran;
   tables Destination / nocum;
run;
```

d.

```
proc freq data=ia.sanfran;
   tables Destination*DepartDay;
run;
```

2. Validating Data with PROC FREQ (Optional)

a.

```
proc freq data=ia.mechanics;
   tables Gender JobCode;
run;
```

What do you notice about the values of the variable **Gender**? There is a **B** and a **G**.

What do you notice about the values of the variable **JobCode**? There is a missing value.

b.

```
proc freq data=ia.mechanics;
   tables Gender*JobCode;
run;
```

What are the **JobCode** values for the invalid values of **Gender**? The **B** is a MECH02, the **G** is a MECH03.

3. Creating Basic Summary Reports

a.

```
title;
proc means data=ia.sanfran;
   var CargoRev TotPassCap;
run;
```

b.

```
proc means data=ia.sanfran maxdec=2;
   var CargoRev TotPassCap;
   class Destination;
run;
```

4. Requesting Specific Statistics through PROC MEANS (Optional)

```
proc means data=ia.sanfran min max mean maxdec=2;
   var CargoRev TotPassCap;
   class Destination;
run;
```

5. Creating HTML Output (Optional)

```
ods html file='means.html';
proc means data=ia.sanfran min max mean maxdec=2;
   var CargoRev TotPassCap;
   class Destination;
run;
ods html close;
```

6. Creating a List Report

```
title 'Employee Salary Data';
proc report data=ia.employees nowd;
   column Division City Salary;
   define Division / order width=20 'Division Name';
   define City /  width=13 'City Based';
   define Salary / format=dollar14.;
run;
```

7. Creating a Sorted List Report (Optional)

```
proc report data=ia.employees nowd;
   column Division City Salary;
   define Division / order width=20 'Division Name';
   define City / order width=13 'City Based';
   define Salary / format=dollar14.;
run;
```

8. Creating a Summary Report

```
title 'Employee Salary Data by Division / City';
proc report data=ia.employees nowd;
   column Division City Salary;
   define Division / group width=20 'Division Name';
   define City / group width=13 'City Based';
   define Salary / format=dollar14.;
run;
```

9. Adding a Grand Total to the Report

```
title 'Employee Salary Data by Division / City';
proc report data=ia.employees nowd;
   column Division City Salary;
   define Division / group width=20 'Division Name';
   define City / group width=13 'City Based';
   define Salary / format=dollar14.;
   rbreak after / summarize ol dul;
run;
```

10. Creating a One-Dimensional Frequency Report

```
title 'Counts by Division';
proc tabulate data=ia.employees;
   class Division;
   table Division;
run;
```

11. Creating a Two-Dimensional Frequency Report

```
title 'Counts for Operations Divisions';
proc tabulate data=ia.employees;
   where Division contains 'OPERATIONS';
   class Division City;
   table City all, Division all;
run;
```

12. Creating a Report on an Analysis Variable

```
title 'Average Salaries for Operations Divisions';
proc tabulate data=ia.employees format=dollar10.;
   where Division contains 'OPERATIONS';
   class Division City;
   var Salary;
   table City all, Division*Salary*mean all*Salary*mean;
run;
```

13. Creating a Report Using HTML (Optional)

```
ods html file='tabulate.html';
proc tabulate data=ia.employees format=dollar10.;
   where Division contains 'OPERATIONS';
   class Division City;
   var Salary;
   table City all, Division*Salary*mean all*Salary*mean;
run;
ods html close;
```

Chapter 10   Introduction to Graphics (Optional)

10.1 Producing Bar and Pie Charts

Objectives

- Produce high-resolution bar and pie charts.
- Control the statistics displayed in the chart.

3

Graphically Summarizing Data

You can use bar or pie charts to graphically display the

- distribution of a variable's values
- average value of a variable for different categories
- total value of a variable for different categories.

4

Vertical Bar Chart

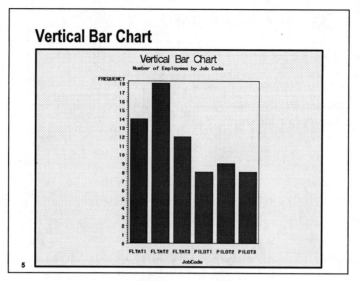

Horizontal Bar Chart

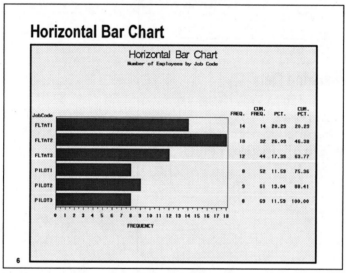

Pie Chart

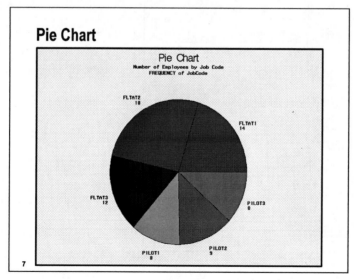

Specifying a Chart

When using the GCHART procedure,

- specify the physical form of the chart
- identify a chart variable that determines the number of bars or pie slices to create
- optionally identify an analysis variable to use for calculating statistics that determine the height (or length) of the bar or the size of the slice.

By default, the height, length, or size represents a frequency count (N).

8

The GCHART Procedure

General form of the PROC GCHART statement:

PROC GCHART DATA=*SAS-data-set*;

Use one of these statements to specify the desired type of chart:

HBAR *chart-variable . . . </options>*;

VBAR *chart-variable . . . </options>*;

PIE *chart-variable . . . </options>*;

9

Chart Variable

The chart variable

- determines the number of bars or slices produced within a graph
- can be character or numeric.

10

Vertical Bar Chart

Produce a vertical bar chart that displays the number of employees in each job code.

```
proc gchart data=ia.crew;
   vbar JobCode;
run;
```

JobCode is the chart variable.

11   c10s1d1

Vertical Bar Chart

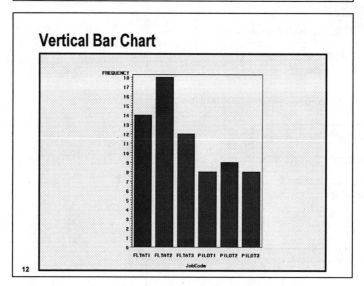

12

Horizontal Bar Chart

Produce a horizontal bar chart that displays the number of employees in each job code.

```
proc gchart data=ia.crew;
   hbar JobCode;
run;
```

JobCode is the chart variable.

13

c10s1d2

Horizontal Bar Chart

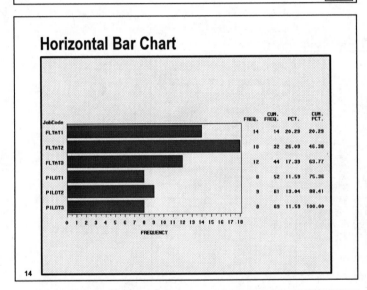

14

Pie Chart

Produce a pie chart that displays the number of employees in each job code.

```
proc gchart data=ia.crew;
   pie JobCode;
run;
```

JobCode is the chart variable.

15

c10s1d3

Pie Chart

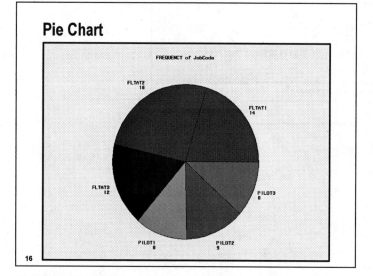

16

Character Chart Variable

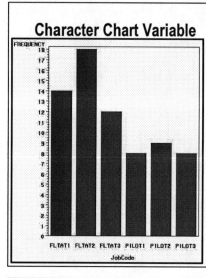

If the chart variable is character, a bar or slice is created for each unique variable value.

The chart variable is **JobCode**.

Numeric Chart Variable

For numeric chart variables, the variables are assumed to be continuous unless otherwise specified.

Intervals are automatically calculated and identified by midpoints.

One bar or slice is constructed for each midpoint.

18

Numeric Chart Variable

Produce a vertical bar chart on the numeric variable
Salary.

```
proc gchart data=ia.crew;
   vbar Salary;
run;
```

Salary is the chart variable.

19

c10s1d4

Numeric Chart Variable

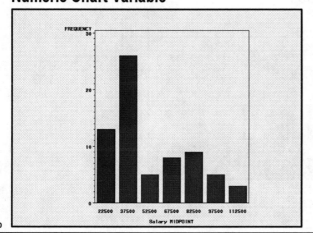

20

The DISCRETE Option

To override the default behavior for numeric chart
variables, use the DISCRETE option in the HBAR, VBAR,
or PIE statement.

The DISCRETE option produces a bar or slice for each
unique numeric variable value; the values are no longer
treated as intervals.

21

Numeric Chart Variable

Produce a vertical bar chart that displays a separate bar
for each distinct value of the numeric variable **Salary**.

```
proc gchart data=ia.crew;
   vbar Salary / discrete;
run;
```

Salary is the chart variable, but the DISCRETE option
modifies how SAS displays the values.

22   c10s1d5

The DISCRETE Option

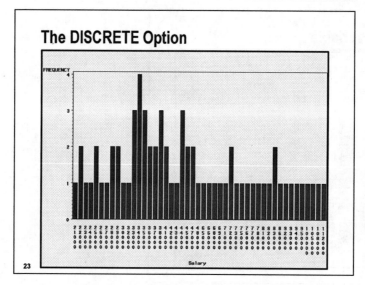

23

In this example, using intervals instead of discrete values produces a more
meaningful chart.

    The DISCRETE option is typically used for numeric chart variables that have
only a small number of distinct values.

Summary Statistic

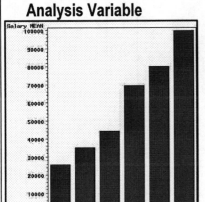

By default, the statistic that determines the length or height of each bar or size of pie slice is a frequency count (N).

Analysis Variable

To override the default frequency count, you can use the following HBAR, VBAR, or PIE statement options:

SUMVAR=*analysis-variable*

TYPE=MEAN | SUM

SUMVAR= and TYPE= Options

SUMVAR=	identifies the analysis variable to use for the sum or mean calculation.
TYPE=	specifies that the height or length of the bar or size of the slice represents a mean or sum of the *analysis-variable* values.

If an analysis variable is
- specified, the default value of TYPE is SUM
- not specified, the default value of TYPE is FREQ.

Using an Analysis Variable

Produce a vertical bar chart that displays the average salary of employees in each job code.

```
proc gchart data=ia.crew;
   vbar JobCode / sumvar=Salary type=mean;
run;
```

27   c10s1d6

GCHART Output

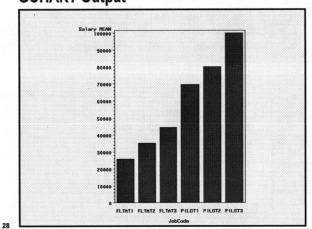

28

RUN-Group Processing

PROC GCHART supports RUN-group processing, which means

- the procedure executes the group of statements following the PROC statement when a RUN statement is encountered
- additional statements followed by another RUN statement can be submitted without resubmitting the PROC statement
- the procedure stays active until a PROC, DATA, or QUIT statement is encountered.

29

Pie Chart

Produce a pie chart that displays the total salary of employees in each job code.

```
proc gchart data=ia.crew;
   pie JobCode / sumvar=Salary type=sum;
   format Salary dollar8.;
run;
```

30   c10s1d7

Pie Chart

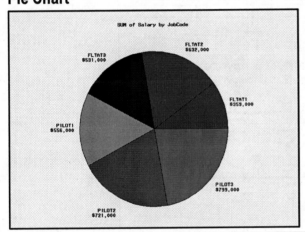

31

Pie Chart

You can use the FILL= option to specify whether to fill the pie slices in a solid (FILL=S) or crosshatched (FILL=X) pattern.

```
   pie JobCode / sumvar=Salary type=sum
                 fill=x;
   format Salary dollar8.;
run;
```

32   c10s1d7

✎   PROC GCHART supports RUN-group processing, so it is unnecessary to resubmit the PROC GCHART statement.

Pie Chart

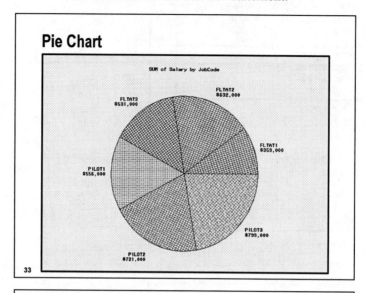

33

Exploding a Pie Slice

You can highlight individual slices of a pie chart by moving them away from the rest of the pie with the EXPLODE= option.

```
   pie JobCode / sumvar=Salary type=sum
                 fill=x explode='PILOT3';
   format Salary dollar8.;
run;
quit;
```

34   c10s1d7

✎   A QUIT statement was added to the PROC GCHART code to enable SAS to stop processing the procedure.

Exploding a Pie Slice

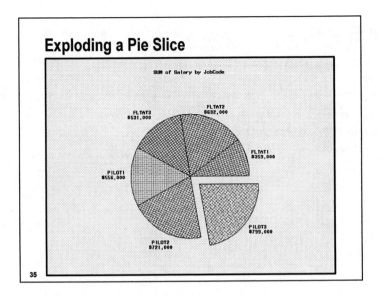

35

10.2 Enhancing Output

Objectives

- Specify a graphics device.
- Incorporate titles and footnotes with graphs.
- Enhance graphs using color, fonts, and different size titles and footnotes.

37

Defining the Graphics Device

To specify the graphic device, use the GOPTIONS statement.

General form of the GOPTIONS statement:

> **GOPTIONS** *graphics-options*;

38

The GOPTIONS statement is a global statement that can be placed outside of DATA and PROC steps. Initially, the GOPTIONS statement must be submitted prior to the GCHART procedure for the options to be in effect for that graph. Once the statement is submitted, it is in effect for the entire SAS session.

Graphics Device Option

The DEVICE= (or DEV=) graphics option in the GOPTIONS statement specifies the graphics device.

Examples:

Graphics Device	GOPTIONS Statement
HP Deskjet Printer	goptions dev=HPD
HPLaserJet Driver	goptions dev=HPL
GIF Driver	goptions dev=GIF
Tektronix Driver	goptions dev=TK1
Portable Document	goptions dev=PDF
PostScript Driver	goptions dev=PSL
Windows Metafile Driver	goptions dev=WMF

39

There are many device drivers available. A list of device drivers can be found in the **sashelp.Devices** catalog.

Adding Titles and Footnotes

You can use TITLE and FOOTNOTE statement options to modify the characteristics of text strings.

Selected Options:

```
COLOR=color | C=color
FONT=type-font | F=type-font
HEIGHT=n | H=n
```

40

COLOR=   names the color to use for the text that follows the option. The default depends on the device.

FONT=   identifies the font to use for the text that follows the option. Valid font names include SWISS, DUPLEX, SIMPLEX, BRUSH, and SPECIAL. The default is SWISS for TITLE1 and the hardware character set for all other titles and all footnotes.

HEIGHT=   specifies the height of the characters in text that follows the option. Units of H=n can be in CELLS (default), inches (IN), centimeters (CM), or percent (PCT) of the display.

All title and footnote options must precede the quoted text string.

Title and Footnote Options

Examples:

```
title color=green 'Number of Pilots by Job Level';
title font=brush color=red  'March Flights';
title height=3 in  font=duplex 'Flights to RDU';
footnote height=3 "IA's Gross Revenue by Region";
footnote height=3 cm 'Average Salary by Job Level';
footnote height=3 pct 'Total Flights by Model';
```

41

Exercises

1. Producing Vertical Bar Charts and Pie Charts

Use the **ia.personl** date set and a WHERE statement to produce the charts requested below for the ticket agents (**JobCode** values of TA1, TA2, and TA3).

```
where JobCode in ('TA1', 'TA2', 'TA3');
```

a. Produce a vertical bar chart that displays the number of male and female ticket agents (**Gender** values are M and F).

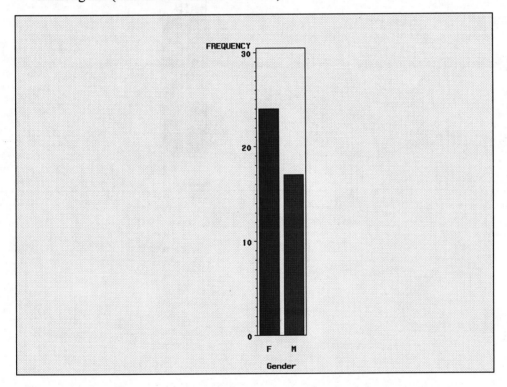

b. Enhance the chart by adding an appropriate title that displays the text in blue with the DUPLEX font.

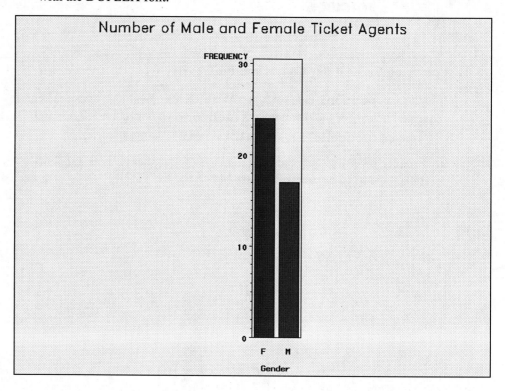

c. Compare the average salaries of each ticket agent job level by showing a solid pie slice for each of the three **Jobcode** values. Add an appropriate title that displays the text in red with the SWISS font.

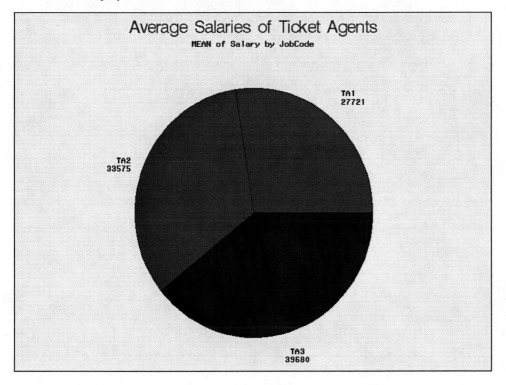

d. Enhance the pie chart by filling the pie slices with crosshatched lines and exploding the slice represents the TA3 value of **JobCode**.

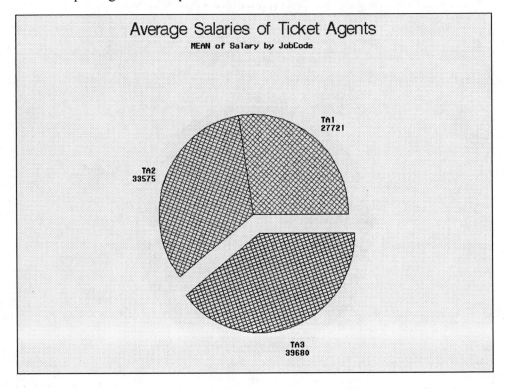

2. Producing a Horizontal Bar Chart (Optional)

Use the **ia.chicago** data set to produce a horizontal bar chart that displays the total number of passengers boarded (**Boarded**) each day of the week. Create a new variable, **Day**, which contains the day of the week, where 1 represents Sunday, 2 represents Monday, and so on.

- Place an appropriate title on the chart.
- Use the label **Day of the Week** for the variable **Day** and the label **Passengers** for the variable **Boarded**.

If the chart did not generate seven bars, add the DISCRETE option to the HBAR statement and generate the chart again.

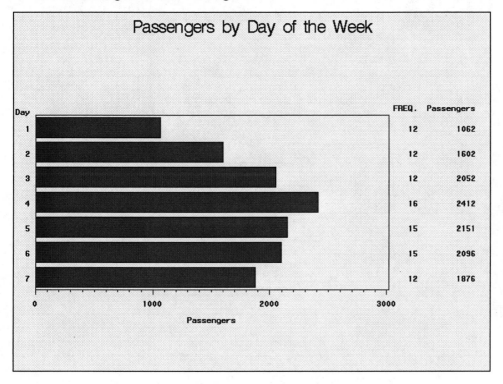

10.3 Producing Plots

Objectives

- Produce plots.
- Define plotting symbols.
- Control appearance of the axes.

44

The GPLOT Procedure

You can use the GPLOT procedure to plot one variable against another within a set of coordinate axes.

General form of a PROC GPLOT step:

```
PROC GPLOT DATA=SAS-data-set;
    PLOT vertical-variable*horizontal-variable </options>;
RUN;
QUIT;
```

45

The *vertical-variable* specifies the vertical axis variable. The *horizontal-variable* specifies the horizontal axis variable.

You can

- specify the symbols to represent data
- use different methods of interpolation
- specify line styles, colors, and thickness
- draw reference lines within the axes
- place one or more plot lines within the axes.

    PROC GPLOT supports RUN-group processing. Use a QUIT statement to terminate the procedure.

Default GPLOT Output

Produce a plot of number of passengers by date for flight number 114 over a one-week period.

```
proc gplot data=ia.flight114;
   where date between '02mar2001'd and
         '08mar2001'd;
   plot Boarded*Date;
   title 'Total Passengers for Flight 114';
   title2 'between 02Mar2001 and 08Mar2001';
run;
```

46   c10s3d1

Default GPLOT Output

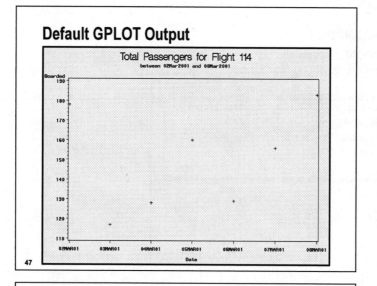

47

SYMBOL Statement

You can use the SYMBOL statement to

- define plotting symbols
- draw lines through the data points
- specify the color of the plotting symbols and lines.

48

SYMBOL Statement

General form of the SYMBOL statement:

SYMBOL*n* options;

The value of *n* can range from 1 to 99.

If *n* is omitted, the default is 1.

49

SYMBOL Statement

SYMBOL statements are

global	once defined, they remain in effect until changed or until the end of the SAS session.
additive	specifying the value of one option does not affect the values of other options.

50

SYMBOL Statement Options

You can specify the plotting symbol you want with the VALUE= option in the SYMBOL statement:

VALUE=*symbol* | **V=***symbol*

Selected *symbol* values are

PLUS (default)	DIAMOND
STAR	TRIANGLE
SQUARE	NONE (no plotting symbol)

51

SYMBOL Statement Options

You can use the I= option in the SYMBOL statement to draw lines between the data points.

I=*interpolation*

Selected *interpolation* values:

JOIN	joins the points with straight lines.
SPLINE	joins the points with a smooth line.
NEEDLE	draws vertical lines from the points to the horizontal axes.

52

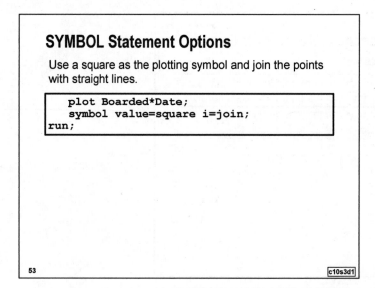

PROC GPLOT supports RUN-group processing and is still running, so it is unnecessary to resubmit the PROC GPLOT statement when submitting other PLOT statements.

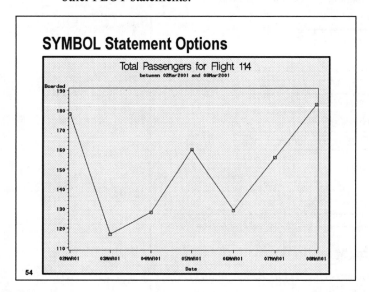

Additional SYMBOL Statement Options

You can enhance the appearance of the plots with the following selected options:

WIDTH=*width* **W**=*width*	specifies the thickness of the line.
COLOR=*color* **C**=*color*	specifies the color of the line.

55

Color and Width Options

Show the line in red with double thickness.

```
    plot Boarded*Date;
    symbol c=red w=2;
run;
```

56   c10s3d1

Color and Width Options

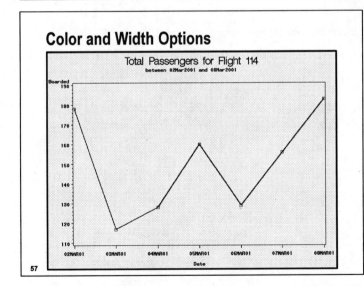

57

✎ The line appears in red with a width of 2.

Modifying the SYMBOL Statement

Set the attributes for SYMBOL1.

```
symbol1 c=blue v=diamond;
```

Modify only the color of SYMBOL1, not the V= option setting.

```
symbol1 c=green;
```

58

Cancel SYMBOL Statements

You can cancel a SYMBOL statement by submitting a null SYMBOL statement.

```
symbol1;
```

To cancel all SYMBOL statements, submit the following statement:

```
goptions reset=symbol;
```

59

Controlling the Axis Appearance

You may modify the appearance of the axes that
PROC GPLOT produces with

- PLOT statement options
- the LABEL statement
- the FORMAT statement.

60

PLOT Statement Options

You can use PLOT statement options to control the scaling
and color of the axes, and the color of the axis text.

Selected PLOT statement options for axis control:

HAXIS=_values_	scales the horizontal axis.
VAXIS=_values_	scales the vertical axis.
CAXIS=_color_	specifies the color of both axes.
CTEXT=_color_	specifies the color of the text on both axes.

61

PLOT Statement Options

Define the scale on the vertical axis and display the axis
text in blue.

```
   plot Boarded*Date / vaxis=100 to 200 by 25
                       ctext=blue;
run;
```

62   c10s3d1

PLOT Statement Options

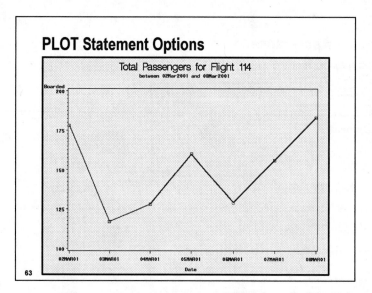

The line appears in red with a width of 2, and the axis text is blue.

Adding Labels

Place labels on the axes.

```
plot Boarded*Date / vaxis=100 to 200 by 25
                    ctext=blue;
label Boarded='Passengers Boarded'
      Date='Departure Date';
run;
```

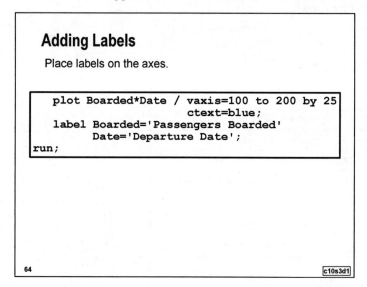

Adding Labels

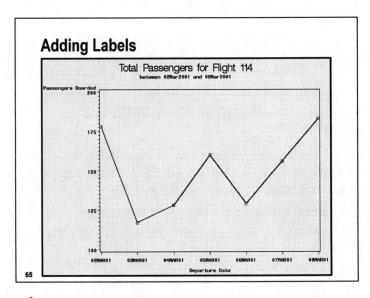

65

The axis text color is blue.

Exercises

3. Producing a Two-Dimensional Plot

The data set **ia.delay** contains dates and delays in minutes for International Airlines flights. Use the data set and an appropriate WHERE statement to select flights to Copenhagen (**Dest='CPH'**) and produce the plot described below:

- Plot the delays on the vertical axis and dates along the horizontal axis.
- Adjust the scale on the vertical axis to start at −15 and end at 30 with a tick mark every 15 minutes.
- Display the title **Flights to Copenhagen** in red.
- Display the points as red squares.
- Use the NEEDLE interpolation technique to connect the points to the horizontal axis.

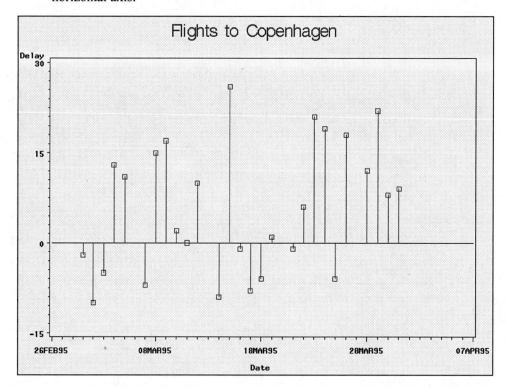

10.4 Solutions to Exercises

1. **Producing Vertical Bar Charts and Pie Charts**

    a.

```
proc gchart data=ia.personl;
   where JobCode in ('TA1', 'TA2', 'TA3');
   vbar Gender;
run;
```

    b.

```
proc gchart data=ia.personl;
   where JobCode in ('TA1', 'TA2', 'TA3');
   vbar Gender;
   title c=blue f=duplex 'Number of Male and Female '
                         'Ticket Agents';
run;
```

    c.

```
proc gchart data=ia.personl;
   where JobCode in ('TA1', 'TA2', 'TA3');
   pie JobCode / sumvar=Salary type=mean;
   title c=red 'Average Salaries of Ticket Agents';
run;
```

    d.

```
proc gchart data=ia.personl;
   where JobCode in ('TA1', 'TA2', 'TA3');
   pie JobCode / sumvar=Salary type=mean fill=x
                 explode='TA3';
   title c=red 'Average Salaries of Ticket Agents';
run;
```

2. **Producing a Horizontal Bar Chart (Optional)**

```
data chicago;
   set ia.chicago;
   Day=weekday(Date);
run;
proc gchart data=chicago;
   hbar Day / sumvar=Boarded type=sum discrete;
   label Boarded='Passengers';
   title c=blue 'Passengers by Day of the Week';
run;
```

3. Producing a Two-Dimensional Plot

```
proc gplot data=ia.delay;
   where Dest='CPH';
   plot Delay*Date / vaxis = -15 to 30 by 15;
   title c=red 'Flights to Copenhagen';
   symbol i=needle c=red v=square;
run;
```

Chapter 11   Additional Resources

11.1 Resources

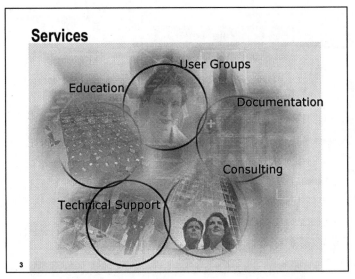

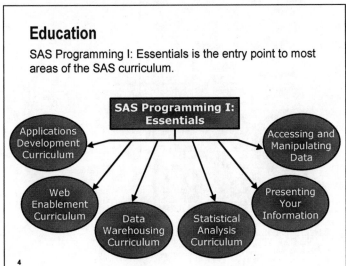

Next Steps

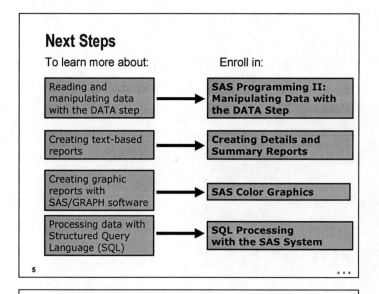

To learn more about:

To learn more about:	Enroll in:
Reading and manipulating data with the DATA step	SAS Programming II: Manipulating Data with the DATA Step
Creating text-based reports	Creating Details and Summary Reports
Creating graphic reports with SAS/GRAPH software	SAS Color Graphics
Processing data with Structured Query Language (SQL)	SQL Processing with the SAS System

5

Education

Computer-based:

- e-Learning

Conferences:

- Data Mining Technology Conference

6

Education

Refer to the SAS Training Web site for more information on these classes and the broad curriculum of courses available.

support.sas.com/training

7

Consulting Services

Services provided:

- knowledge transfer
- application development
- analytical consulting
- implement business solutions.

8

Technical Support

Goals:

- Provide support to our users to solve any problems they encounter when using SAS software.
- Free unlimited support.
- Local support at each site - designated SAS consultant.

World Wide Web Services:

- Report/resolve problems
- Frequently asked questions
- SASware Ballot suggestions/results
- Download zaps/fixes/patches
- Upload code/data
- Search SAS notes
- Alert notes.

9

Technical Support (North America)

- Problem Tracking System

Telephone: 9:00 a.m. until 8:00 p.m. Eastern Time, Monday-Friday
(919) 677-8008

E-mail:

support@sas.com - report problems

suggest@sas.com - software suggestions

Web: **support.sas.com/techsup/**

10

Documentation

Documenting the SAS System:
- Reference Guides
- Getting Started Guides
- User's Guides
- Companions
- Changes and Enhancements.

Current products and services:
- Publications Catalog
- Solutions @ Work
- Books by Users
- On-line Documentation
- SelecText.

11

Documentation

Reference guides:
- SAS on-line documentation
- Delivered on a CD-ROM
- Shipped free with software
- Single copies available
- Hardcopy books to purchase.

support.sas.com/documentation

12

SAS Documentation

SAS documentation is also available in hardcopy.
Some useful references are
- *SAS® 9.1 Language Reference: Concepts* (order # 58940)
- *SAS® 9.1 Language Reference Dictionary, Volumes 1 and 2* (order # 58941)
- *Base SAS® 9.1 Procedures Guide, Volumes 1, 2, and 3* (order # 58943)
- *SAS® 9.1 Output Delivery System: User's Guide* (order # 58966)
- *The Little SAS ® Book: A Primer, Third Edition* (order # 59216)
- *SAS® 9.1 Companion for Windows* (order # 58942)
- *SAS® 9.1 Companion for UNIX Environments* (order # 58950)
- *SAS® 9.1 Companion for z/OS* (order # 58938)
- *SAS® 9.1 Companion for OpenVMS Alpha* (order # 58951)

13

User Groups

Benefits:

- Enhance your understanding of SAS software and services.
- Exchange ideas about using your software and hardware most productively.
- Learn of new SAS products and services as soon as they become available.
- Have more influence over the direction of SAS software and services.

14

International Users Groups

SUGI (pronounced soo-gee)
> SAS Users Group International. Annual conference held March or April in North America.

SAS Forum International (formerly SEUGI)
> Annual conference held May or June in Europe.

SUGA (SAS Users Group of Australia)
> Annual Conference held August or September in Australia.

15

Regional User Groups (RUGs)

SESUG	Southeastern United States
NESUG	Northeastern United States
MWSUG	Midwest US
SCSUG	South-central US
WUSS	Western US

All RUG conferences are usually held in September or October.

16

Other Users Groups

Local   City or area user group. Often hold multiple meetings per year.

Special Interest Industry-specific user groups.

In-house   Single organization or company user group.

Worldwide   Most countries have their own users groups.

support.sas.com/usergroups

17

Newsgroups

There is a newsgroup called **comp.soft-sys.sas**. This is a bulletin board for users to post questions, answers, and discuss SAS software.

To view this newsgroup, use any newsgroup viewer, such as **groups.google.com**.

18

Newsgroups

This newsgroup is also gated to a listserv. To subscribe to the listserv, send e-mail to any of the mail servers:

- listserv@listserv.uga.edu   University of Georgia
- listserv@vm.marist.edu   Marist University
- listserv@listserv.vt.edu   Virginia Polytechnic University
- listserv@AKH-WIEN.AC.AT   University of Vienna

The subject line is ignored and the body should contain the command: subscribe sas-l *your name here* .
For example, subscribe sas-l Tom Smith is how Tom Smith would subscribe.

19

Additional Information

Access the SAS Web site at **www.sas.com** to learn more about available software, support, and services and to take advantage of these offerings.

20

Wrap-Up

Do not forget to

- fill out your evaluation
- deposit your name badge in the container provided by your course coordinator
- pick up your diploma.

21

Thank you for attending **SAS® Programming I: Essentials**.

We hope that the topics you have learned in this course have provided you with a good foundation and that you will put them to good use.

22

Appendix A Index